CELESTIAL GIFTS
BOOK SERIES

ANGELIC MYSTICISM

A Complete Guidebook

of Esoteric Teachings & Practices

to Experience the Divine Angelic Energies

Georgios Mylonas
GEOM!*

Important Note

The recommendations made in this book should not be considered a replacement for formal medical or mental treatment. A physician should be consulted in all matters relating to health, including any symptoms that require medical attention. Anyone who has emotional, mental, or physical problems should seek professional consultation before attempting any of these practices. While the information and the suggestions in this book are believed to be safe and accurate, the author cannot accept liability for any harm as a result of the use or misuse of these practices. This book is intended as general information and for educational purposes.

First English edition 2024

© Georgios Mylonas

GEOM!*

Georgios Mylonas
Teacher and author on methods of energy healing,
personal development and spiritual advancement

The School of Reiki, Athens
www.energiesoflight.com
www.universityofreiki.com
www.reikiathens.com
e-mail: reiki@reiki.gr

ISBN: 9798882649455

Ten percent of the proceeds from this book go to charity.

PART I: ALL ABOUT THE ANGELS

PART II: CONTACT WITH ANGELS

Contents

Contents

INDEX OF EXERCISES, MEDITATIONS AND TECHNIQUES

Contents

Contents

Contents

Dedication

This book is dedicated to all mystics of humanity, no matter when they lived on this most beautiful Earth, no matter where they are in the Great Now.

It is also dedicated to the inner mystic, the mystic within; the seeker of mysteries, of the truth, of the essence; to the mystic within you.

This book is dedicated with the Highest Love!

Gratitude

Are there adequate and sufficient words in the human language to express true thankfulness to the Angels, those incorporeal celestial, spiritual beings, the transcendental heavenly spiritual energies, intelligences, and powers of the Cosmos, of the whole of Existence?

May this work be the true, meaningful, and substantial thankfulness!

Activation and Attunement of this Book:

Infinite Light and Infinite Love!

For Everyone!

For You!

How to proceed with this work

The book that you now hold in your hands will lead you on an extraordinary—probably ecstatic—journey of self-discovery, self-healing, illumination, and enlightenment, as well as collective planetary healing and enlightenment, since the part affects the whole. It is a journey beyond imagination and expectation. You may not yet be fully aware of how many wondrous powers a human being hides inside him...in his heart, his soul, his spirit, or in his mind, this perfect instrument of consciousness. You may not yet be fully aware of the infinite wonders, the miracles the universe conceals—the enormous universe, the external just like the small universe-inside-the-universe, that inner universe of human existence. Are you prepared?

Initiate and embrace this journey with an open and pure mind; with an open and warm heart; with faith, trust, and love! These three powers make the world move; they birth and create the world. It is about a leap—a huge leap of consciousness beyond and above what is already known and familiar, beyond and above what is visible and apparent. It is a leap to the unknown. Engage in it with faith, trust, and love, and bear in mind that only good can come out of it—the Highest Good! You will see what can be seen only from the big picture, the great prism, a superior level of existence and awareness—the deepest, broadest, and most elevated level. It is a level of existence and awareness more macrocosmic, more hypercosmic—a level that, when we finally experience it, we exclaim, "Yes, this is how it should be done. In the end, everything was for good. It was all for the best!"

Introduction: Celestial Gifts

In a period of deep and intense spiritual work, I "heard" with my internal senses-the senses of the soul and spirit-the Angels saying that some small angelic books would be written, several heavenly gifts comprising one collective work. Each would be a different, parallel, and complementary path to come closer to the Angels and receive their help and support, their knowledge, their wisdom, and their love, to heal and improve-as much as it is possible and as much as we desire-our life on Earth.

These books would be called Celestial Gifts, and they were very soon ready and written in mind and spirit. They were put on paper in a short period of continuous inspiration and nonstop automatic writing, with no second thought, hesitation, judgment, or difficulty. A smooth flow of words coming straight from the heart and soul was all it took-just like the Angels would want it to happen, Angelically.

The material of Celestial Gifts includes positive affirmations and healing decrees; symbols of energy and spirit; secrets, tips, and techniques of spiritual connection and manifestation; energy invocations and prayers; Angelic meditations; and creative visualizations. These are keys and tools to inspire, guide, help, and support a person in his personal and collective path-beautiful and open gates of light, bridges of heavenly light! The Angels have given their assurance and proof that this is so-angelic assurance and angelic proof. But you now take on the most important proof of all: the proof of personal experience. To believe, experience! Experience to believe!

Enjoy these beautiful and luminous spiritual tools and keys, the gifts of Heaven. Celebrate with your entire being! Improve your life, and make it more radiant and illuminating, starting today...starting now! See the Light of Love and the Love of Light rising again within your beingness, rising to new crystal clear heights.

With Infinite Joy, Infinite Gratitude, and Infinite Love!
Infinitely Infinite.

Alpha and Omega

Leaf through this book; it contains a piece of heaven! It contains a large and generous, over-abundant and luminous piece of spirit, of paradise, of wholeness and transcendence. A piece encoded, enriched, attuned, empowered, energized with Light and Love – and even more Love and even more Light. As much Love and Light, as much spiritual energy and power that a text – a book – can possibly hold and contain; the Word, a human being...

Leaf through the book! How do you feel? Love it! Study it! Meditate on it! Place it near you or even under your bed when you sleep: it is a source of pleasant energy and uplifting positivity! Read it from beginning to end, read it from end to beginning, read it randomly and intuitively or simply read the parts and points that most interest you and draw your attention. How do you feel...?

With Love toward All and with Love toward You! Our precious, unique, sublime, divine beings!

You Are Love and You Are Loved, from Alpha to Omega!

Primary Questions

How are you? How do you feel?

Are you ready to open up, to receive, to be exposed to new information? To take a glimpse or a good look into a brand new world? Can you see the Cosmos, the Reality, with different eyes, refreshed, anew? Are you willing to become wide open, to accept, to wonder, to doubt, to discover, to recognize, to believe, to move beyond, to transcend? Are you willing to release, to embrace, to synthesize? To listen, to see, to sense, to feel, to experience? Not just with your known and familiar aspects, but also by using your unfamiliar and unknown ones. Not just the known, but also the unknown aspects of life; the esoteric, the hidden, mystical, wondrous side of life; of the world, of the existence, of All-That-Is, of the Total, Supreme and Absolute Divine.

Are you ready, willing, open to receive new information, new knowledge, new ideas, new inspiration, new insight, new awareness? To open and receive the New – what was formerly Unknown. And is it truly unknown? Or is it closer, more familiar, apparent, and visible than you have ever imagined?

Are you open to possibilities, to probabilities? Open to questions and answers? To answers that in their turn bring forth even more questions?

The journey has begun and you are already moving...

You are moving forward and you are moving upward!

ESOTERIC PRACTICE

Opening the Mind

This is an initial simple exercise for opening the mind and for mental expansion.

Imagine that your mind is opening. That your mind is opening, growing, expanding. As simple as that; just imagine it. Can you?

Feel that your mind, your mental perception, your mental strength and capability open, grow, expand. They are developing, evolving, illuminating. Now, there is more space, there is abundant space to receive new knowledge. Superior, deeper, and substantial knowledge. You can apprehend all things, now. You can perceive everything. Nothing is difficult for you. Everything has become easy and simple. You possess a great, open, luminous mind! You are a great, open, luminous being with a great, open, luminous mind! Nothing is difficult for you, now. You can understand all things. You can perceive everything. Everything is easy, everything is immediate, everything is direct, everything is simple. You have a new, greater and higher mental perception, comprehension, ability and power!

Stay in this expanded, wide-open, bright state. This wonderful, open, and bright state of the greatest and highest knowledge, of the highest and greatest perception and of the absolute, total, and perfect understanding of all and of everything!

I Open Myself to Knowledge, I Love Knowledge – Always – I Perceive, I Understand, I Expand, I Evolve Anew!

MEDITATION

Angelic Path

Sit comfortably, breathe deeply, and relax. Just relax; let go.

Visualize a path... a beautiful path...

See yourself walking on this path. It is a wonderful path through the forest, a most serene and peaceful forest...

The trees are so vibrant and the air is so refreshing... Life!

Breathe deeply the air, the oxygen, the trees and the forest, all the life, and the positivity.

You are following this wonderful path, through the exquisite green scenery of Mother Nature.

It leads you to a most serene and beautiful lake.

The lake is completely calm and you can see the white clouds of the sky reflected on its calm surface.

Joy, so much joy! Your heart blooms.

Look around. Observe the flowers: they are all around, in all colors.

Look at them; smell them.

Their velvety colors, in all the colors of the rainbow, their delicate light fragrances, the divine aromas. You rejoice!

Listen to the different sounds of nature. All the melodies.

Breathe. Feel.

Feel the soft breeze; it is so invigorating.

Feel the sweet warm light of the sun on your skin and on your face.

Such a delight.

You enjoy. You experience and enjoy with all your senses, with your entire being.

Beauty! Everything is immensely beautiful.

Breathe. Breathe deeply.

A warm ray of white-golden sunlight touches you.

You feel surrounded by this warm white-golden sunlight.

You feel totally safe and completely protected.

You are purified and energized, energized and purified even more.

The white-golden light protects you, purifies you, energizes you, more and more.

It permeates you, it fills you within, it brightens and illuminates you. Light!

The white-golden light empowers you, uplifts you. Light!

Breathe. Breathe deeply. Light!

Gradually, you find yourself elevated, transported to an even more beautiful and wonderful place.

It is a White Realm. A Higher Dimension.

You are there!

On this White Realm, on this Higher Dimension.

You are so happy to be there!

Angels. There are Angels. Angels all around you. Close to you.

Loving Angels of Pure Light are all around you, close to you, right next to you.

Breathe. Breathe deeply.

You are so happy to be here!

More and more, you are having this wonderful celestial experience.

More and more, experience, see, listen, feel.

Experience, enjoy the light, the serenity, the beauty, the harmony.

The light, the purity, the positivity, the vitality.

Experience, enjoy the Love.

Pure, Angelic, Spiritual Love. Total Love, True Love, Supreme Love.

The Angels' Presence.

Breathe. Breathe deeply.

So much energy, life, love, light! Of such quality, quantity, intensity.

Truly, an Angelic Experience!

You are in bliss, ecstatic, euphoric, yet completely peaceful, tranquil, and serene.

Breathe. Breathe deeply.

You feel more and more revitalized and rejuvenated, renewed on all levels.

Completely revitalized, totally rejuvenated, perfectly renewed. On all levels.

Slowly, you come back. You return easily, gently. You return completely.

Breathe. Breathe deeply.

Feel that you are your most clear and pure self, your most bright and enlightened self, your most authentic and true self, your most joyful and peaceful self, your most healthy and balanced self, your most brilliant and radiant self. Feel that you are your best self, your greatest self, your highest self... You Are Yourself.

You feel it, you feel it deeply, truly and completely, and you are indeed!

You Are Yourself. Love Thyself!

Continue your wonderful day in the highest light and love and in the most angelic way.

Heavenly Calling and Welcome!

How brave and how nice of you to come to the sublime, transcendent, luminous world of angels, the most angelic world of All! An unknown, enigmatic realm, mysterious and mystical, apocryphal and hidden... a secret of seven seals. A world that exists somewhere out there, faraway, in the heavens... or perhaps right here – so much closer – within us? On second thought... would that be possible? Could both be true? A faraway world (far beyond our known universe) and simultaneously a world so close (closer than our thoughts, closer than our own breath), an angelic world that exists up in the heavens, just as deeply within us, existing within you and me, within us all.

Oh, but it is a divine, a supreme, a sublime world, just like the state you experience when you are in love. When you are crazy in love, unconditionally, totally, absolutely, completely in love. It takes you that far, it takes you that high. But, contrary to earthly love and romance, it doesn't let you fall, ever. It is a world that is purely spiritual, radiating pure beauty to our life, a transcendent sense of pure bliss. A world that not only offers beauty and bliss to us, but is a dimension of light, a spiritual dimension that bestows meaning, direction and purpose... how very few things in life can actually offer these! Comfort, support, and loving care in all of our times, especially in the most challenging times. Truly, isn't this the most beautiful and wonderful of all the worlds? The most pure, loving, and bright? The most Angelic of all, just like its name indicates!

I joyfully and warmly welcome you again and so do the angels! However, the welcoming from the angels is not ordinary; they welcome you with a fervent hug, a most luminous and bright hug, a hug of celestial and heavenly love – a hug that goes far beyond the human hug, resembling the fiery, golden, life-giving, all-encompassing and all-reaching energy of the Sun.

In the following pages you will find all the usual – and some not so usual – questions you have been asking about the spiritual realm and about the angels. What are those heavenly creatures, those immaterial, spiritual, transcendental beings? How do they help us and in what ways? Can we be aware of them and can we connect and communicate with them? Should we do something like this? Is it a good thing to do? How and why will we do it? You will find the answers to all these questions. You will also find many exercises, meditations, and techniques to explore these matters and discover your own answers, through your own experience. This book is a most complete and comprehensive guide to the angelic esoteric study, both in theory and practice.

It is important to read and proceed with an open mind and, above all, with an open heart. Give yourself a chance to receive, perceive, and understand. To feel and experience. Keep only what seems true and real, things that are useful and beneficial for your heart and soul. Keep, assimilate, comprehend, feel, and experience only what makes your life better, more beautiful and happy, complete, and free...that is, Angelic! Focus within, on the source that exists within you; focus on the imperishable and eternal divine element. It exists within a human being; it exists within every human being and all human beings. Focus on your inner heart, the heart of your heart, the soul of your heart, your spiritual essence, presence, and beingness. Feel and listen, carefully and devoutly, to your own primordial wisdom.

With Love... let's get started... and love is the best possible start!

"In the beginning was Word"... and then came the questions!

PART I

All About the Angels

What Are Angels?

Angels are true spiritual beings, real, heavenly creatures. They are immaterial beings and pure consciousnesses that carry out divine purposes and acts. One of their duties is to convey messages from human beings to the Highest Spiritual Power, the Divine (ultimate reality and supreme source of everything), and, vice versa, from the Divine Dimension – the purely spiritual – to the human plane. Angels are most known to people as messengers of the Divine and their name comes from the Greek word "angelos" which means "messenger." Nevertheless, angels have countless other duties and tasks, attributes and characteristics, qualities and powers. Transferring messages between the human and the divine realms and encouraging direct communication between human beings and the spiritual plane of existence is only one aspect, a very small fraction of angels' qualities. However, it is a first step to understanding angels and their world.

How can I approach the Angels? How can I picture them?

Imagine the most beautiful, luminous, free, ethereal spirit that you can think of... can you even consider it? Can you imagine, feel, or even perceive it? The most beautiful, luminous, free, ethereal, energy, essence, and intelligence that you can think of... can you think of it, can you imagine it? Even remotely, approximately, vaguely? Nice! Now, multiply by 1,000 what you imagine, feel, or think of... you have an angel! The most beautiful, luminous, free, and ethereal energies, essences, intelligences, and consciousnesses that can exist!

ESOTERIC PRACTICE

"Imagine": a First Angelic Approach

Sit comfortably.

Gently, close your eyes.

Take a few deep slow breaths.

Inhale deeply from the nose and exhale slowly from the mouth.

Count ten slow, deep, conscious breaths, full of energy, positivity, and life.

Relax.

Ask from your body and mind to let go, relax, and loosen up.

Imagine and feel being in a calm state of perfect Harmony and Serenity.

You experience more and more this calm state of complete, total, and absolute Harmony and Serenity.

Bring into your mind the word "angel."

"Angel"...

What do you imagine an angel looks like?

Let your mind and your senses free, completely free...

You possess a great mental ability and limitless imagination...

You are highly open, sensitive, and intelligent...

Imagine what a being of pure light looks like. Higher light, infinite, transcendental, spiritual, celestial, and heavenly light.

Imagine a being of pure love. Higher love, infinite, boundless, existential, universal, and cosmic love.

Imagine a being of supreme and infinite wisdom and intelligence, a being of infinite and supreme power and energy.

Bright, radiant... Loving, wise...

Can you imagine it?

Can you assume something like this, to approach it even as a thought, an image, or a feeling?

Stay with it a little longer.

Allow these thoughts, this energy, to create more thoughts and feelings, to lead you, to direct you, to guide you.

Allow these thoughts, this energy, to show you, to reveal.

Bring more of your awareness into your thoughts and feelings.

Become fully conscious and aware. Attentive, sensitive, observant.

Observe anything you sense and feel, anything you hear or see in your mind's eye.

Engage in this exercise your entire being, your mind, your heart, your soul, your body.

Imagine, think, and feel with your whole self.

Whenever you can, bring your awareness back to the word "Angel" and focus on it...

"Angel"...

You are always in the calm state of absolute, total, and perfect Serenity and Harmony.

After a while, bring your attention to your body. Take a few deep and slow breaths, make a few small movements, awakening your body, and open your eyes.

How are you? How do you feel?

Write down your experience and your observations.

Stay attentive, aware, and conscious throughout this and the coming days and observe carefully, with great perceptiveness, sensitivity, and intelligence everything around you.

Do angels truly exist, or do they just exist in the mind of daydreamers and people with great imaginations?

Yes, angels truly exist; they are higher, incorporeal, spiritual beings. They are entities and consciousnesses, energies and presences, forces and intelligences of pure spirit. Certain people enjoy the great blessing and the supreme privilege of being able to perceive them! Just think about this: if truly superior, purely spiritual, otherworldly, unknown, and transcendental beings do exist, who would be able to perceive them? Or at least, come near to this?

Surely it would be people with great courage and boldness, as it takes boldness and courage to let go of what is known, apparent, familiar, and secure, even if it is for a short while. It would be people of great imagination. After all, human imagination did create the greatest philosophies, sciences, arts, and all discoveries and inventions that make human life easier and in many respects better. People who juggle between reality and fantasy, the real, the unreal, the surreal, and the hyper-real – beyond the "real" as we know it. Between the rational, the irrational, and the hyper-rational – beyond the rational; between the visible and the unseen, the obvious and the hidden, the apparent and the substantial. People who are fiery, open-minded, restless, adventurous, seekers, and researchers. They have a generous piece of "heaven" within them, a glowing light within their hearts and minds. They are awakened to their true nature: to look behind, above, and beyond what is apparent and known.

As we grow and evolve, we all become this kind of person, all of us, with no exceptions. You and me and everyone. And we will all enjoy the great blessing and supreme privilege of perceiving this larger magnificent Reality, including angels themselves. Words cannot do justice to the experience, but it is sheer happiness.

I am not religious, but I consider myself being on a spiritual path. Do I have to believe in angels?

You don't have to "believe in something." Just keep your mind open; keep this precious instrument of your consciousness open to the possibility and receptive to the probability. Reality, Existence, is probably endless and possibly infinite, therefore inconceivable by the human mind. We are a grain of sand on top of another grain of sand (planet Earth) at the edge of the universe (we don't even really know where we are!) Isn't it quite possible that other entities and intelligences much more superior (to say the least) and advanced might exist in this Reality? In our universe or even beyond?

Would these superior and advanced beings that possess higher intelligence, greater consciousness, and are more total, whole, and complete be like us? Would they necessarily have a body? A material form? Would they have a beginning and an end? Would they experience physical life and death? Would they be limited by space? By matter? By time? What would these beings be? It's inconceivable and it's hard even to imagine something like this but it's worth trying to have a glimpse!

You may also approach what we call "angels" as being the natural forces, the cosmic forces of nature. You may see angels as the cosmic creative energies and powers of the cosmos, which possess and experience consciousness, a greater or higher kind of consciousness, awareness, intelligence, and perception than humans. After all, human beings are a latter miracle of creation, a younger wonder, in the immense space-time ocean!

It is also essential to note that angels do not belong to any religion, because angels do not have a religion. Religions are man-made creations and systems; however, this doesn't mean they are of a lesser value, beauty, and inner essence. Angels pre-existed mankind and, therefore, all religions! References to angels – references to higher, spiritual, light-beings – occur not only in all of the religions of the world, but also in many independent esoteric, and spiritual paths and philosophical systems. It is not necessary for a person to be religious, in the strict formal sense, in order to perceive or feel the presence of angels. But a person has to be spiritual. And all human beings are Spiritual, already, in themselves, since they are Spirits and Souls in the form of human beings, Spirits and Souls manifested in matter, on the physical reality, on Earth. As we all are Spirits and Souls, angels are close to all of us. The question is: are we close to them? Are we aware that we are Spiritual, already and in ourselves?

A Question for Thought, Meditation, and Further Study

Where are you? Do you know where you are? Where do you stand time-wise and space-wise in the universe and in the world? Where are you physically but also energetically, spiritually, consciously, existentially in the Greater Reality?

Ask yourself: "Where am I Physically... Energetically... Spiritually... Existentially... Within Reality..." and then simply enjoy some moments of relaxation, silence, and tranquility. Stay there... maybe you are already always there, at the most perfect place. At the most perfect point in the Grand Scheme of things. At the one point, the only point!

ESOTERIC PRACTICE

Angels in Various Religions

Do your own research to find all the references to angels within your religion. If you are not religious yourself, then research the major religion of the society you are part of. In the case of Christianity, write down passages from the Bible, the Old Testament, and the New Testament that describe or mention angelic beings. What are they, how do they appear, and for what purpose?

Expand your research by studying texts from other religions as well, since great knowledge, wisdom, truth, value, and essence are to be found in all religions of the world. Discover references to similar celestial spiritual beings, forces, and energies. Spot possible similarities and differences. It is indeed an intriguing and fascinating study!

Why are angels not visible to people?

Angels are not visible to humans because they have a higher frequency, vibrating higher than matter. They exist at a higher vibrational level of existence, in a superior energetic field, what we humans call "spiritual plane." It is as if angels are on another floor in the big "building" of the Ultimate Reality, which expands beyond physical matter and includes it. In this Great Building (or is it a "Tree"?) of Reality, imagine angels inhabiting a higher floor, from where they are able to visit all the other floors below (other planes, worlds), including the physical universe and the Earth... they enjoy a great view (knowledge, wisdom) and freedom. "It feels good to be in heaven"!

A Question for Thought, Meditation, and Further Study

Is there a reason why angels are not visible to humans? If angels were indeed visible, could the Divine Plan be served and fulfilled? In a relaxed state, reflect on this.

If we don't see angels, how do we know that they exist?

We know from the experiences of certain people, mystics, meditators, and spiritual teachers that have ascended to higher "floors" – something that we will gradually understand and do ourselves. And from angels that visited (descended to) the human "floor" due to special circumstances or needs, or to fulfill a certain purpose.

What is the purpose of angelic visitations and appearances?

The angels are represented throughout the Bible and various religious texts as spiritual beings between God and man. They carry messages, heal, praise, protect, purify, support, worship, and comfort.

There have been stories throughout our everyday lives of unexplained rescues by angels who appear in time of need and trouble but also of angelic appearances in visions, insights, dreams, and in altered states of consciousness. Angels are at work in our lives, protecting us, warning us, supporting us, healing us, enlightening us, providing us with answers, guiding us, and even talking to us. Angels are not some beings that appear only in religious books and paintings; their visitations and their beneficial, healing, rescuing, and often life-changing appearances have been directly and personally experienced by a great number of people in all times and places of the world.

A Question for Thought, Meditation, and Further Study

What is the purpose of angels? What is the purpose of their existence? In respect to God, All-That-Is, the Divine Creation and the Divine Plan? In relation to mankind? In relation to you, specifically, individually, personally? Why do angels exist? What is their purpose? Relax and think about it.

ESOTERIC PRACTICE

The Work and Purpose of the Angels

Reflect and meditate on the previous question.

Make a list and write down a total of thirty angelic purposes that you can think of or imagine: that will consist of ten cosmic purposes regarding All That Is and Creation, ten purposes regarding humanity, and ten purposes regarding you, personally (you may refer to specific circumstances in your life).

Use the following phrases to help you and inspire you.

The angels exist to...

Angels can...

Angels help in...

Angels created...

Angels function as...

Angels offer...

Angels work as...

God created angels for....

God created angels as...

Angels offer to human beings...

Human beings receive from angels...

Angels helped me when...

Angels provide me with...

Angels support me when...

Relax, take your time, and make your own list with the cosmic, human, and personal purposes of angels. Thirty purposes in total – or more, if you are inspired to write more. Place your list of angelic purposes near or under your bed and go to sleep.

How many angels are there?

No one really knows with absolute certainty. As strange as it may seem, there have been attempts by scholars and spiritual seekers in the past to count them! It is most probable that the number of angels is infinite.

A Question for Thought, Meditation, and Further Study

How many angels do you think there are? Reflect, count, assume, guess. In a meditative, relaxed state, can you intuitively think of a number? Write it down. It may prove useful in the future!

ESOTERIC PRACTICE

Reading in a More Holistic/Spiritual Way

How do you read a spiritual text? Do you read it with your mind? With your heart? Superficially or substantially? Partially or wholly? With an aspect of yourself or with your entire being?

Attempt to read not only with your mind, mentally, but also with your heart and your entire being, spirit, and soul. Experience what you read. Feel the words not only as concepts and images in your mind but also as sensations and real experiences deeper within your body and spirit. Read from the higher levels of your soul, through the wisdom and power of your core, the wisdom and warmth of your heart. Your soul, your heart, your essence already know everything, being attuned to the Absolute and Ultimate Reality, the Divine Reality. Let your heart guide you to discover what it already knows at the deepest and highest level, to discover every single thing once again from the beginning!

Where Do Angels Live?

Angels reside in the infinite spiritual dimension, the dimension of the transcendental light and pure Beingness. It is the sixth dimension of the Great Reality, a plane of absolute wholeness, bliss, and freedom. In this dimension of infinite pure light, there are unlimited possibilities. The Light is the Alpha and Omega that has the Power and the Ability to create Everything (isn't everything that exists essentially energy, vibration and light?) The Light creates not only physical matter and all of its manifestations – the universes, galaxies, stars, planets and all physical beings – but also what exists before those: laws, archetypes, ideas and forms, which were first described by Plato, the most known and highly influential Greek philosopher, one of the greatest teachers of all times.

The sixth dimension, namely the Plane of the Six Dimensions, creates and permeates whatever exists: existence itself, all the worlds, the material world, and everything within it. Therefore, the dimension of the Pure Spirit, of the Spiritual-Transcendental Light, of the Unlimited Powers and Possibilities is everywhere, at all places and it is also here. Imagine this spiritual dimension, the six-dimensional Reality, like the Supreme Aura of the entire Existence and of the World. Imagine that this Supreme Spiritual Aura not only envelops and surrounds Existence and the World, but also permeates it and fills it. It Is It. Spirit surrounds, embraces, envelops, permeates, and fills Existence, All-That-Is, the World, and the Universe, and It Really Is All of These. Everything that exists originates, emanates, and emerges from this spiritual essence, the supreme and ultimate spiritual basis and frame of all.

The dimension of Spirit, the six-dimensional plane of Reality, has a most high energy frequency and vibration and, for this reason, it is not directly perceived by human beings. Our common senses are made of physical matter and they are destined to perceive matter and the physical world. The spiritual realm is not directly visible to us through our senses.

Human beings are created in the image and likeness of the Supreme Authority and Power, and as spiritual beings, they always seek the higher, what is real, the truth. Due to their spiritual nature, they have the potential to align with and enter consciously the more expanded and higher planes of reality, the sixth dimension, the spiritual dimension that includes the angelic realms. This becomes possible through enorasis (clairvoyance) and ecstasy, through spiritual out-of-body-journeys (which are even more amazing than it sounds!) and transcendental experiences that are achieved through meditation, prayer, spiritual practices, etc. This is not mere imagination or self-suggestion, although it can begin like that. It is the genuine experience of higher states of awareness, higher levels of energy, and higher-than-the-ordinary everyday consciousness – namely: super-consciousness.

People may have transcendental experiences unintentionally, during intense pain (agony, despair), extreme events (accidents and near-death experiences), or conversely during intense emotional and physical pleasure (euphoria, ecstasy). During such experiences, people may perceive angelic presences or lights; they can leave their body and arise to higher dimensions of existence (the fourth and fifth dimension), or to the spiritual dimension (the sixth dimension). These are experiences of transcendence, liberation, expansion, ecstasy, euphoria, and utmost wholeness. Often, these experiences are of such a transformative nature that the person enters the path of spiritual quest and self-improvement for good. It is said that these experiences are most wisely planned by our Higher Self, our Spirit, and Soul, for our spiritual awakening and the expansion and growth of our consciousness.

Do angels have a human form and human characteristics?

Angels don't have a human form or characteristics. They are pure consciousness, energies of the Spirit, manifestations of the Divine. They are rays, powers, qualities, expressions of the Divine. Nevertheless, angels can take a human form at will.

Note: On the mental level and the energetic realm of our imagination, we can also take any form we wish – no matter if we don't actually do it, as we are not yet accustomed to this extraordinary aspect of our mind and consciousness! Taking different forms, expressing different aspects and qualities, being different things, even on the mental state, through intention and imagination, is actually a process of attunement. In other words, attunement is the process of becoming temporarily something different, turning yourself to another frequency, energy, taking another expression, manifestation, form. Practicing energetic and spiritual attunement is an excellent method for the most powerful form of healing on all levels.

Do angels have wings?

The wings are symbolic and of a deeper spiritual meaning. Angels are often depicted as having wings, as a symbol of the freedom that they experience and enjoy. They can be wherever they can think of, since they travel through the power of will alone. This resembles our dreams, where we can travel freely with no physical limitations and boundaries. We are already where our thought goes in an instant, without effort. In our dreams, we can be wherever we want, meet whomever we want, and experience anything we wish. The freedom we experience, while we sleep, is close to the freedom angels and pure spiritual beings enjoy fulltime.

Apart from the dream state, we humans may experience this kind of higher freedom during meditation, and this time, more consciously and at will. It is an amazing feeling to fly, and if you have experienced it during your sleep, you can experience it even more vividly during your deep meditative practice!

This freedom, to fly without wings, to fly in an effortless blissful way, is completely ours after our earthly life. Following the death of our physical body, which is a liberating, expanding, and uplifting experience, we ascend to higher wonderful planes of luminous exquisite existence. We enter a warm loving world of light, peace, joy, and utter freedom. Our whole being rejoices and celebrates. We are total, we are complete, we are whole. We are our spirit fully. Our spirit is our freedom and it is our divine wings. On the spiritual dimensions of Reality there are no limits and we are free, free to fly to ever higher levels of love, light and bliss!

Do angels have a gender?

Angels are not male or female – or rather, they are both male and female as they express all qualities of spirit. They are able to express and manifest the power, the authority, the protection, the stability of the spirit (male qualities), and also the love, the affection, the beauty, the healing care, and the sweet flow of the spirit (female qualities). Perhaps we perceive angels (e.g. the archangels or our guardian angel) as male or female according to what they want to convey to us, or depending on the circumstances and our needs at the time.

A Question for Thought, Meditation, and Further Study

When do you think angels appear as female and when as male? What is the reason that they appear as male or female or why we perceive them as such? Do they also appear as little children and for what reasons? Contemplate these questions.

ESOTERIC PRACTICE

Discovering the Characteristics of Angels

Sit comfortably and close your eyes.

Take a few slow deep breaths and relax.

Ask yourself with your inner voice:

"What are angels?"

Wait a little.

Observe any answer that comes to you.

Observe any idea, image, or sensation you might have.

You can hear, see, or feel the answers.

Continue with the following questions:

"Where do angels live?

What do they look like?

Do angels have wings?

Are angels male or female?

What is the purpose of their existence?

What are their qualities?

What roles and duties have been assigned to them?

How can they help mankind?

How can they help you personally?

What can you do for angels?

What advice and guidance can angels give you?"

After each question, wait a bit and observe anything that comes in mind.

Imagine that you are able to receive answers to all your questions.

Be open and receptive. Totally open and completely receptive.

Write down the answers.

If you cannot receive answers, simply repeat the exercise over the following days or when you feel like it.

This particular practice will give you important tools to enhance your intuitive perception; it will initiate your angelic connection, and increase your spiritual awareness and self-improvement.

Why Were the Angels Created?

The answer to this question lies far beyond the human intellect, reason, and understanding. It would be related to the reasons why the Divine Beingness, the Absolute Reality, created the angels. And who in this world can claim to know the mind of Ultimate Reality, the Divine Mind?

Nevertheless, there can be an attempt to answer the question of why the angels were created, based on esoteric sources, great spiritual teachers, and mystics:

1. Angels were created to worship, praise, and honor God/The Divine (according to religious scriptures).
2. God/The Divine created Angels to express and share His Infinite Love, Bliss, Ecstasy, and His Creative Will and Power (this is a more esoteric answer).
3. Angels were created to participate, help, and fulfill the Divine Plan and Purpose: they build the universes, they create the worlds and everything that exists. Angels are considered as the creative forces of spirit (this is also a more esoteric and mystical answer).
4. A human-centered answer would be that angels (or at least some of them) were created to accompany and support human beings in their long and rough journey, the transition from matter to spirit, from the limited "ego" to pure "beingness," from the lower energy of fear to the higher energy of love, from unconscious karma to conscious freedom, from darkness to Light, Illumination, and Enlightenment, from misery and limitation to Transcendence and Theosis (Divine Unification and Oneness).

A Question for Thought, Meditation, and Further Study

If you were to create an angel – and, do not worry, this is only a hypothesis and not a blasphemy! – for what purposes would you create one? Make a list of the qualities and tasks that you would assign to your wonderful celestial creation! Be for a day, in your imagination, just as a playful game, an angel co-creator!

Why were human beings created?

As we ourselves are spiritual consciousnesses inhabiting human bodies within the physical world, it is much easier to seek an answer to this question than the previous one! Again, according to esoteric seekers, mystics, and great teachers, mankind was created so that the Divine, The All-That-Is, the Ultimate Reality could temporarily and on one level experience the separation of matter and spirit, to experience individuality. The individual "self" that starts evolving within the unity of existence. The individual "I" that tries to find, discover, understand what it is, through the contrasts of the material world: day-night, female-male, strong-weak, healthy-ill, pleasant-unpleasant, joy-pain, love-hatred, security-fear, good-evil, comprehensible-incomprehensible, known-unknown, present-past.

Through the human experience – and what an extra-ordinary experience this is! – in the world of separation, the realms of "Good and Evil," the level of physical matter, Spirit is able to expand, broaden, grow and understand itself more as Oneness and Wholeness, as Complete, Perfect, Infinite, Eternal, and Divine! The Spirit is realizing itself experientially, actually, and externally. With all its senses, within the tangible and specific time-space realm. It is realizing itself through man, through me and you, through us...

The weirdest part? We ourselves chose this! We wished for it and we wanted it! And still do! Because... take a deep breath... We Are the Spirit and the Spirit Is Us! We Are One. You and me and all people, wished and wanted to understand, experience, expand and broaden ourselves more. On new levels, to new horizons, heights, and depths. In new ways and forms, even in the most dense and difficult of worlds. Even in conflict, in contrast, in separateness, in duality.

As the great mystics and seekers taught, the Light cannot understand, experience, perceive the Light, itself, its beingness, within the Light! So the Light decides to create darkness to comprehend and perceive itself more clearly and vividly. It is our very own journey of human existence, an intimate journey of self-consciousness, that declares, "I am, I exist, I am me, I am here and now!" Of self-awareness that asks "Who am I? What am I? Why? What is the meaning and purpose of it all?" A long and hard journey of self-knowledge, self-improvement, self-growth, self-acceptance, self-actualization, self-transcendence, self-love, and self-enlightenment. We are still going, always moving forward and upward and we are on a good path... the best possible path, the Divine one!

A Question for Thought, Meditation, and Further Study

If you were to create a human being, what would be the greatest gift that you would give to your creation? How far from you would you "allow" your creation to reach, how much would you allow it to experience? What would you like your creation to experience?

ESOTERIC PRACTICE

You as Creator of Your Journey on Earth

Imagine: what if you were the one to create your own existence, your own life, your own self? What would be the reasons for this creation and what would be its purpose?

Make a list of the experiences that you would wish your creation to encounter, i.e. you, yourself on Earth. You can include roles and challenges that you wish to face, professions and jobs you would like to have, people you would like to meet and connect to, places you would like to visit and live in, feelings and situations you would like to experience. Make a list of the things you would like to see, experience and learn on Earth, just as the list of "important things to see and do" that you prepare before travelling to a new place!

This exercise will assist you in thinking and perceiving yourself and your life experiences from a greater and higher perspective, to be more spiritually aware and self-conscious.

Where do we get information about angels?

We find information about angels from various sources such as:

- Personal experiences of people, many of which simply "occurred" without effort, as a divine intervention e.g. life-saving intervention of a guardian angel.
- Spiritual experiences of people who engage in spiritual practices (meditation, etc.), esoteric seekers, and mystics and their recordings.
- Religious texts like the Old and New Testament of the Bible and also sacred texts from all religions.
- Kabbalah, the esoteric and mystical part of Judaic tradition, offers in its spiritual teachings valuable insight into the world of angels.
- The New Age, the spirituality of the 20th and the 21st century, which draws knowledge from all spiritual paths and traditions, both western and eastern, has taken a special interest in angels. Contemporary writers such as Doreen Virtue, Elizabeth Clare Prophet, Diana Cooper, Gustav Davidson, Richard Webster, Hazel Raven, and many more have opened the door to the angelic realms by providing us precious knowledge with their writings, helping us connect with the angels in easy and practical ways.

Do I have to accept everything I read in books about angels? Do I have to believe what the – relevant to the subject – teachers say about angels?

No, you don't have to! But keep your mind open and your heart even more open! Aim at experiencing your own truths by following your own esoteric path. Study in depth and diligently apply your exercises, listen attentively to your intuition and your inner guidance and draw your own conclusions. Trust and believe, but also doubt and search. Both ways are essential and necessary. A truth that is not personally experienced is a useless, a dead truth. Individual, personal, direct experience turns truth into a living reality.

A Question for Thought, Meditation, and Further Study

What are the benefits of doubt? What can research, comparison, rejection, or differentiation offer us? And, on the other hand, how can we benefit from faith, acceptance, confirmation, or recognition? Are you inclined to one side more than the other? Come to the golden mean!

Are angels superior beings to humans?

Within the Divine Beingness and Reality, every single thing has its own unique and specific place, role, value, and purpose. Everything has its own righteous, supreme, and perfect place, role, value, and purpose. There is no separation between inferior and superior. Both angels and humans are pure transcendental consciousnesses and eternal perfect souls. In the plane of the sixth dimension, the dimension of spirit and light, you wouldn't distinguish one from the other since they both are manifestations of the Absolute/the Divine. They are heavenly children, spiritual rays, beings and entities, spiritual essences, and presences with infinite and unlimited possibilities. Angels and human beings are sacred cells on the divine body, divine units of infinite love and wisdom!

From a human perspective – how we people perceive things through our physical level – angels do have greater freedom and consciousness of Who/What They Are and of what they can do. Angels have higher vibrational frequency; they move and function from a superior, more expanded plane of perception, action, and existence. However, people have chosen a harder path, through the plane of physical matter, the world of duality and separation, in order to fulfill the Divine Plan and Purpose; a difficult journey that humans themselves as eternal spirits have willingly chosen and joyfully planned and co-created. Mankind has actualized a bold and distant journey of consciousness. Nevertheless, spiritually and in their essence, Angels and Humans are siblings.

A Question for Thought, Meditation, and Further Study

If angels are "superior" to human beings, in what ways would that be true? In what characteristics, aspects, and areas you think angels are superior? At the same time, in what ways could human beings be "superior" to angels? Take some quiet moments to reflect on this.

The idea of angels attracts me and at the same time it scares me. Is that normal? How do I overcome my fear?

It is in the nature of human beings to fear the unknown. However, people need to discover and awaken the strength and the boldness that also exist within them so they can enter the plane of higher knowledge and esoteric experience – that is, if they want to move away from the limitations of their "ego" and further from what they have so far learned and conquered. Again, it is in the nature of man, the constant thirst for knowledge, experience, discovery, growth, evolution, re-creation. All the paths of Enlightenment and Theosis pass through the angelic realms, since Angels are an absolutely essential and precious part of the Divine Reality, the Divine Beingness in its most beloved and wise, sacred, and holy manifestations.

A Question for Thought, Meditation, and Further Study

If you are scared of angels, reflect on what it is that you are truly scared of. Is it worth being afraid? How can you overcome your fear? Perhaps to stop being afraid is simply a decision, a turn, a new perception? Make a truce with Angels and the invisible spiritual side of Existence. They are full of Good!

ESOTERIC PRACTICE

Overcoming the Fear of the Spiritual Element

Most people are afraid of the spiritual element and the spiritual realm, of spirituality in general. They are even afraid of the angels – *especially* the angels! In the same way, they are afraid of anything good and positive: love, abundance, truth, honesty, freedom, power, happiness! Although they actually desire all those positive and beautiful things in life, their ego revolts against the changes, their lower self feels more comfortable with what they already know: the small, the limited, the poor, the selfish. Our deeper and essential need for liberation, love, truth, brightness, and happiness should try its hardest and fight a hard "battle!"

If you feel that in some lesser or greater degree, on some or more levels, you are afraid of the Good, of the Spiritual (which is the Source of all positivity and of all and every good that exists), and of the angels (the embodiments of all good and positive energies), but at the same time you want to move forward in your spiritual development, then you can try the following exercise.

With your eyes open, just consider the following:

Think of how, in the universe and in life in general, there are two opposite forces: love and fear.

Where there is love, fear doesn't exist. Love negates fear, just as light negates darkness.

Where there is fear, there is lack of love.

When you love, you are not afraid and when you are afraid, you cannot truly love!

Fear is limiting; love is liberating.

Fear paralyzes you; love mobilizes you.

Fear makes you stagnant and miserable; love makes you flow and flourish.

Is it worth to live in fear, out of fear?

What is the reason and what is the purpose of living in fear?

There is no reason or purpose worth living in fear.

You don't deserve to live in this state; you are worth more than that, much more.

You are worth of living in love, in a state of love.

You, now, have another chance to realize, decide, and choose to live more with love, more in love, more out of love, more on love.

You have a chance to realize, decide, and choose to think, feel, express, and experience more love.

To be more love.

It was love that was taught by the greatest teachers of mankind, not fear.

The Divine, the angels, the spiritual plane, and spirituality are love, all love and only love.

They are full of good, all good and only good!

You can free yourself from fear.

Face and speak directly to you fear. Confront it. Ask from your fear to walk away, to abandon your body and your entire being.

It is possible and it happens. It is happening right now.

Imagine fear walking away, vanishing from your body and your entire being.

Fear has no place within you or within your life.

Now, ask love to fill you, to completely fill your entire body and mind. Your whole self, your being.

It happens, it is possible.

You love the energy of love, you love to love and you love Love.

Love is your new state of being.

Affirm your loving intention aloud or silently:

"I leave fear behind and I enter the higher energy of pure love! I fear no more, I only love and I truly love to love, I love Love! I heal myself and I replace all fear with love! I reach a place of fearlessness about all positive and good things, states, and energies. Fearlessness about the True, the Real, Angels, Spirit, the Divine. My love for spirituality, the spiritual side of existence and all its angels grows in each moment! Only good comes from my loving relationship with spirituality, the Angels and Spirit and I fully enjoy it to the deepest degree! I receive and experience all the positive and good things that Love offers in such a divine abundance!"

Take a few deep breaths.

You are now full of love and you are fearless!

You affirm it, you believe it, you feel it and you know it deep within. You absolutely deserve it, you choose it consciously, you conclusively decide it. And So It Is!

You are fearless, full of love!

From now on, Love equals Spirituality and Spirituality equals Love.

Love equals Spirit and Spirit equals Love.

Love equals the Angels and the Angels equal Love.

I am not sure if I believe in one God, in a supreme being that watches over us, or in "beings with wings!" Is there an alternative way to perceive the information about angels?

Yes, you can see it from the perspective of angels being the Virtues of Man, his superior ideals, his highest, most beautiful and loving expressions and manifestations. You can also approach, think of, or perceive God as the Totality and Wholeness of Existence, of the Cosmos and the Universe, of All That Exists, all known and unknown things. The Total, Absolute, and Supreme Reality.

Thus, when you attune to angels, you resonate with the most beautiful, supreme qualities and virtues a person can create and manifest in their life. From this perspective, each spiritual practice (meditation, invocation, prayer) can help and inspire us manifest our higher and greater potential, to restore, recharge, and reprogram our minds in order to positively affect all that we are and all that we can be.

A Question for Thought, Meditation, and Further Study

There are various ways to look at a topic, an issue, or a situation. For example, an apple can be approached and perceived in many ways. It can be seen, smelled, and tasted. A child, an adult, and an animal perceive the apple in different ways. Similarly, a poet, a painter, a physicist, a chemist, and a philosopher, they all perceive and consider the apple differently. Everyone has something diverse and possibly unique to say about the apple. These are parallel perspectives, interpretations, and levels of information. The same applies to angels. Could you consider and approach the topics of angels, Spirit, and the Divine from various perspectives? Can you perceive alternative ways of understanding and interpretation? Could these ways, instead of negating, be complementary and possibly enhance and enrich each other? Take some minutes to think about it.

Are angels a substitute for God?

No, angels do not substitute God. On the contrary: they reinforce our love, our bond with

God. Angels are divine rays, pure forces, and intelligent energies of loving light that direct and show the way to God, the Divine. Angels uplift us to the Highest and Supreme Reality, to the Highest and Supreme Consciousness. They connect us to the Total and Absolute Spiritual Unity and Wholeness of All-That-Is. Angels are a most precious part of Divine Beingness; they fulfill specific duties; they are unique and irreplaceable just like human beings are.

To think about the angels is to think about God, the Divine, in all of its angelic, holy, and sacred forms. The Divine Source and Power does not take offense, if we think of, invite, and connect to our celestial siblings! On the contrary, that is what It has in Its mind and in Its heart for us; that is what we are – divinely – meant and urged to do!

Do angels understand the human language?

Languages were created by human beings to communicate thoughts, feelings, and meanings. Angels can understand the entire spectrum of all human languages because they directly perceive what we emit, our auric field, an energy field of vibrations, light and colors, which is created from our thoughts, feelings, and actions. When we radiate joy, love, gratitude, appreciation, pure selfless thoughts, and other high-frequency feelings, angels are naturally and instantly drawn energetically to us.

A Question for Thought, Meditation, and Further Study

Can you imagine the language of angels? What does it consist of? Sounds, colors, energies? Is it a language of the mind, of the heart, of the spirit? Could you approach the language of angels? Can you be open to it? To attune to it? To communicate with the angels?

Are there incarnated angels, angels born as human beings?

It is quite rare for a human being to have an angelic origin. There is a possibility that a human being might have had angelic duties before or during their current incarnation. Angels do not need to take on human form, as they are able to fulfill their tasks in their incorporeal, more free spiritual forms. However, angels can, for a short time, assume a human form, in order to help or to fulfill a specific earthly purpose. Or even just for fun! Yes, Spirit can have a sense of humor; it was it that created it in the first place!

A Question for Thought, Meditation, and Further Study

If there are incarnated angels, – that is angels in human form – who do you think they are? Can you "spot" someone? Are you thinking of someone that fits the description?

Are there human beings that became angels?

Yes, at the end of the long earthly journey, a human being can become an angel or follow other paths, such as to become a spiritual teacher or to unite with the Divine while preserving their individuality (their individual journey).

A Question for Thought, Meditation, and Further Study

Would you like to be an angel? If you were an angel, what kind of angel would you be?

Do angels evolve?

We do not really know. It is quite possible that angels follow their own distinct celestial evolution by serving Creation.

A Question for Thought, Meditation, and Further Study

What do you believe? Do angels evolve? If yes, in what ways? Or perhaps they are absolutely evolved, perfect already and always?

Do angels feel fear, anger, sadness, jealousy, hate, or any of the other negative emotions?

No, these feelings correspond to very low vibrational levels, below the sixth dimension of reality, the realm of absolute spirit and transcendental light in which angels reside.

Do angels have free will?

Angels do not have free will in the sense that we humans do, to choose between right and wrong and good and evil. It is more like angels possess the supreme will and intention, the Divine one.

Who are the most important angels?

The most important angel is the one closest to us and this is not by mere chance. This angel is our guardian angel, the most important angel for our soul. Our guardian angel accompanies us, protects, supports, and guides us through our entire earthly life. They are our spiritual guide and partner, connected intimately, directly, specifically and exclusively with us. Our guardian angel is the Divine's most precious and personal "gift" to each one of us!

Following our guardian angel, the very next angel in importance (with respects to our earthly journey, since all angels are absolutely important and cannot be compared to each other) is Archangel Michael, the archangel who is best known to man. He is as close as it gets to the Divine and at the same time the closest angelic being to humanity. Archangel Michael is the Power of God, of the Divine, manifested in form and action. His name means "God is my Power," or "Great God," and he protects and guides all humanity. Archangel Michael fights and defeats the evil and usually he is depicted holding a sword. He is the Light that negates darkness. His element is fire, one of the highest elements in nature, the mastery of which fueled the entire human evolution. Archangel Michael is probably the highest, most direct, and well-known manifestation of the Divine on Earth.

The angels that come next in importance and closeness to humanity are the Archangels

Gabriel, Raphael, and Uriel. Also known from the Hierarchy of Angels are the Seraphim and the Cherubim. The Kabbalah tradition, esotericism, mysticism, sacred texts, and spiritual researchers have offered a lot of additional information about angels. New Age contemporary philosophy with its broad horizon embraced the information about angels from the all traditions and popularized it, making it more accessible to a large number of people.

A Question for Thought, Meditation, and Further Study

Do you believe that you have ever seen, sensed, or met an angel? Perhaps, that an angel has helped you, protected you, guided you, warned you, supported you, or healed you at any given time in your life? Who was it? Take some moments to think about it and meditate on this heaven-sent experience.

ESOTERIC PRACTICE

What do you know about the four archangels?

Take a piece of paper and make four lists; one list for each of the four major and most known archangels: Michael, Raphael, Gabriel, and Uriel. In each list write down pieces of information you know about each archangel and the information you will discover from your ongoing research. By attributing different characteristics and elements to each archangel, you will have the chance to feel clearly their different energies and qualities.

Who are the supreme angels and archangels?

From a human perspective, we do not and cannot really know. The highest angels, the supreme energies of light and consciousness, vibrate in such high levels that they vanish into the infinite light. They completely merge into the transcendental dimensions of Divine Beingness. Man is not able to resonate with such supreme vibrational frequencies of light, as perhaps it is energetically impossible; it would be like landing on the sun with our physical body!

What we do know is that all the known archangels – Michael, Raphael, Gabriel, Uriel – are supreme, almighty angels of the highest, infinite spirit and the ecstatic Divine light! Archangels are the bright gates to the Divine. They are far more important, great, multidimensional, and luminous than anything we can possibly perceive, understand or experience from a human perspective!

We also know that the first celestial sphere in the angelic hierarchy consists of the Seraphim, the Cherubim and the Thrones that are considered to be the highest angelic beings, energies, and super-consciousnesses. Furthermore, Archangel Metatron, Shekhinah, and Elohim (based mostly on Kabbalistic sources) are considered celestial beings of the highest light and of absolute creative power, close or next to the Divine Throne (Divine Consciousness); it is possible that this is a symbol of their absolute and complete divine consciousness and the total awareness of All-That-Is, participating in the boundless cosmic bliss, oneness, ecstasy, wholeness, and perfection of the Divine.

A Question for Thought, Meditation, and Further Study

How do you imagine the highest angels? How do you imagine the highest energies, consciousnesses, intelligences, and forces of the universe and of the cosmos? Close your eyes for a few moments and think about this supreme angelic reality!

Are there "fallen" angels?

Yes, fallen angels do exist but they are a minority group within the greater angelic family.

We do not know the exact reasons for their existence and there are various points of view. It seems that fallen angels are necessary and valuable for the Divine Purpose of the Whole and they are an essential part of the Divine Plan. People should not be afraid of the fallen angels but try to understand the purpose and nature of their existence. Fallen angels are no worse than the negative elements, the fears, and flaws of humans. We can say that fallen/dark angels are the representation, the embodiment of the human flaws, of the negative energies, thoughts, and feelings (both individual and collective). They are nothing more, nothing worse.

The "demon," the devil, the enemy exists within us in the form of our lower, negative self. It is the selfish one, the greedy, the hurt, who wants to retaliate the hurt; the one that doesn't forgive, the one denying compassion and love; the inconsiderate, the intolerant; the one who depends, attaches and clings; the materialist, the arrogant one. The separated, the conflicting one. The jealous and the hateful, the fearful, the sad, and the miserable one; our shadow. This is the demon that we need to expel and overcome. At first by understanding, comforting, accepting, loving, and healing our lower self, all of our parts. With the support of the forces of light that are infinite, eternal, overabundant, all-wise, all-loving, and all-powerful, we will gradually and eventually transcend our "demons."

It is truly an amazing and wondrous process and the essence, purpose, and meaning of life itself; of life on Earth, of being human. Gradually, through a great variety and diversity of human and earthly experiences, experiencing many lives, roles, and lessons, all people, with no exception, actualize this purpose of life. The transcendence of their ego and lower self, the illumination of their shadow. All human beings are primordially destined to their complete and total enlightenment and, finally, to Theosis, the complete unification of their individual consciousness with the Divine Beingness.

Don't fallen angels have a separate entity from human beings? Aren't they separate and independent of man, his lower self, and his ego? Don't they exist "out there"?

Fallen angels are separate entities from human beings; they exist in the lower astral plane (the lower planes of the fourth dimension), but it through us resonating with them through our own low vibrations of negative thoughts and feelings that we attract our "demons" – we invite and experience them and we may even choose to walk together with them (to be attached to them). It all comes down to our own choice, our own energy field (our thoughts, feelings, and actions), our own consciousness. At the same time, there is a greater reality which is almost unconceivable to the human mind and yet is experienced by the mystics and the spiritually awakened, conscious, and enlightened human beings. This greater reality is that God, the Divine, is within us, as our divine essence and core, and it is far superior to all the darkness and negativity that exists in the world.

A Question for Thought, Meditation, and Further Study

What is the reason that fallen angels exist? Why do negative feelings, negative thoughts, negative actions, negative choices exist in the first place? Why is there darkness and evil?

Are angels a new trend? Or perhaps now there are more angels on Earth?

If angels are becoming a new trend, this is something wonderful and exquisite! It is about time that something so illuminating, beautiful, and positive becomes a trend!

However, it's not only a matter of trend; humanity emerges into a new stage of consciousness reflected in a transforming spiritual awareness that will lead to collective spiritual growth and advancement. The soul's awakening to its true nature will bring transformation to the collective psyche of humanity. Humanity reaches adulthood after experiencing a violent adolescence; it is ready to get out from its self-inflicted limitation and its existential selfishness. Humanity is ready to connect to, communicate, and work together with its siblings on a universal, cosmic, and spiritual level. The flame of humanity's spiritual quest is always burning and it is burning ever brighter.

I notice that angels and spirituality are widely commercialized. There are many books, meditation CDs, magazines, cards, posters, crystals, workshops, and so on. Isn't all of this commercialization a superficial and even disrespectful approach to important topics such as angels and spirituality?

The current mass conception of spiritual matters and their increased commercialization show that spirituality is more popular than ever on a collective scale. Commercializing aspects of spiritual traditions is a means of sharing more information, ideas, and energies. This was and is the wish and purpose of mystics and spiritual teachers. The mass availability of spirituality can cover various needs and give ease and comfort, joy and happiness, artistry and beauty, purpose and meaning. It is wonderful that angels are a part of this interest for spiritual matters and because of that their voice is reaching to us.

Consider the opposite: would it be better if there were products and services for all matters except the spiritual ones? Can spirituality be inspired without teachers – human beings who have advanced before us? Workshops and seminars, books and CDs are ways to make their teachings available. And you need to give something of yourself in order to receive. You need to travel to meet these teachers, offer your time, attention, focus, love, and dedication. You often need to offer money, for their time and effort, since they too are human beings living in this material dimension with all that it entails. You need to offer money in order to read books and receive sessions and seminars that offer you knowledge and skills, which illuminate you and brighten your life. Money and commerce are not negative per se; they can be used and they are indeed partly being used for good; they make our life easier and they serve our needs.

In our days, the astonishing abundance of the Earth and of the spirit is expressed with a plethora of books and other products that offer us precious, useful, practical, beautiful elements and moments... it is something we have been longing for, both on a spiritual and on a material level; we have been yearning for such a long time to receive this abundance. This overabundance of knowledge and all good things on all levels!

Like all things in life, similarly in commerce, in products, and services, whether we offer or we receive time, energy, money, products, or services, there is a higher way to do so: the pure, the enlightened, the spiritual way. We need to act with love, respect, and awareness; to have good intentions and act for the common good; to act without attachment and dependency; with freedom, wholeness, and oneness; to act authentically, genuinely, responsibly, and with integrity. It takes decisive and conscious choice, the practice of discrimination, to apply our full intelligence, our reason and intuition and to be able to find the balance between the two. The ancient Greeks expressed the effort for equilibrium with "*metron ariston*," meaning "all good things in moderation." If we can think and act in such a higher way, then spirituality will no longer be a part of our material life but, on the contrary, our material life, including the issues of money and commerce, will become a part of our spirituality.

Is belief in angels a superstition of the past when scientific research and knowledge had not yet advanced?

No! The universe, the cosmos, and existence are full and overabundant with life, energy, intelligence, and consciousness. There are an infinite number of different forms of life, energy, intelligence, and consciousness in the universe. Even more so in other worlds, on other planes of reality, and other dimensions! Angels are higher energies, forces, intelligences, and consciousnesses. They do exist! When human beings realize and accept it, once they open up to the possibility of their existence, they directly experience and see for themselves this spiritual reality. And vice versa: when human beings experience and see for themselves this spiritual reality, they open up, realize, and accept the existence of angels!

Is there any chance that science will ever recognize and prove the existence of angels?

When it comes to answer questions regarding the future, the answer is: "sure, why not!" That would be extremely interesting! At the same time, if this does not happen, does it really matter? Can science prove Love? Can it prove its subjective personal unique experience; can it do justice to it? Does this make love "inferior" or "less real" than the things science can study, measure, and prove? Does this make Love "less love"? No! Love is Love, a true and real experience and therefore a truth and a reality in itself.

Does the belief in angels arise from the fear of man for the unknown? Or is it perhaps the fear of death? Or is it the hope for a better life?

Our fears and hopes certainly play a role but there is much more to it. Truth is that we are not alone in this world and in the universe. Just because someone or something is not visible to us or not perceivable by our earthly/physical senses, it doesn't mean that it does not exist. The universe is full of life, intelligence, and beings, both material and immaterial. Life is full of life! Perhaps the belief in angels partly comes from man's existential fears or from the hope for something higher (eternal life, transition to other planes of existence after death), but that doesn't mean that other forms of life or incorporeal beings do not exist.

The universe and existence are far greater, more creative, inventive, vivid, intelligent, and diverse than we can ever imagine, expect, hope, or fear. Our human mind and all its capabilities, including imagination, fear, and hope, are an infinitesimal part of creation and the universe. We can't even begin to imagine what is out there in the greater scheme of things! As the Divine, Reality, Existence, and All-That-Is are immanent and mirrored in man, being created "in the image and likeness of God," man has the sense, the primary notion, and essence of the divine and the whole within him. The greatest fear or the greatest hope both have their limitations; they cannot produce the infinite. The eternal, the perfect, the infinite have existed before humanity. These states or concepts were not created by man; they were discovered by man through fear and hope and, above all, through his spiritual growth and expansion of consciousness.

Keep in mind that reality is far more rich and multidimensional than what we can ever think of or perceive. Nothing is as it appears to be, since this world, the universe, is a world of appearances, a world of phenomena. Phenomena are by their nature wonderful and beautiful to perceive, experience, and study yet they are a mere aspect of Reality.

So, angels and spirituality, believing in other dimensions, God, etc. are not just creations of the human mind?

Similarly to the previous question, be aware of the fact that the human mind and consciousness are a manifestation within the universe, within the existence, within the Sublime, the Transcendent, the Absolute Whole, which is infinite, unlimited, and unknown. Although the part contains in essence the whole, it is not superior or more intelligent than the whole. An analogy can be found in the connection of our cells to our whole body. A cell (humanity), although a unique and precious part of the body (total reality, the divine), has in its essence the whole body within itself (divinity), but it is not greater or superior than the whole body. There are so many other cells (other energies, intelligences, and beings, such as the angels) and the whole of the body (total reality, divinity) is far greater, full of wonders and miracles, transcendental and unknown to the cell. The fact that the cell thinks, philosophizes, and meditates about other cells and the whole body is a gift of the whole body's far superior intelligence and consciousness.

Isn't it an exaggeration to give spiritual attributes and characteristics of consciousness to the material/physical universe?

It could also be the other way around. Perhaps the universe gave spiritual attributes and characteristics of consciousness to us. Taking it even further, it could even be that Spirit/Consciousness gave us earthly, physical, and material attributes!

How can I convince myself that angels truly exist?

You can't! I am kidding... (sort of)! However, I can share my personal experience and research, and that of many others as well: it is the direct personal experience and contact with angels that can convince you. Only the experience is strong enough. So, instead of asking how you can convince yourself, ask how you can experience the energy and presence of angels!

How can I experience the energy and presence of angels?

The book you hold in your hands contains all the secrets of angels, not just in theory but also in practice! It contains the true experience of angels! Read the book a few times thoroughly and carry out the exercises. Don't read superficially. Read deeply. Reflect and think about everything you read. Become open, attentive, receptive, and sensitive. Become more aware. Pause, relax, and meditate. Study and meditate on a daily basis. Practice all the techniques diligently. There is no way you will not experience the energy and presence of angels!

How many times should I read this book?

One time is not enough! Read it a few times. You will notice that each time you read the book, you will discover new things, new layers, and develop a deeper understanding. You will increasingly be able to vividly experience the spiritual dimensions and Divine Reality; the higher energies and frequencies as well as the higher beings and intelligences that we, from our narrow perspective and limited point of view, simply call "Angels"!

Where does the material of the answers and meditations of this book come from?

The material of the book comes from two sources of knowledge:

The inner and the outer source.

The inner source is the internal wisdom and knowledge that we all human beings possess (as we are made in the image and likeness of the Divine) within the deepest depths and at the highest heights of our existence and beingness.

Many years of daily esoteric study and research, as well as working intensively with spiritual practices such as introspection and concentration, meditation and visualization, prayer and invocation, and many energy healing techniques have provided me with insight and a wealth of personal experiences concerning the spiritual, including our beloved angels.

The outer source of knowledge that gave the material of this book comes from external re-sources, a variety of books written about angels, old and contemporary books of a religious or spiritual nature. A great number of mystics and spiritual teachers who have devoted their lives to the study of Spirit and of the angels have made this possible.

At the end of the book, you can find a comprehensive bibliography on the topic of angels.

ESOTERIC PRACTICE

Angelic Promenade

Take a serene walk outdoors. Select a natural place where you can find peace, such as a garden, a park, a forest, a lake, the mountain, or the beach.

Walk slowly, in a relaxed and meditative way, in any direction you feel drawn to. Observe, notice, be aware, notice all the elements. Pay attention to them, respect them, greet them, and enjoy them to the fullest with all of your senses. Soak in all the details of the surrounding environment – the light, the water, the sun, the sky, the colors, the sounds, and the smells. Touch the grass, the flowers, the plants, and the trees. Feel their vibrancy and aliveness.

Bring the angels in your mind; think about them. Talk to them mentally, ask the angels to surround and accompany you... to guide and bless you... open up, become receptive and ultra-sensitive... feel their love and their light while you walk... angelic love and angelic light. Think about it and attune to its frequency... feel Mother Earth, Mother Nature... the consciousness of Mother Nature, of Mother Earth, its beloved powerful energy...

As you continue your walk, feel more and more that you are taking a spiritual walk, a walk of light, peace, healing, and love... an angelic walk. As you walk, cleanse your feelings and thoughts, let them go and at the same time, regenerate your body and spirit, completely energize yourself.

Take deep breaths, full of life and vitality... breathe in and accept and receive all the goods that Mother Nature and Mother Earth offer... all the goods the angels bestow upon you... nature is sacred, nature is divine, a Sacred Divine Mother, your Sacred Divine Mother... with the angels above you, around you and by your side... such a heavenly earthly experience!

ESOTERIC PRACTICE

Angelic Bath

This specific technique is recommended for deep energetic and spiritual purification/catharsis and it is highly beneficial for both body and mind; it regenerates, invigorates, and rejuvenates the body, the mind, and the psyche.

Fill the bathtub with warm water. Throw in two to three fistfuls of natural unrefined sea salt and a few drops of an essential oil of your choice (lavender and rose are wonderful). You can also add elixirs and your favorite crystals, such as a clear quartz or a rose quartz.

Call upon the Angels of Light; ask them to bless and charge the water with their bright angelic qualities and energies. Soak in the water; stay for 15 minutes or more. Relax and enjoy the experience.

Alternatively, you can also call upon the Angels of Light while taking a shower. Ask them to bless and infuse the water with their pure angelic qualities and energies and feel the water rinsing you in body, mind, and soul. You can also gently scrub yourself with natural unrefined sea salt.

Whether you are taking a shower or a long warm bath, relax and meditate while you are within the element of water. Invite and feel the light, care, and love, in the company of your angelic friends. Relax and let yourself feel and absorb deeply the vital healing energies.

Apply the technique of the Angelic Bath whenever you want to cleanse and purify, regenerate and rejuvenate yourself. It helps you assimilate, absorb, and integrate all higher energies, especially following some healing/energetic/spiritual work, such as intense and deep meditation.

Note: *The combination of warm water and meditation might lead to very deep relaxation. Make sure you stay safe in the water.*

ESOTERIC PRACTICE

Angelic Altar

The Angelic Altar is a place of spiritual focus for meditation, introspection, relaxation, prayer, and for all healing, energy, and spiritual work. You can create the altar in a part of your house that you feel is appropriate, perhaps in a beautiful and positive spot where no one will disturb you and you can have privacy.

Place on your Angelic Altar objects that have spiritual meaning and value or special energy. For example, icons of saints and angels, spiritual books, prayers, candles, healing crystals, or other objects with energetic and healing properties, frankincense, incense sticks, and so on.

Relax for a few minutes, then bring your hands in a prayer position and dedicate your altar to the Highest Good, the Highest Plan, the Divine, and its angels. Call upon the angels to watch over your personal altar and to bless it. Visualize a shower, a stream, or a waterfall of pure bright light and spiritual energy to flow over your altar, infusing, energizing, and activating it. Repeat the process of dedication for two more days.

Now you have your own altar; a pure energetic place of focus, relaxation and meditation, for praying and for the healing of your mind and spirit. You can communicate and align with your essence, the spiritual dimension of existence, the Source, and its all-luminous and hyper-luminous, all-loving and hyper-loving angels!

ESOTERIC PRACTICE

Angelic Box

Choose a large box that you like where you can place objects related to your spiritual work. Within it store books, notes, prayers and symbols, spiritual images and icons, crystals, and other energetic spiritual objects that inspire you.

Name your box "Angelic Box" and wholeheartedly dedicate it to the angels. Draw or write on the inside or outside part of the box energy symbols or spiritual concepts and words.

Hold the box in your hands and visualize or feel bright angelic light surrounding your box. Ask the angels to energize and charge it with all the highest spiritual qualities! Feel the loving healing light filling your box.

Inside the box you can place notes with your wishes or goals or notes with the names of people who ask for help and support. It is a tiny angelic room, full of energy, light, and love! Handle it with care, tenderness, respect, and love! In this angelic space, welcome the people (by placing the notes with their names) that need support, your own goals and wishes, and your favorite energy healing and spiritual objects.

Every now and then, lovingly hold the box in your hands and energize/charge it with the help of angels, while you visualize and feel the bright angelic light overflowing the box.

ESOTERIC PRACTICE

Angelic Diary

In your path of personal growth and improvement, it is necessary to keep a diary, an Angelic Diary of energetic and spiritual thoughts and experiences. It will be a diary of spiritual development and evolution, your own spiritual biography.

Take a notebook that you would like to use for this purpose and hold it in your hands. Relax for a few minutes, then bring your hands in a prayer position while still holding the diary between your hands. Dedicate your diary to the Highest Good, the Highest Plan, the Divine, and its angels. Call upon the angels to charge and bless the diary with angelic qualities and illuminating energies. Repeat the process of dedication for two more days.

After this process, use your diary to write down your spiritual experiences, your thoughts and feelings, everyday events, dreams, prayers and meditations, ideas and inspirations, drawings and symbols. You will now have a complete and comprehensive Angelic Diary of your personal growth, self-awareness, and self-actualization. You can express and manifest yourself, your deeper being but also you can study, compare and remember. Your utmost interesting Earthly-Heavenly-Divine Journey will be recorded and documented!

PART II

Contact with Angels

I don't believe something until I see it with my own eyes. I am skeptical about believing in angels!

Being a skeptic is a good thing! If you cannot see something, how can you believe in it? Experiencing something has higher value and meaning than learning it parrot-fashion or pretending that you believe in it. When you experience, see, and live something, will you believe? Maybe not... keep a door open to the unknown and the incorporeal, to see beyond what it appears to be; a door open to the transcendent, to the possibilities and probabilities. Angels want us to become explorers of heaven, of the unknown and transcendent, to be courageous and brave. Faith takes courage. So does love. And so does insight. It takes courage for one to do the leap of consciousness to reach personal growth. Freedom, knowledge, and awareness require boldness and courage! Dare and you will only lose what you don't need – what limits you. Dare and you will win whatever you desire. You will get everything that you deserve and that belongs to you, everything that is offered to you.

How can I proceed if I am skeptical?

Try reciting the following affirmations three times each, slowly, with intention. The affirmations can "vibrate" your being, create new possibilities and opportunities, and call forth an energetic opening, an expansion of consciousness and perception. You can also create your own affirmations and repeat them each morning and evening. Affirmations have a way to inspire and motivate you.

Affirmations:
I keep my mind open to receive... everything is possible!
I keep my heart open... I am safe and everything is love!
I am willing and I want to discover what exists beyond the apparent.
I am willing and I want to be open to the unknown!
I am willing and I want to discover what people call "angels," "spirit," "God!"
I am willing and I want to discover what the inner planes, the higher dimensions, and the heavenly worlds are!
I connect, continuously, daily, with my essence, the divine element within me, my higher self, and soul.

I perceive better and I perceive more!
I look in the eyes of whatever is out there.
I look beyond the veil.
I remember.
I want to evolve! I want to be enlightened! I am ready for an energetic leap. I actualize the leap of consciousness! A leap of faith and trust!
I have all the courage and the strength that I need to acquire new information and knowledge!
I turn fully to the Light and to Love. I see, I feel, I hear, I perceive, and I experience clearer than ever.
The Higher Power knows. I let myself to the Higher Power.

If the angels would say something, what would that be?

They would tell us that they love us. They love us truly, deeply, substantially, unconditionally, without judgment and limitations. Angels love us wholly, purely, and luminously. They love us in an impersonal/existential/cosmic way, just as the sun loves a flower. They also love us in a most intimate, close, and personal way, like a mother loves her child.

Angels would tell us that they are always near us.

Angels would also tell us that we are divine creatures, divine beings, with divine powers and unlimited creative potential. We discover and we unfold gradually our consciousness, our spirituality, and our divinity. Our journey on Earth and in the space-time continuum is temporary; we have chosen it from a divine point of view, and it is all worth it! Our higher essence is never in danger of being lost and nothing earthly can diminish it. We are "angels" (eternal spirits) "disguised" as humans. We are not humans having spiritual experiences; we are divine consciousnesses and spiritual presences that are having human experiences... it is true; things can be deceiving!

I don't want to experience more pain, fear, insecurity, sadness, or conflicts in my life! Can angels help me with that?

Angels cannot stop the flow of life and that flow includes all the lessons gained from all the negativity, pain, darkness, difficulties, obstacles, contrasts, conflicts, and diseases that we experience. As we gradually become awakened and evolve, the painful and negative part of our life loses its power and becomes smaller. Our consciousness expands and occupies more and more space in our life and our being. We become more conscious, and thus more spiritual; we act with more awareness, wisdom, and love; we experience more light, power, harmony, serenity, unity, freedom, wholeness, our true nature, our essence, and purpose. We receive our life lessons in additional ways, in more intelligent and less painful ways. Gradually, we begin to receive our lessons in a more positive way and not only in the hard, painful way. A spiritually awakened and conscious person experiences broadness of thoughts, feelings, actions, reasons, choices, situations and not just the limited unconscious ones. Angels don't deprive us of happiness or pain. They shine as bright examples of absolute freedom, joy, wholeness, wisdom, and love so we humans can learn from them and follow our most conscious, spiritual, whole, and higher nature.

How and in what areas can the angels help us?

Angels can help us to connect with the Spiritual, the All, the Divine, the Highest Source and Oneness, the Transcendental Principle and Power. Furthermore, with their guidance and protection, their empowerment and upliftment through their energies (qualities of the spirit, like joy, freedom, love, vital energy, etc.), they enhance our spiritual growth and accelerate our spiritual evolution. Angels bring messages from higher realms, they give answers to our questions, they guard and protect us from danger, encourage and comfort us in times of need, and inspire and heal us with their benevolent energies. Angels can help us with all our problems, challenges, and daily life. Literally all! Their energy is beneficial and useful on all levels of our existence and in all areas of our life. Angels are the Light, the Higher, the Good in action, the Good manifested, the vibration, the energy, the essence of Good. And Good is Truth, Love, Awareness, Wisdom, Wholeness, Freedom, and Bliss.

Why don't angels always help us?

Angels are always helping us: it is the Divine Help manifested in angelic form and action!

However, angels can't intervene into our lives without our permission. Human beings were given the gift of free will, and the angels cannot go against our wishes, choices, or the various forms of limitations we live with: energetic, mental, and emotional. They cannot go against the law of Karma, either: the concept of an action that causes an effect, the law of cause and effect, that keeps Everything in Order and Harmony. Karma is the quintessence of the Divine Justice in the Universe: we receive and experience what we have created individually and collectively, consciously or unconsciously. Karma teaches us to take self-responsibility as it makes us feel responsible for our actions in every situation. Angels, together with the universal law of Karma – and not against it – help us to become awakened, to actualize the higher powers and potential of our spirit and soul that are: Pure Love-Wholeness-Freedom.

So, angels always and continuously help us. However, there might be some karmic lessons, or some mental and energetic limitations (which we should lift or heal first) as well as our free will, which is sacred. Our first step is to put our intention and permission out to the angels. If we want help in our lives, all we have to do is ask! God, Spirit, and Angels can offer us assistance if we use our free will to call upon them directly and clearly. "Ask and it shall be given to you."

A Question for Thought, Meditation, and Further Study

Are you clear on what you want and where you are headed? Are you asking angels what you truly desire? Are you asking clearly and precisely? Is there a possibility that angels answer your requests in ways different than the ones you expect or perceive?

Why don't angels help me even when I ask them to help me?

Angels help you in ways that you don't imagine or you don't see, yet. Divine guidance comes in various forms. Angels make suggestions and offer guidance via intuition, synchronicities, thoughts, impressions, hunches, etc. You can listen to their suggestions or ignore them and in either case, angels will continue to guide you with ultimate love. If you were at the end of your life and looked back, you would exclaim, "Yes! There was a reason, a purpose for everything! It was for the best!" Part of the beauty of life is found in what the future holds (the unknown), in the element of surprise, in the continuous quest for answers, in change and in the flow of life.

What can I ask from the angels?

We can ask angels anything we wish, from the smallest request to the most important. We can ask for love, romance, good work, comfort, healing, health, strength, independence, freedom, life free from addictions, friendship, vitality, wellbeing, abundance, delight, joy, serenity, calmness, relaxation, rejuvenation, creativity, communication, companionship, beauty, optimal body weight, protection, purification, self-awareness, self-improvement, enlightenment, guidance, inspiration, ideas, answers, and solutions. We can ask something for ourselves or on behalf of another person, of the Earth, of our planet. We can ask all good things for ourselves, our friends, our family, our "enemies" (if there are any), for people that we don't know, even for animals and plants.

The angels are always there, waiting for us to ask for their help and guidance, ready to offer us with unconditional love. Whatever we ask, it needs to be for the Good, the Highest Good. It may be that we know what the Highest Good is, or we have a hunch, or perhaps we don't see it yet. The Highest Good is that which includes everything and everyone, the common good, the good that can be perceived from a broader, a higher spiritual perspective. It is the Good from a higher state of awareness and consciousness. Always ask for the Highest Good in everything and that everything is for the Highest Good.

A Question for Thought, Meditation, and Further Study

Would it be possible that the Higher, Broader, Total Good is different from your requests and desires at this moment? That it is different from what you expect? Could it be that situations and things appearing in the present as "negative" or "bad" are part of an overall, broader, higher good that is not yet visible to our human perspective? Could it be that your "Highest Good" is higher than the "specific good" that you expect and desire?

Is it right to ask the angels so many things for ourselves? Isn't it a sign of selfishness, vanity, and greed?

Distancing ourselves from the Abundance, Wholeness and Completeness of God, of the Divine and its angels is what causes selfishness, vanity, and greed – and not the other way round. Selfishness and greed have their roots exclusively in fear. God, the Divine, the Source, Spirit, and its angels are Light, Life, and Love. Light, Life, and Love remove you from fear, selfishness, and greed; Light, Life, and Love lead you to freedom, generosity, altruism, compassion, and selfless service. The more we ask, the more ardently we ask and when we ask with ever growing awareness, love, faith, will, and strength, the closer we get to the Creative Powers of our True Self, the Powers of Manifestation of our Spirit. The closer we come to the angels, the Spirit, and the Divine itself.

Another perspective to answer this question is:

Think of all the selfish and greedy people. They are materialists, bigoted, superficial, ego-centric, driven by vanity, spiritually non-conscious. They are detached from the essence, the spirit, the angels, and the higher consciousness, the Source, the All.

Now think of all the great teachers, the masters, the saints, and those close to the angelic realm. They manifested the Perfection, Completeness, and Abundance of Spirit and the Divine; they were one with Its infinite power, infinite wisdom, and infinite love. They manifested all the possibilities and all the gifts, countless blessings. It is their example we want to follow!

Is it possible that when we ask and wish for things to be different in our lives we lose satisfaction, fulfillment, and gratitude? Isn't it important to be grateful for what we have in the present moment?

Of course it is natural and rightful to desire, ask, create, attract, communicate, and express more of the good things of the world, such as Abundance, Love and Joy. But it is best to do that without being attached to the results and to our expectations, without basing our worth and happiness on our desires, requests, and creations. It is best to keep our completeness, freedom, power, serenity, and balance intact. They exist within us in our core, our essence, no matter what we do. It is what we are. Thus, whatever we desire, ask and create is an extension, an effect of our completeness, our power, our freedom, our value, our happiness, and not a prerequisite or something that complements and rewards them. They are purely resulting from our existence; they are divine creations on the material plane of what we are spiritually: divine consciousnesses.

At the same time, it is spiritually wise, beneficial, and proper to be satisfied and happy with what we already have, with what we already are, with what we have accomplished, with what we experience, with what is. To be able to experience gratitude in the present moment.

The one way does not negate the other. We can (and we should) act, be, and exist both ways: to express gratitude, satisfaction, and completeness for what we already have, and to express gratitude, intention, and openness for what we desire for the future. And again, we do so without attachment, without dependency, just acting from the point of our higher consciousness, freedom, and wholeness, and from the infinite creativity that exists within us.

Is it right to ask angels for help on behalf of someone else?

When acting for the Highest Good of All, from a place of love, respect and humbleness, honesty, and benevolence, we can ask all the good things for any person in the world. Just as our true, honest love and unconditional care for others is an uplifting service and not a burden on others, in the same way, asking for their Health, Abundance, and All Good Things is the spiritually desired and rightful thing to do. In fact, it is the spiritually necessary thing to do.

How should we talk to angels?

We can talk to angels through our thoughts, through images, or through the power of love. By using words and affirmations, invocations, and prayers we can talk to angels out loud like they are right in front of us, or just silently in our mind. We can even write down our thoughts on a piece of paper.

We call upon the angels with love, friendship, "openness," and receptiveness, but also with respect, humbleness, and a sense of awe and sacredness. It is as if we speak to our best friend, our dearest companion, and our loving parents. We communicate directly, without fear, freely, openly, and with love. And we will receive back in the same way.

Which angels should we talk to?

To whomever we wish! We can address our Guardian Angel and the four most known Archangels: Michael, Gabriel, Raphael, and Uriel. We can also talk to the rest of the Archangels: Chamuel, Sandalphon, Metatron, Zadkiel, Jophiel, and others. To the orders of angels: the Seraphim, the Cherubim, the Thrones, but also to special groups of Angels, such as the Angels of Healing, Angels of Abundance, Angels of Protection, Angels of Love, Angels of Romance, Angels of Arts, Angels of Nature, and many others.

Is it right to invoke angels for small and everyday matters?

If you call upon angels with a sense of true friendship and deep love, with humbleness and gratitude, it is right and appropriate!

Is it safe to do spiritual work with angels?

Yes it is absolutely safe. In essence, it is a "collaboration" (connection, attunement) with the Spiritual, the Transcendent, the Divine Element itself, the everlasting and perfect – and nothing in the world is safer than that. Actually, it is the definition of true safety!

What keeps me from seeing, hearing, feeling, or experiencing angels, the spiritual dimension of life and the Divine?

What keeps you from experiencing the spiritual plane and from communicating with the angels is fear, your ego, and your judgment. You are well trained to be continuously judgmental of yourself! You need to control and monitor your ego. It is only a part of you, the lowest part in your entire being. Banish the judgmental side of you ("don't judge, so that you won't be judged"). Let go and move past your fear. You deserve your higher self, your higher being (infinite, selfless, illuminating, free, complete). You deserve love, safety, intelligence, power, boldness. That is what you deserve to experience in your present and your future. Sacred, precious qualities that will connect you with what your soul is seeking for. Remember:

your soul is thirsty for completion, wholeness, freedom, and bliss and only the higher, the spiritual, the divine element can quench your thirst. Angels are the way.

Can my health improve from working with energy healing and spiritual methods?

The energetic and spiritual methods and practices should not be considered a replacement for formal medical or mental diagnosis and treatment. However, they can help a person to return to wholeness, to a primary harmony and balance, and to energize the deeper powers and the self-healing wisdom of the soul and of the body. Those who practice spiritual and energetic methods experience increased serenity and peace, clarity, and lucidity, states that promote the optimal and the good on all levels of existence.

What do angels love the most about human beings?

Angels love benevolence, selflessness, compassion, generosity, creativity, joy, playfulness; an open, warm, pure, radiant heart; the honesty, the genuineness. Above all, angels love goodness.

How can I connect with angels?

By calling upon them every day; by thinking of them when you go to sleep and when you wake up each day!

How can I bring them closer to me?

You are the one that will come closer to angels by elevating the frequency of your vibration and your energetic field: clean and purify yourself physically, emotionally, and mentally. Clean your space physically and energetically. Illuminate and harmonize yourself and your space with energetic techniques and more light and vital energy: use focused intention, positive thinking and affirmations, prayers and invocations, meditation and visualization, energetic and spiritual symbols, etc. Use whatever you consider pure, luminous, and good, whatever expresses and uplifts you to a higher level of consciousness, to a higher plane of existence. Do this esoteric work on a regular basis.

How can I communicate with angels?

You can communicate by using everyday energetic and spiritual practice: with deep relaxation, deep breathing, meditation, and visualization; by developing your psychic and spiritual gifts and by making your internal senses more perceptive (insight, intuition, clairaudience). You can also use invocations, prayers, symbols, and other techniques. You can frequently bring yourself in an inward state of receptiveness (imagine you are ready to receive), by opening up and trusting angels with a pure mind and heart and by observing everything carefully, with increased sensitivity and awareness.

ESOTERIC PRACTICE

Awakening the Higher Senses

Awakening the Higher Senses

You can practice the following exercise to develop your internal higher senses, the abilities and powers of your mind and spirit, your psychic and spiritual intelligence and perception.

Close your eyes and take ten deep breaths. Feel the breath filling your entire body; breathe through every cell of your body. Relax your body and mind, let go of any tension. You can call upon the angels, the Pure Bright Light and the Pure Radiant Love of Heaven and Spirit.

Clairaudience

Imagine that you can hear the angels. You are able to hear with your higher senses; you are able to hear the spiritual messages, truly and substantially. Stay in this state for a few minutes.

Clairsentience

Imagine that you can sense the angels. You are able to feel with your higher senses; you are able to feel spiritual states, truly and substantially. Stay in this state for a few minutes.

Clairvoyance

Imagine that you can see the angels. You are able to see with your higher senses; you are able to see spiritual images, truly and substantially. Stay in this state for a few minutes.

Spiritual Knowledge / Claircognizance

Imagine that you are able to know things about the angels and from the angels. You are able to use your higher mind; you are able to know spiritual information, truly and substantially. In an automatic, inner, higher way. Stay in this state for a few minutes.

Complete the exercise by gently moving your body and slowly opening your eyes.

Carry out this exercise at least seven times in the following days.

How can I become aware of angels or angelic energies around me?

Many people perceive angelic presences and energies during meditation, dreams, prayer or in a state of deep relaxation, higher consciousness, and ecstasy. It can happen when people are in a natural surrounding and also in a state of emergency or grave danger.

We may perceive angels and their energies in different ways: as a change in temperature (either as a cool sensation, a coolness, a cool breeze, or as a warm sensation, a flame, a burning). We may experience shivers, goose bumps, waves passing through our entire body, vibrations, pulse, the feeling of being touched or pinched. At other times, an angelic presence is seen as flashes of light, sparks of colors, light spheres, clouds of light. An angelic presence may be heard as a voice in the distance, a sound, a whisper, the faint sound of bells or chimes, or the sound of water. We may also "hear" an angelic message within our mind in the form of thoughts or intuition, or in the form of a sudden knowledge. We may even catch a glimpse of a figure. Or we may feel joy, euphoria, serenity, release, have tears in our eyes, yawn, laugh, become dizzy, or lose touch with the ground.

All of the above are considered common signs of angelic visitations. It is important that we don't get scared and instead we welcome angels with awe and joy, with love and gratitude. This will lay the foundation for our relationship with angels, a relationship that will offer us meaning, guidance, and momentum in our lives.

Is it true that only gifted and clairvoyant people communicate with angels?

Yes, but all people are gifted and clairvoyant! They are just not aware of it yet, or they have not dared to try it! It is never too late to try and the best moment to begin something is Now!

I observe how the clouds sometimes take angelic forms and shapes. Am I seeing angels?

Those signs are heavenly – literally and metaphorically! Your consciousness recognizes what you are been taught spiritually!

I found a feather on the street! I have the feeling that it is a good sign!

Yes, indeed! It means that angels surround you with their loving energies. You are being guided and looked after!

Are there more angelic signs to look for?

Yes, there are countless signs from angels, Spirit and the Higher Realms! Open your eyes and your mind, and learn to recognize them – you can!

How can I become aware of angelic signs?

Ask from your inner/higher self to bring them in your path. Start observing the signs of angels and Spirit around you. The more you recognize them, the more they will appear to you and offer you guidance and advice for your development and course of your life.

Can animals feel the presence of angels?

We don't know for sure. It is likely that when the angelic presence is powerful, animals can feel it. If you have a pet, observe its reactions when you call upon the angels, or invite the angels through drawing angelic symbols or meditating.

Can children feel the presence of angels?

Yes! Babies and children have a special pure connection with the spiritual and angelic realm! You had also a direct connection with your guardian angel when you were a kid! Do you remember that?

Is it good to encourage children to connect and communicate with angels?

Spiritually, on the whole it is the best, wisest thing to do! Angels are the absolute good and the ultimate intelligence of the universe and of the spirit! It is vital that we don't interrupt the communication of children with angels by discouraging or disproving them, as they grow up. Many parents adopt such behaviors because they are afraid of their children getting lost in their imagination and wishful thinking, becoming weak, unbalanced, ungrounded, ineffective, and dysfunctional in the present material reality.

The contrary is true: a person who is not in contact with the spiritual side of life – their essence, truth, wisdom, power, and source – has great difficulty to adjust and function in this material reality, to be truly balanced and grounded. The majority of humanity is in this state. Effective, successful, and most importantly, happy individuals have nourished their spirituality and have been in harmony and unity with their spirit, the unknown, immaterial, higher element. They are the ones who have had great sensitivity, faith, and love in their hearts and in their lives.

Can I become an angel after my earthly life?

This will be decided by the higher wisdom and the higher power of the Divine. By having completed your karmic commitments, your earthly karmic lessons (all your experiences on Earth are karmic lessons your soul needs to learn), you may ascend and become an ascended master, a teacher of light. This way you can offer guidance, knowledge, wisdom, and power to many people from a higher, wider plane. You will experience greater freedom, bliss, and wholeness than in your incarnation as a human being. You will be spiritually as the sun in the sky! All of us, one day will come to know this planet very well, after having visited it for so many times, and we will ascend and become "stars" in the "sky" – ascended teachers in the heavens!

Am I worthy of contacting the angels?

Yes, you are worthy and we are all worthy. Not only do we all have value and worth, but we are ourselves the value and worth. I Am Value and Worth and You Are Value and Worth. You and I are all beings of spiritual essence; we are pure, free, immaterial souls and consciousnesses, divine rays of the one Divine Beingness! We deserve all the good things of heaven and Earth. We deserve all the love, wisdom, and power we can receive. The point is: are we receiving them? Or do we believe that we don't deserve them, closing our hands, minds, and hearts to them?

I am ashamed of certain things I have done in my life and I feel guilty about them. Will the angels judge me?

No, angels do not judge us. You are judging yourself; your conscience is doing it. Your conscience knows right from wrong and it is natural to judge yourself, but don't overdo it. Your conscience (your inner voice) helps you to grow through your mistakes and to learn from them. The Spirit, the Angels, God/the Divine are Light and Love. Only Light and only Love. All Light and all Love. They do not judge. They don't have time to judge (just joking!), their joy is to create and offer life and infinite possibilities!

Do angels watch us during our private moments?

Many people have this concern because we have connected our private moments with shame, guilt, and fear instead of naturalness, simplicity, and purity. Angels do not watch us in our private moments – at least not the way we imagine. They see the energies we emit, the colors and vibrations of our emotional states; the lighter, brighter colors and vibrations of joy, peace, euphoria, satisfaction, and fulfillment, but also the heavier, darker colors and vibrations of fear, anger, and sorrow. In the case of negative, painful emotions, the angels see the energy we emit and they "wait" for us to ask for their help so they can fill us with their pure heavenly healing light. We do need to take steps in the right direction, by recognizing the need for help and by specifically asking for it. Angels cannot intervene without our consent. In any case, angels do not judge us because they don't think or function as human beings. Thank God for that!

Is it a blasphemy to talk to angels and invoke them into our life?

No, angels belong to God, to the Divine. They are its manifestations and projections; they are divine qualities and powers – the most luminous, sacred and beloved ones! And even more so: angels are Light, Sacredness and Love!

Do we have to worship the angels?

No, the worship and praise of all beings, of both humans and angels, should be addressed to God, to the Divine; to the One, Perfect, Supreme, Total, Absolute Source. We openly recognize the angels, we respect and appreciate them deeply, and we feel awe, joy, great love, and gratitude for them.

Why don't angels help us solve our problems? Why don't they save dying children? Why don't they heal the sick? Why don't they just fix the negative and bad things of this world?

This may be the greatest mystery of all times. The greatest philosophical, metaphysical, religious riddle: why is there evil and suffering in the first place? No one can fully apprehend it, understand it, or explain it. Rationality, morality, and humanity – they all fail to answer the question of why suffering exists. It is an irrational paradox and a paradoxical irrationality, even from a spiritual point of view. Isn't it true that "God is Love?" Isn't the Divine all-powerful and able to heal all the suffering of the world? Why did the Divine create suffering or allow it to be created? Why does evil exist? What is the purpose of its existence? Are we living in a cold, blind, chaotic, violent, and hostile universe? Are we a species that is almost mentally deficient, self-destructive, and uncompassionate, a species without love and respect for other beings, a species obsessed with power, control, and money, full of egoism and conflict? Is there anything more than that?

If we approach the question about the purpose of suffering from a higher, broader, and deeper perspective, the answer would be related to the Law of Karma and the soul's desire to physically experience itself through the separation and the duality (good/evil) of the material world. As to "why don't angels intervene to the suffering of humanity?" the answer would involve the Law of Free Will of people, but also, their self-limitation on lower levels energetically, mentally, consciously. For more information about that, see the answer to the related question about the guardian angel.

There is another question that is raised and it is even more important than the previous one: "Why don't humans help to solve their own problems? Why don't we save the children that die unjustly? Why don't we cure the sick? Why don't we fix all the wrongs of the world? Why do we keep on hurting ourselves, animals and our planet?" Who may answer such questions? We live on this planet; the responsibility is ours. We are the ones to answer those questions. It is not the case of a metaphysical, philosophical, religious question but of a real, actual, and concrete question. It exists all around us, it continually asks us: "Why?"

Reflect on the following piece of advice (and also a promise): take the weight of humanity on your shoulders, all the wrongs, all the harm, as if you are the only one responsible for it. As if you are the only one who is able to help or do something about it. And heaven will open. Heaven will take on your weight.

Note: Check also the answer related to this topic in the chapter about the guardian angel.

How do angels view all the negative and bad things happening on Earth, such as wars or injustice?

Most likely angels perceive everything that happens on Earth without judgment. They understand that everything we experience is based on our own free choice in the present or in the past, consciously, unconsciously or super-consciously (from higher levels of consciousness), individually or collectively. We have chosen our experiences; we have desired, caused, and created them. All negative things in the life of human beings are not negative elements of life, existence, the world, or the Earth; they are negative things of human beings. They don't exist separately: they exist to, with, and from human beings. They are called negativity, harm, injustice, wars *of humans*.

Angels understand that all harm constitutes human karma, the effects of false, selfish, greedy, envious, dark ways of thinking and acting. Harm is the result of limited mentality and intelligence on all levels of existence: spiritual, mental, emotional, and social. Celestial beings understand that harm and suffering are not only the results of karma and limited intelligence, perception and consciousness, but also essential – although really hard – lessons for the soul to learn on the material plane. Our higher self (our soul and spirit) experiences the lowest levels (energetically, consciously) so that it can create, co-create, discover wholeness, freedom, illumination, love, happiness, awareness, and oneness, even at the far side of the spirit: the material, the earthly plane. It is the biggest descent followed by the biggest ascent!

Angels stand as the highest, manifested forces of the absolute and infinite good; they stand as teachers, protectors, guides, spiritual siblings, friends, and companions to all people who will call upon them for help, either in times of great need, pain, fear, sorrow, and despair, or through spiritual insight, perception, and awareness of their existence and the potential and gifts that such divine beings can bring. Angels do not judge; they stand as the ultimate good, ready to overwhelm our lives if we choose it... when we choose it. When we realize it, dare to do it, ask for it, allow it, pursue it.

To discover angels in the heavenly and spiritual realm, it is to become aware of your own nature, the angel within you, your spiritual self. If all people did that at the same time, life on Earth would become a true paradise and all harm would cease to exist. Starting from change in our individual everyday lives, we can bring a complete collective, social, and global change. Change does not begin from the angels; angels are the path and the destination. Change begins from within. Not from the whole but from the one.

What do angels think about sexual intercourse? Or about money?

Questions related to what angels think of earthly affairs are hard to answer. We can assume, or imagine how they see things by taking as a starting point the way great, wise teachers of humanity perceived earthly affairs.

When two people engage in a consenting sexual act with love, passion, communication, joy, and pleasure for both, the sexual act becomes a sacred creative process that gives life, vitality, emotional and physical wellbeing, and balance. It releases, supplements, rejuvenates, invigorates, and uplifts. If someone could see the energies emitted by a couple in love... it would be a feast of light and colors, with intense healing features! The sexual act is the primal, most important, supreme means to Life; when it is combined with consciousness, awareness, joy, communication, and love, it becomes a means to Fulfillment and Freedom, Happiness and Illumination. The sexual act has the potential of awaking each one of our cells, to make it feel alive, experience joy and satisfaction and to make each cell emit its most high and pure light.

When it comes to money, a great teacher (possibly the angels, as well) would see it as a neutral energy that can be used by our lower self or our "higher beingness." Money can be used selfishly or unselfishly with a giving attitude, for joy or hurt, for happiness or misery, for good or for bad. Money in the hands of consciously spiritual (or spiritually conscious) people can be a means to happiness for all. It is better if we see money as a source of good – it offers us countless comforts, chances, and possibilities – and we don't become attached to it. It is better if we use it meaningfully, with generosity but also with prudence and moderation – finding the right balance in all situations. From the way we use money we can learn about ourselves, about others, and about life in general. As with all things, we use it from a state of love; we use it with love and for love (that is, for the good)!

Is there a chance that I will lose my sanity if I practice meditation, study esotericism, or communicate with angels and other incorporeal beings?

Unless you are suffering from a serious mental disorder, then you are not at risk of going crazy! It is doubtful that people with severe mental illnesses are able to see or hear celestial beings. Usually, they see things that are ugly, negative, or scary. On the contrary, getting involved with spiritual/esoteric matters and of course angels, connecting and studying them, may bring important mental benefits and comfort to people who are dealing with mental illnesses (always as a complement to the appropriate psychological and medical treatment). God, the Spirit, and the angels do not reject any human being and offer their love generously to all humanity. Love brings only good! Angels, being the higher, pure, positive vital forces of existence and of spirit that they are, only empower, balance, purify, and heal our existence (all its parts, all its levels). Angels are only beneficial to our mind and soul and they support us in all possible ways. In essence, they are our wise and all-powerful siblings, our older siblings (indeed, they were created first!). They are Positivity, Illumination, Good, Beauty, Perfection in a most elevated spiritual form.

The fear of going insane derives from the darkness within us and not from our ever-bright light that knows no fear. Fear is an expression of our insecure, earthly, lower self that needs to become attached to people and material things, that likes the known and the predictable, in order to feel a bit good occasionally but never good enough. A slight dose of humor and "craziness" – and spirituality is the biggest insanity in a human being's life (or perhaps a human being is the biggest insanity of the spirit?) – can work miracles in our lives... only machines are exclusively "logical," though they have been evolved as well to include a bit of unpredicted "craziness!"

Is it possible that I may stray from the path of righteousness, the path of God, if I communicate with angels?

No there is no such possibility. Angels accelerate and assure your journey to the Divine, to God. Angels are the path to the Divine Source, and the Divine Consciousness communicates with us through its angels. Are we, as human beings, open to listen and follow the angelic path to God?

Could the whole "angels" thing be a case of auto-suggestion?

As soon as you begin to receive messages and the healing energies of angels, as soon as you begin to perceive the presence of celestial beings and their illuminating qualities around you, heaven and Earth will begin to play a "game" with you: they will show you – and prove you in ways that you can't imagine – that angels are not just impressions and creations of your mind. They are not an auto-suggestion but a process and a plan of astonishing truth, essence, beauty, and perfection beyond the human mind and anything familiar.

Is there a chance that I will call an angel of light and a fallen angel will come instead? Or that a fallen angel will appear e.g. as a guardian angel or Archangel Michael?

Based on my experience, I find it rather difficult. Darkness rarely appears as light. Usually it appears as what it is. Nevertheless, if the opposite occurs, human beings can distinguish and single out the lower/dark/negative energy from the higher/luminous/positive. We can feel it directly and intuitively and recognize it. Light is pleasant and lucid while darkness is not. Joy and love are satisfying and feel good, while fear, sorrow, and anger are not. The same goes for spiritual planes, spiritual energies, and spiritual beings.

If you have doubts over the origin and the quality of an energy or an incorporeal presence around you, you may repeat three times the following affirmation:

"If you belong to the Light, I welcome you with love; you may stay! If you belong to the darkness, you must leave right now! Only Divine Light and Divine Love exist here and nothing lower than that!"

You can also repeat this declaration if doubts occur during your spiritual practice. Repeat and affirm the declaration three times, out loud or silently, and observe what is happening and how you feel. You may also use any prayer that you find helpful.

Remember that the Light protects and guides you everywhere and always. Your true essence, your soul, is Light! You are superior to darkness – absolutely and at all times!

Have supreme faith, absolute confidence, and perfect trust that the evil, the dark and the inferior can NOT touch you, affect you, or stand in your way. That is how strong the power of the Divine Will and the Divine Guidance is, and you are completely one with it!

Your intention is fundamental, primary, and important in every energetic and spiritual work. It is the base and the frame of the work. If your intention is based on Love, the Good, Offering, Selflessness, Healing, then all the energies (including the angels) will be aligned with that.

Is it right to invoke angels and their names without a serious reason?

The more we invoke angels from deep within our hearts and souls, with gratitude, joy and love, for our own good and the good of others, the more we manifest the light of our spirit, our soul, and our true self. Angels are happy to manifest their superior pure energies and qualities on the earthly plane at every chance. By asking the angels' assistance, we and angels, earthly and heavenly beings of light, co-create a better life for everyone. This is totally acceptable, favorable, and desirable by the higher planes.

How do I know that I'm communicating with a real angel and that I am not making it up?

In the beginning it might be a part of your imagination. After a while, you will be able to understand if it is your imagination and to what degree...yes there are percentages of subjective-objective, imagination-reality. Not everything is black or white! As time passes, your experience and receptiveness will grow, and you will gradually understand when you are surrounded by angelic presences and their divine loving energies! It is an incredible experience of delight, mellowness, and transcendence and one that is impossible to reject, hide, doubt, or forget!

Does relying on angels mean we become irresponsible?

Angels do not take the responsibility for our thoughts, feelings, actions, decisions, and choices. By thinking of angels, calling upon them and tuning into their energies, we receive the heavenly power, guidance and direction that we deserve as spiritual beings made "in the image and likeness of God." The responsibility is exclusively ours to take in all situations. Either we are stuck in materialism, separation, and our ego, or we are open to the higher, cosmic, spiritual energies and forces, and on their side, since they already and always are on our side. The responsibility and the choice are ours at all times.

Is it enough to invoke the angels and be on a spiritual quest? Does this make us ineffective in our everyday life and reality?

Spirituality – the pursuit and practice of the spiritual side of our existence – offers us great joy, meaning, value, beauty, and power in our everyday life. Nevertheless, this incredible power needs to be grounded in decisions, choices, and actions. We need to always use our full potential: we are multidimensional beings with thoughts, feelings, visions, imagination, insight, intuition, instinct, creativity, will, speech, writing, movement, drive, energy, vitality.

Why shouldn't we use our full potential with awareness, discernment, and wisdom whenever it is necessary and to the right degree? This is how a whole and complete, authentic and liberated, conscious and enlightened being would act.

I have heard that there are angels for everything, even for the traffic and for finding a parking space! Angels for the weather, angels for several situations, and angels for all kinds of objects. How is it possible that there are angels helping with such mundane earthly matters and situations? Angels that watch over animals and birds, forests and seas, angels for all jobs and occupations, and angels for poetry, friendship, romance, pregnancy and more. Are there really angels for everything?

There are countless angels, angels for every situation, whether it be small or big, important or "insignificant," permanent or temporary, substantial or superficial, material or spiritual, visible or invisible. The entire Being, the entire Existence, the entire Universe are angelic, spiritual, and Divine. The All That Is, the Whole is angelic, spiritual, and Divine. By invoking the angels that correspond to small, material, everyday matters, we recognize the essence and the transcendence of that situation. It is as if we recognize the spirituality and the divinity even in these everyday things. Everything is energy, light, divinity. Everything is One and One is in Everything. Everything is Divine and the Divine is in everything, – even though it transcends everything and it is many things more, many things higher – it is the transcendence, the beginning, the source, the wholeness itself.

Thus, the rain, the snow, the sun, the Earth, the soil, the water, the houses, people, cars, professions, the roles we "play" in life, motherhood, birth, childhood, old age, benevolence, offering, feelings, thoughts, situations, objects... they all have a spiritual nature and essence, a higher aspect. They are one with the spirit, with the Divine, they are parts of the All, parts of the One. Divine parts.

By invoking angels that are related to these earthly elements, it is as if we recognize the higher self or the higher aspect of them, the spirituality, the Divinity, the All and the One behind them, within them, and beyond them. By talking to the angels of the rain, of the sun, of objects, of feelings, of thoughts, of deeds, of professions, of roles, of groups and of all of life's situations, you recognize the great wholeness, the great oneness, the great spirituality, and the ultimate Divinity. Now, here and here, in the now. You are reconnected on a conscious, individual, earthly, material level with the splendid, supreme, and ultimate Reality (what we call God, the Divine).

Remember: everything, even the negative aspects of life, the difficulties, the darkness, they all belong to a greater Light, to the Wholeness and Oneness of Existence and of Being, they belong to the Divine Source. Fill your life with spiritual awareness and consciousness and you will be attuned to the whole, the spiritual, and the divine... unconditionally, unlimitedly, like never before!

What are the names of those angels?

In some studies and books on angels, you can find the names of angels assisting with various matters and situations of human lives, ranging from natural phenomena to human characteristics and qualities. It is not necessary to mention all the names, or to remember them. The names may give an insight to the celestial kingdom (the spirituality of existence).

We can call upon the angels associated with any quality, situation, or circumstance directly and freely. We can invoke angels related to an element of nature (water, rain, snow, sun, etc.), angels related to a place or location (city, forest, country, etc.), angels related to a certain profession (doctors, lawyers, etc.), angels related to an activity (sleep, play, etc.), and angels related to a situation or experience (joy, abundance, love, romance, motherhood, birth, etc.), without using specific names, just by calling upon the angels of the condition we want help with.

ESOTERIC PRACTICE

Angels in Everything

The Divine and the celestial beings are everywhere and everything has a divine nature. Whenever you are in trouble, facing a difficult situation, recognize that there is an angel that corresponds to it and invoke this angel. Acknowledge the spiritual and the divine element in each action, thought, feeling, place, profession, role, and deed. Each and every moment acknowledge, be aware, invoke, tune into, connect to. It is the best you can do and it is more than enough.

What is an angelic invocation?

An invocation is a form of energetic prayer with a specific structure and repetitions of powerful words that will uplift your consciousness and your energy field. With the invocations you call forth the celestial beings, you recognize and honor them, you give thanks and express your gratitude, and, at the same time you state and affirm ideal, positive situations (your wishes) and timeless, universal spiritual truths. For example you can affirm that "All Is One," or "God Is Love," or "I AM a Spiritual Divine Nature and Essence" etc. An invocation creates and emits great spiritual energy and vital power, acting upon the etheric double (our own aura and the aura of the Earth), which affects all levels of our being: our body, mind, and spirit, as etheric vitality is the force that creates and sustains all of our bodies.

Where can I find angelic invocations? Can you give me some examples of simple angelic invocations?

You can find a complete guide to angelic invocations in the book entitled *Angelic Invocations* in the same series as this one (*Celestial Gifts*)! Included in the book are invocations of all angels and archangels, invocations related to all issues and situations of our human lives.

Here are some examples of simple and short invocations. Repeat each invocation slowly and consciously, a few times. Use them as much and as often as you want during the day:

"Beloved Angels of the Spirit, Light and Love, come to me now!"

"Beloved Angels of the Spirit, Light and Love, thank you for being by my side!"

"Dear and Beloved God, send Your Angels to …… (name of the person) to protect, guide and heal him/her!"

"Beloved Angels of Heaven, we are one, I love you!"

You can always create your own invocations as long as they are absolutely positive and illuminating; they are created with the purest of intentions and expressed – with angelic inspiration – from your heart, the divine wisdom that exists within you.

What are the Angelic Symbols?

Angelic Symbols are symbols of high vibrational frequencies with specific energetic characteristics, manifesting and expressing angelic energies and qualities. They are absolutely pure, luminous, and powerful symbols for spiritual empowerment, upliftment, and healing of our being. For example, when we use the symbol of Archangel Michael, when we think about it, visualize it, draw it, either energetically (in the air with our palm/finger), or on a piece of paper, it manifests – within and around us – the vibration and the energy of Archangel Michael. This energy (burning, fiery gold or red) provides Protection and Guidance, Catharsis and Purification from lower frequencies (negative energies and influences). The symbol emits the energy of the archangel and everything it offers.

Symbols can go beyond words since they have a deeper influence to our subconscious and to our higher consciousness. They are sacred gifts, sacred tools, and sacred keys crucial to our spiritual and esoteric path, as they advance and empower every energetic and healing work. Symbols also awaken the sacred and the mystery, the esoteric, the mystic, the seeker within us.

Where can I find Angelic Symbols?

You can find a complete guide of Angelic Symbols in the book entitled *Angelic Symbols* in the same series as *Celestial Gifts*. Working with energetic symbols is totally safe, deeply healing, and highly illuminating and it offers multiple benefits! Symbols speak to our subconscious and to our higher consciousness and offer potentialities and activations where human language reaches its limits.

In which everyday matters can the angels help me?

There are many different, parallel, and interconnected ways of approaching the topic of angels. There are also various things that angels can assist us with and we can request their help for.

We can ask the angels for everything as long as we ask with respect and love, and it is for our greater good and the benefit of others as well. We can ask angels:

To help us find something we have lost.

To help us remember.

To help us learn.

To help us with our exams.

To help us with our work.

To reach our destination faster.

To have a safe trip.

To have a positive outcome from an appointment.

To be the best version of ourselves.

To achieve a goal.

To complete a project.

To reach and maintain our optimal body weight, an optimal physical appearance, the beauty of our spirit and our true higher self.

To soothe and take away the sorrow, fear, anger, worry, and anxiety.

To strengthen our creativity and inspiration.

To give us ideas.

To improve our communication.

To find our optimal job.

To find a romantic partner.

To bless and improve the relationship with our romantic partner.

To start a family.

To receive guidance on parenthood issues, conception, birth, and raising a child.

To provide abundance.

To help us heal our relationships.

To help us forgive.

To overcome a loss.

To guide and protect us.

To heal us physically.

To awaken our healing powers.

To protect, guide, and heal someone dear to us or another person.

To assist with social matters.

To help people in need.

To heal animals and plants.

To bring peace on Earth.

To heal the Earth.

And many other issues.

What are the exact steps in order to receive the help of angels?

There are specific invocations and energy symbols (in the books from the series *Celestial Gifts*) and also esoteric knowledge, exercises, meditations, and a lot of information in the book you now hold in your hands. All these tools are related to your connection with your spiritual essence and your soul, the Divine Source, the Divine All. They are related to your spiritual awakening and advancement, the development of your inner wisdom, the catharsis and purification, your healing, your upliftment and enlightenment, your spiritual transformation, and your happiness on all levels. This is the intention and the purpose of the material offered in this book and also in the other two books (*Angelic Invocations* and *Angelic Symbols*).

If you want to ask angels for help with a certain issue in your daily life, like the things mentioned in the previous question, then this is simple and independent from your overall spiritual/esoteric practice:

Close your eyes; let your heart be filled with love and faith and ask what you want!

"Beloved angels, please help me with/to..." (or whatever fits your request).

Repeat your request a few times, keep your eyes closed, take some deep breaths, and relax to feel and experience the energy.

Just ask and it will be given to you!

What is an Angelic Meditation?

It is a meditation during which you call upon and connect to angels, your guardian angel or the archangels. It is a way of attuning to angels mentally, energetically, and spiritually. It may include gradual relaxation, deep slow breathing, clear and strong intent, a prayer or invocation, and a visualization. The Angelic Meditation may have a specific form and structure, it may be taught by a certain teacher, spiritual system, or a book. It may also be a meditation that we create and practice on our own, according to our internal guidance and inspiration.

What can meditation offer me? Why should I meditate in the first place?

Why do you breathe? Just as you breathe without having to think about it consciously or without having to control your breath, in a similar manner you are constantly meditating: you don't realize it; you do it unconsciously. You are lost in thoughts and images, in sensations and feelings, in daydreaming and fantasies, in the past and in the future, in higher and lower levels of consciousness.

To decide consciously to invest your time and energy in meditation, it means that you slow down and experience inner peace in the midst of your daily turmoil. You "pause" time and experience deep levels of rest. You experience the silent void that is more fertile and complete than anything else; you experience being more in the present, in your "here and now." Meditation is to go consciously through this process of introspection, self-reflection, and restructuring.

Meditation is the ultimate means, tool, path and journey of consciousness, a chance to purify, improve, upgrade, restructure, enlighten, release, uplift your energy, your thoughts and feelings, yourself, your being, what your emit, create or experience, your own life. It is the ultimate tool, the greatest gift, the perfect path that leads to True and Substantial Happiness! Happiness = wholeness = freedom = wisdom = authenticity = essence = oneness. You can reach all these things through meditation, introspection, self-observation, focused thought and positive envisioning, conscious breathing, receptiveness, and going with the higher flow.

Do you really need more reasons to meditate?

The most intelligent, wonderful, special, talented, creative, wise, unforgettable people and teachers of humanity were fully committed to meditation! They had their own way of tapping into the pure wisdom, power, and love that abundantly (and fearlessly) exists within them, within their Divine Source!

Is there some kind of preparatory process that I need to follow prior to working with energies, angels, or doing any spiritual work in the form of meditations, invocations, or other spiritual practices?

You can use meditation, invocations, or energy techniques practically everywhere and always, at any given moment and under any circumstances. You don't need any preparation or special effort. They emanate from your being, your soul, your will, your love, and your inner wisdom. However, following a ritual preparation (conscious, gradual, and consistent) will deliver the message of this esoteric practice to your subconscious, will prepare you, will elevate your frequencies, and make your experience even more deep and intense. So, even though preparation is not a prerequisite, it definitely has its benefits. Engage in the process of preparation with love, trust, and joy. Preparation is a part of the esoteric work and meditation. It is a form of meditation, as well. So, do it meditatively!

How to prepare yourself for meditation or any other spiritual work:

– To cleanse, purify, and bring yourself in a state of harmony, serenity and receptiveness, take a nice shower or indulge in a relaxing bath. Use plenty of coarse salt as it purifies your aura and your etheric field. You can rub it on your skin with soft circular movements or add it (three to four fistfuls) to your warm bath water. Soak in the water and relax for 15 minutes or more. Then, rinse your body with water and feel the water cleansing you on all levels: physically, energetically, emotionally, mentally, and spiritually. Your intention is enough.

– Cleanse your space physically as well as energetically. Make it as clean, tidy, beautiful, and harmonious as you can.

– Energize and scent your space with pure essential oils. Choose an essential oil (or a mix of them) that relaxes you or consult with an aroma therapist or an aromatherapy book.

– Light a few white candles. As you light the candles, dedicate them to the angels, the Divine Source, the Higher Self or the Highest Good (or to all of these elements – they comprise a unity). Attention: always keep the candles away from flammable objects and do not leave the candles unattended.

– Affirm (mentally or out loud) that you and your space are 100% clean and luminous on all levels! Repeat at least three times and feel that it is so!

– Say a prayer that expresses you at the moment. Fill your heart with faith and love, say the prayer slowly, with intention, being aware, and meaning each word. Repeat the prayer three times.

– Alternatively, you can use an invocation in a similar way (or just ask angels to surround you).

– For even deeper relaxation, it may help to have soft and serene music, like new age music, meditation music (or yoga, reiki, massage music, etc.), sounds of nature (birds, waves, etc.) or classical music. You may of course prefer silence and quietness.

– Have some pieces of paper to write or to draw on. Use a colored pen that you like (or choose a color that intuitively draws you)

You feel ready and you truly are! Have a wonderful and superb esoteric, energetic, and spiritual work! With Love!

How do I put into practice the meditations, the visualizations, and the exercises described in this book?

You will find various meditations, visualizations, techniques, and energetic and spiritual exercises, some simple and others more complicated, included in this book.

To practice a meditation or any other spiritual technique, follow the instructions below:

– Sit comfortably, with your back straight.

– Read the text three to four times.

– Read slowly and meditatively.

– Feel the words and their meaning. Feel the qualities, the vibrations, and the energy of the text, of the words and of their meaning.

– Open yourself; be receptive and sensitive.

– Observe your body and your feelings. Observe what you perceive with your inward and outward senses.

– Feel like a child discovering the world: without past, without prejudices, without blinders and limitations, without judgment. Feel innocently, purely, like a child filled with awe, yearning, passion, hope, and joy.

– Be kind and respectful to yourself. Let go of your expectations. Don't judge your effort; there is no success or failure (everything is an accomplishment). Just go for it, meditate!

– The mere reading of a meditation (or of the entire book) constitutes meditation, a meditative experience, an esoteric, enlightening, purifying, healing, liberating, uplifting process. The reading of a meditation gives you all the benefits that the meditation abundantly offers.

– After reading three to four times the spiritual practice you want to carry out (each reading connects and attunes you deeper to the meaning of the practice), close your eyes and repeat the meditation/spiritual practice in your mind. There is no need to repeat it exactly as you read it; you may follow your own version according to your needs, your intuition, and your inner guidance and inspiration. Remember that you have infinite inner wisdom; allow it to manifest itself.

– You can open your eyes and read passages that you like. Or, while reading the meditation, you may close your eyes, to recreate and experience it as a visualization or an insight in your mind and spirit.

– Use your intention and your imagination. They are sacred abilities of the spirit, privileges of the human consciousness, almighty powers of creation.

– Meditate creatively, inventively, trustfully, and joyfully. With sensitivity, faith, and self-confidence. Let go of your fear. Fear only limits you. Free yourself!

– Remember that anything you feel or don't feel during your spiritual practice is good (even nothing is good!). Meditation needs practice. Dedicate 10 minutes each day to your meditation practice. After a few days, you will find yourself enjoying and experiencing the meditation directly, deeply, and intensely. You will reap the benefits of meditation in no time.

– Take some slow and deep breaths before the meditation and after its completion. Breathe in through your nose and breathe out through your mouth, blowing the air gently. Take 10 breaths before the meditation in order to relax and open up and a few more at the end to assimilate the energies and ground yourself. During the meditation, whenever you feel like it, breathe deeply to release unnecessary negative thoughts and feelings and to strengthen your energy and your light. Deep breaths will enable you to experience higher vibrations and qualities. Not only is your breath the vehicle of your life, but it has purifying, invigorating, and stimulating properties, too.

– Make a list of your favorite meditations. Practice each meditation once a day for at least one week to ground, manifest, and experience its power and purpose. Alternatively, you may dedicate a weekend to carry out more meditations, techniques, and exercises.

– Drink a glass of water before and after meditation to help your body's cleansing process.

– If you need grounding, to feel that you are fully back in the here and now, or to function and adjust to your surroundings after your spiritual practice, just rest, sleep, or take a shower/bath. You may also engage in physical activity or take a walk in nature. Choose natural, light, colorful food from Mother Nature, and try to avoid processed, artificial, dead food.

– Remember there is no wrong in meditation!

Finally, as we have already mentioned earlier, all the texts of the book can function as meditation since they bear spiritual energy and knowledge! Approach each text as meditation and experience it substantially and deeply!

Are there any success tips for practicing and experiencing meditation?

Yes, there are! When you meditate:

1. Use your entire potential, your whole being: your mind, your imagination, your envisioning, your intention, your faith, your body, your breath, your heart, and your soul.

2. Experience and feel everything deep in your heart, deep from your heart.

3. Meditate with trust, faith, spiritual self-mastery, and self-confidence.

4. Discard fear. Fear is the opposite of life, light, and love. Fear indicates deficiency and not completeness.

5. Meditate joyfully! Joy is sacred!

6. See meditation as a game! Play, experiment, approach it with innocence and purity, curiosity, and courage!

7. Foster compassion, kindness, humbleness, and respect to the sacredness of Life and Existence, of the Self and of Beingness.

8. Become sensitive and observe with awareness each and every thing.

9. Bring yourself to a state of receptiveness and openness. You are open to receive all the gifts that the universe has to offer.

10. Surround yourself with serenity and harmony. Suppose you are surrounded only by serenity and harmony.

11. Surround and fill yourself with love; selfless, spiritual, illuminating love. Do the same for the entire Earth and humanity. Send love everywhere. This is a true healing practice that acts on all levels and even affects matter!

12. Intention is the "alpha" and "omega" in meditation and in every energy work, practice, and technique. What is your intention? Do you want peace, serenity? Healing? Spiritual growth? Insight, channeling, deep meditation? Do you want bliss? Do you want to travel to

other dimensions, and connect with angels? Are you looking for answers and guidance? Do you want to help a person in need? Intention is your driving force, your primary principle, and your spiritual basis. It leads the way and it mobilizes you (subconsciously, consciously, and superconsciously!). Have clear intentions and wait to see them taking action, functioning, and manifesting. It is as if you plant a seed in a spiritual soil.

"My intention is to experience the deepest, highest, most substantial meditation that I can experience! To become the great spiritual meditator that I can be!"

Last and most important? Enjoy it!

Can you suggest some simple but effective Angelic Meditation?

Remember that meditation is a true spiritual fulfillment, a rejuvenation and upliftment for our spirit, an invigoration and deep healing. It is a simple and natural process just like deep sleep, and you can learn it with some practice.

A simple, short and beneficial Angelic Meditation is the one that follows below.

MEDITATION

A Simple and Complete Angelic Meditation

Sit comfortably with your back straight and gently close your eyes.

Take some deep breaths and feel your belly expanding with each in-breath. Inhale through the nose, exhale through the mouth, slowly and gradually, without haste. Feel and enjoy every deep breath. You are breathing in energy, oxygen, life. Imagine your lungs and your body being filled with energy, oxygen, and life.

Relax: ask your mind and your body to let go and relax as much as possible...

Imagine you are in a state of Serenity and Harmony... Serenity and Harmony surround you... only Serenity and Harmony...

With your intention, bring Light all around you... visualize (see and feel) the Light filling every cell of your being. You are inside the Light... Vital Light, the Light of Life, Bright Light, clear, pure... it becomes more and more luminous, pure, dazzling, more and more white. You see and you feel it more and more... the pure and radiant light surrounds you, permeates, and fills you up... feel the light cleansing you, purifying you... The light empowers you, uplifts you... the radiant light illuminates you, it fills you up... the light is all around you, the light is inside you... it is truly happening... you see and you feel it... white light all around you, white light all inside you... stay in the pure, vital, radiant and wonderful White Light!

Call upon the angels... wait... call on them again... from your heart... see and feel yourself pure and radiant, clean and luminous, full of energy, full of power, full of wisdom, full of love!

Invoke the angels once more and feel their presence surrounding you...how do you feel? What do you see? What do you hear? Talk to them; communicate from your heart with respect, humbleness, gratitude, joy, and awe! Feel their presence intensifying, feel your connection growing stronger! Light, light all around you and light all inside you. Stay in this high and illuminating state and energy; enjoy the absolute serenity and harmony...

When you are ready, conclude the meditation: thank the angels, the light, and the energy, take a few deep breaths, gently move your body and open your eyes. Feel your soul and your body smiling, your entire existence rejoicing, like one big smile! The energy of joy is sacred, angelic, and Divine! It brings good (and it is good) to all levels of existence!

Dedicate even just 10 minutes every day to this meditation and put all your love into it: you will benefit substantially on all levels of your being and in every aspect of your life. Meditation will bring you in contact with the source within you, your essence, your true nature: you are nothing less than consciousness, soul and spirit, light and love, freedom and completeness!

You may have a notebook next to you so you can note down images, sensations, and experiences that you can refer to later, write down questions and answers, observe, remember, and study the course of your spiritual development.

ESOTERIC PRACTICE

Empowering, Deepening, and Uplifting the Angelic Meditation

You have the chance to intensify the experience of meditation, in order for you to open up to its deeper levels of serenity and wisdom, to tap into its beauty and power, when you use the qualities and the possibilities offered to you by the Angelic Invocations and the Angelic Symbols. You may use one method or the other, or use both.

All the invocations and all the symbols have the ability to enhance your meditative experience as they directly awaken and energize your higher potential and help you to focus on the light of your spirit and your soul. Choose intuitively one or more invocations, and/or one or more symbols (there are no limitations). Choose in relation to the issue you are interested in or you wish to meditate on. Again, you may choose invocations or symbols or a combination of both.

The sequence that you will use the symbols or the invocations doesn't really matter. You may begin with the invocations, or with the symbols; do what feels right for you. Follow your inspiration and your intuition.

Browse through the books of invocations and symbols or check the contents. Choose invocations and symbols for guidance, serenity, or connection with the angels, for healing, for the Guardian Angel, for the issues you want to meditate upon, etc.

Note: There is a specific symbol called "Angelic Meditation" that you may use!

You can find all of the Angelic Invocations and the Angelic Symbols (plus detailed instructions on how to use them) in the books with the respective titles in the series Celestial Gifts.

When I meditate (or use invocations or symbols) I see or feel lights or colors! Am I experiencing the presence of angels?

When meditating or practicing other energy and spiritual techniques, you are opening up to a transcendental, a supreme realm that is filled with beauty, light, and colors! It is full of love, peace, and bliss! Perhaps it is energies, other planes of existence or angels that you see! Welcome and invite these experiences. They are truly extraordinary and sublime!

I don't feel or see anything when I meditate! What can I do?

The answer is simple: meditate more! Meditation needs time, energy, and love just like any activity in your life. You will gain a lot more from meditation than what you invest, that is for sure! So just experiment more (with various meditations) and have faith, trust, persistence, and patience.

What is Angelic Channeling?

Channeling is the process where a human being becomes the receiver (channel) of angelic information and energies. To channel, one needs to be energetically clean and purified, to have uplifted and illuminated oneself, through spirituality and their way of living. With an open heart and clear mind, free from selfishness and judgment, a channel receives information and then conveys it to a written message (automatic writing) or speech (oral channeling). It is an intense, mystical, esoteric process beyond the conscious human mind, which accesses the wisdom and knowledge of other, subconscious or superconscious planes. Besides answers and guidance, angelic channeling may provide spiritual-holistic-deep healing on all levels.

How can I exercise "angelic channeling" and become a channel for the energy and the wisdom of the angels?

You can do that by practicing deep relaxation, meditation, prayers, invocations, and visualizations every day. You can channel the celestial realm by calling upon the angels, becoming sensitive to the invisible, subtle, higher vibrations and energies; by practicing your intuition, your clairaudience (internal hearing), and your clairvoyance (internal vision). By making a leap of consciousness (a leap of faith) to trust the higher, the unknown, and at the same time, taking a brave step to trust yourself, your inner wisdom and power, your psychic inner senses. These divine qualities are present within all human beings, but we need to awaken and cultivate them if we want to ascend to higher planes of existence and being.

Is there a specific technique, practice, or advice about channeling?

Practical advice: Together with all the suggestions mentioned above, dedicate some quality time daily (even 10 minutes!) to bring about a state of calm, tranquility, serenity, silence, and internal observation in order to listen to your angels' messages. Observe and listen carefully. What do angels have to tell you? Simply imagine, imagine freely. After some time, exercise in writing what you listen (or feel or see with your mind's eye). You may also practice in expressing verbally what your feel, listen, or see. You will gain great spiritual wealth from this transforming exercise. Intention has a primary role in verbal or written channeling; it is the driving force but also the base and the frame of work. What is the intention of your mind and your heart? Is your intention to become a channel of the angels' energy, of wisdom, light, love, and healing? Great! So be it! And so it is! Remember that in the spiritual world (and therefore everywhere, since spirit is everything), intention is your compass.

ESOTERIC PRACTICE

Angelic Channeling

Apply the following technique without fear or inhibitions. With love. With trust. Leave the judgment, the limitations, and obstacles behind. Invoke the joy and purity of your soul and spirit! Reach love and trust within you to carry out the technique below!

In this process, preparation plays a significant role. You can refer to the answer on a previous question in relation to the preparation before any spiritual practice. Follow all the steps by cleansing efficiently yourself and your space both on the physical and energetic levels.

After the appropriate preparation, sit comfortably with your back straight and take 10 slow and deep breaths. Breathe in through the nose; breathe out through the mouth. Feel your breath filling your entire body. Ask your body and your mind to relax and let go of any tension.

Visualize white light filling your space.

The white light surrounds you. Let it fill you, permeate you, and illuminate you. Let the warm soothing light fill your space. See, affirm, and feel that your space is filled with pure, vital, spiritual light and you are inside the white light; you are radiating pure, vital and spiritual light. White light everywhere inside you and white light all around you, on all levels (repeat this affirmation a few times). See and feel it, vivid and clear!

Feel great spiritual self-confidence, feel how you are emanating love, wisdom, and power! Pure Bliss!

Affirm that you are 100% one with your higher self, your divine nature, your divine essence, your divine consciousness. You are one with the Divine Source of All, the Grand Principle, and Source of All. You are fully in alignment, fully attuned, and fully united – perfectly and divinely.

Feel the angels coming close to you and around you, inside the pure light and the spiritual love.

You are attuned to the angels' presence; you communicate with them. The angels communicate with you. Are there many or one? Is it your guardian angel or an archangel? Do you see light or colors? Which colors?

What do they have to show, what do they have to tell you?

Can you see, hear, feel?

Affirm that you indeed can see, hear, and feel!

Stay in this state of love and light. Emanate love and light, feel love and light, see love and light, receive love and light.

Thank warmly the loving angels that are close to you and communicate with you!

Now open your eyes, take a pen, and put it to paper.

Start to write; write down whatever comes to mind.

Without judgment, let go. Just write or draw. Experiment. Calmly.

You can also speak the wisdom of angels. Feel that your speech and your writing are fully connected with the wisdom, the energy, the power, and the love of the angels and of the Highest Source.

It is a sacred communication and connection, a sacred transmission and reception.

For the first time, you are in this energetic, spiritual height.

For the first time, you feel the wisdom of the angels and the Source so directly and closely!

You are grounding, manifesting, receiving, communicating such wisdom and power!

Write/speak: you are channeling the wisdom, energy, power and love of the angels and the Source.

Do the above exercise once every week (or more often). It will open and enhance your angelic connection. Your own life, the lives of those around you, everyone's lives will overflow with wisdom and miracles.

ESOTERIC PRACTICE

Facilitating and Empowering the Angelic Channeling

You can facilitate and enhance the process, the flow, and the energy of the Angelic Channeling, even more, in two ways (even one way is enough):

– Angelic Symbols
– Angelic Invocations

You can use either invocations, or symbols, or both.

The following Angelic Symbols are suggested:

Angelic Love
Angelic Light
Angelic Guidance
Angelic Truth
Angelic Insight
Angelic Intuition
Angelic Speech
Angelic Inspiration
Angelic Answers
Angelic Message
Angelic Attunement

You may also use the symbols of the guardian angel and the four most known archangels (Michael, Raphael, Gabriel, Uriel) and other symbols.

The following Angelic Invocations are suggested:

Invocation to the Angels of Knowledge and Wisdom (or Invocation to the Angels of the Akashic Records)
Angelic Invocation for Knowledge and Wisdom
Angelic Invocation for Intuition and Psychic/Spiritual Abilities
Angelic Invocation for Answers
Angelic Invocation for Guidance
Angelic Invocation for Connection with the Angels

You may also use invocations to the guardian angel and the four most known archangels (Michael, Raphael, Gabriel, Uriel) and other invocations.

It is not necessary that you use all the symbols or all the invocations that are suggested. It doesn't matter if you use the symbols first and then the invocations or vice versa. Follow your inspiration and your intuition.

For all the Angelic Invocations and the Angelic Symbols (plus detailed instructions on how to use them) refer to the respective books of the series Celestial Gifts.

What are the Angelic Initiations?

The Angelic Initiations are energetic connections with the angels and the archangels. It is a superior, deep, and intense spiritual process, during which we attune to higher frequencies, energies, and qualities to achieve complete healing, advancement, growth, and enlightenment. Essentially, initiations function as openings giving us the opportunity to receive a greater flow of spiritual energies and information, but also to be aware of and integrate the everlasting spiritual truths. Through initiations we empower our spirit and awake our consciousness. The process of being energetically initiated into the angelic vibrations (or other spiritual initiations) can be facilitated by an earthly master/teacher, a mystic, a person who has reached higher levels of energy, awareness and consciousness, or the angels themselves. All initiations are Divine Gifts that accelerate and advance the process of our return to and our union with the One, the All That Is, the Divine.

What is Angelic Therapy?

Angelic Therapy is a method of healing with the help of the angelic realm. There are various "forms" of angelic therapies – various ways and techniques. Angelic Therapies may involve some, a combination, or all of the elements below: invocations, calling upon the angels (especially healing angels and the most known archangels), meditation and visualization with the angels, prayers, use of energy symbols, energy exercises, breathing techniques, hands on the aura, or directly on the body to transmit the spiritual healing energy. The angelic therapy elements can be combined with reiki – the energy healing technique that primarily involves the gentle touch of hands on the body in order to transmit the universal vital energy – or crystal therapy – a healing technique of laying gems, stones, and minerals on or around the body to reinforce and balance the electromagnetic field of the person.

There are also cases of automatic, "uninvoked" (at least consciously) angelic healing, in which people feel the angelic presence around them, they feel the angelic support as they go through a health issue or they are healed with the help, the intervention or contribution of these loving magnificent celestial beings!

ESOTERIC PRACTICE

Angelic Therapy

Receiving, experiencing an Angelic Therapy can prove to be a lot easier than we believe it to be.

To receive and to fill yourself with rejuvenating, vital energy, with the energy and the light of life that emanates from the Highest Source, the Infinite Spirit and the angels, follow the instructions bellow:

1. Light a white candle and dedicate it to the angels of healing, the highest angels of the supreme spirit, of the supreme love, of the supreme light. Observe peacefully and meditate by gazing at the golden flame of the candle for a few minutes. Relax and let yourself feel calm and serene and empty your mind.

2. Lie down comfortably on your back. Take a few slow, full, deep breaths.

3. Imagine all fear and worries flowing away from your body. Fill yourself with hopefulness and positivity. Feel joy. Be receptive and accepting.

4. Mentally, call upon the angels and ask them to give you healing vital energy and healing vital light. Ask them to heal you on all levels.

5. Affirm three times silently or out loud: "Angelic Healing, Vital Light, on all levels."

6. Place your hands where you need energy/therapy or anywhere: on your head, your eyes, your temples, your throat, your chest, your belly, your hips, etc. Let your palms rest on your body for a few minutes (five minutes or more), channeling light/love/energy to each spot.

7. You can visualize that you are inside a perfect and pure white or golden light (the light of the sun). Feel the wonderful, rejuvenating, healing light flowing abundantly through your hands. The white/golden sunlight is intensified when you lay your hands on the different parts of your body.

8. You may lay your hands on various parts of the body for a few minutes each time, or choose only one spot to lay your hands on. On each spot, you may add to the visualization of the flowing light the following affirmation: "Angelic Healing, Vital Light, on all levels."

9. At the end, place your hands open at your sides and allow the angels to continue the healing and to the flow of light to reach every organ and every cell of your body. Let the light fill your thoughts and your feelings, let the light fill each and every level and part of you. Divine, Spiritual, Angelic, Vital Light on all levels... it is the most precious light that there is, the most perfect light that you have ever experienced!

10. Stay at least 10 minutes in this state.

11. Affirm silently or out loud that you are in the most perfect and optimal state of being that you can be! Affirm perfect health and harmony. Take a few deep breaths.

12. The process is complete. Thank the angels for their support and guidance. Feel gratitude from deep within your heart and soul.
You may continue with your daily activities or go to sleep.

Repeat the angelic therapy at least three times on the following days (or the same day, if necessary).

Therapy of a Specific Area

Place your hands on the specific part of the body where you need therapy or energy. Ask the angels to heal the specific area on all levels. Keep your hands on that spot for at least 10 minutes. Proceed with the rest of the process of the Angelic Therapy as described above.

Archangelic Therapy

To revitalize and boost your physical body with vital, invigorating energy, ask from the Supreme Healing Angel, the Archangel Raphael (whose name means "God heals"), to provide you with pure energy, vitality, and light. Ask for it at the beginning and also during the process and visualize Raphael's pure and bright emerald green (physical healing and harmony) or violet (etheric vitality, life force energy, bioenergy, ether) light. Alternatively, you may also visualize white or golden light (spiritual power, love, wisdom). See and feel the light surrounding and filling you with its energy and flame. Proceed with the rest of the process as described earlier in the Angelic Therapy.

Energetic and Spiritual Empowerment and Therapy

To purify, empower, and heal ourselves on the etheric level (the aura of the physical body) and on the spiritual level (higher levels of the self), ask from Archangel Zadkiel to surround you and fill you with the energy of the violet flame. Ask Archangel Zadkiel, see it happening, and feel it at the beginning and during the process. Proceed as usual.

Mental and Emotional Therapy

To purify, empower, and heal on the mental and emotional level of your being, call upon Archangel Michael (spirit, mind) and Archangel Gabriel (psyche, emotions). Ask the Archangels for mental and emotional healing, at the beginning and during the process. Proceed with the rest of the process.

ESOTERIC PRACTICE

Enhancing the Angelic Therapy

If you wish, you can enhance the experience and the effect of the Angelic Therapy, with the use of the Angelic Invocations or the Angelic Symbols. You may apply any of the two practices (invocations or symbols) or both, in any order you choose, before, during, or at the end of the angelic therapy. There are no rules or limitations. Just follow your inner wisdom.

The following Angelic Invocations are suggested:

Invocation to Archangel Raphael
Invocation to the Angels of Healing
Angelic Invocation for Self-Healing
Angelic Invocation for Healing a Specific Body Part, System, or Organ

The following Angelic Symbols are suggested:

Angelic Love
Angelic Light
Angelic Healing
Angelic Energy
Angelic Health

Angelic Deep Healing
Angelic Self-Healing

You may also use other symbols such as:

Angelic Aura Therapy
Angelic Emotional Therapy
Angelic Mental Therapy
Angelic Spiritual Therapy
Angelic Cellular Therapy

As well as the Archangelic Symbols:

Archangel Raphael
Healing Angels
White Light Angels
Golden Light Angels
Violet Light/Flame Angels

For all Angelic Invocations and Angelic Symbols (plus detailed instructions on how to use them) refer to the respective book in this series entitled *Celestial Gifts*.

See also "Archangelic Techniques: Healing (Archangel Raphael)" in a following chapter of this book.

Can the spiritual work with the angels (connection, meditation, invocations, symbols, etc.) cause some sort of purification? Is it possible that I experience negative symptoms (sensations, thoughts, feelings, situations)?

All the energetic and spiritual means – meditations, attunements, initiations, invocations, symbols, esoteric study, and practice – cause purification and catharsis to the totality of our being, to our whole life. Energetic and spiritual means influence and affect the ground of our existence, our vital energy, and our spiritual substance by uplifting, empowering, and bringing them to the surface. As a result, we may experience various symptoms of catharsis ranging from simple to complicated, with short or long duration, difficult and painful or not. These physical (body) and psychological (thoughts, feelings) symptoms manifest themselves in various ways. We may experience odd circumstances, coincidences, and synchronicity; we may have a cold or experience changes in our sleeping and eating habits; we might become moody, angry, sad, or be in physical pain. We may experience the deterioration of a problem or a situation, or blockages in our personal life and our daily activities. It is as if we remove a thorn (and we do have so many thorns!) from our finger: it may be painful at first but it is for our own good.

The symptoms of purification appear as unpleasant and negative but in reality they are indicators of change, transformation, and transmutation. The symptoms will gradually decrease and we will experience greater health, wellbeing, harmony, power, wholeness, and bliss on all levels. Each time we experience a process of purification – whatever the intensity or the duration and on whichever level – we should welcome it because essentially it is positive and beneficial. We need to let go if we want to receive. There are so many things we need to clear and let go; we have been accumulating quite a heavy load through the years. We need profound detoxification, purification, release, and healing on all levels of being.

If you are experiencing cleansing/catharsis phenomena, focus your intention, attention, energy, thoughts, and feelings on the positive, the good, the optimal, and the luminous. Very soon, you will find yourself experiencing all the good things you desire. The quality of your life will improve drastically! Remember that everything is for the Good!

What is considered the best energy and spiritual practice among meditation, visualization, prayer, invocations, channeling, symbols, and initiations?

Each one of the spiritual practices has its own potential, dynamic depth and breadth. Each of the practices serves a specific purpose and offers a unique set of benefits. Meditation is the art of letting go, of accepting, of observing, of focusing, of bringing tranquility to your body and mind, to experience unity and harmony.

Visualization is a form of meditation, of a rather high energy, which employs the use of imagination. During the process of envisioning images in our minds, we exercise our creativity. Visualization offers energetic, uplifting, empowering, healing, and transformative images that vibrate, charge and influence beneficially our body, our life and our entire being.

Prayer is the art of communicating with the Divine element (spirit, angels, and God) and expressing what you wish or your gratefulness for what you already have. It is a sacred personal communication with the Divine.

Invocation is a powerful energetic process of higher consciousness and awareness, during which you affirm what you desire and you co-create it, together with the forces of light for the higher good of all. In an invocation, we recognize and affirm great spiritual truths. Who/what we are: soul and spirit with infinite gifts and high potential. That everything is light/love/energy. That God/The Divine is Love, is the Grand Source of All and is everywhere. That we are one/in full harmony with The Divine, etc. With the use of invocations we manifest our higher potential and our spiritual essence.

Channeling is the art of allowing yourself to connect with higher consciousnesses and super-intelligences, to receive knowledge, guidance, and wisdom and to express the fruits of this communication orally or in writing.

Symbols provide a clear and direct link of communication with the subconscious and superconscious planes of mind and aspects of our self. Symbols activate archetypes, knowledge, and power on other levels; they awaken our spiritual essence and sacredness, and function as concentrated energies and qualities of light, as keys that unlock the aspects of our higher self and as tools of spiritual (holistic, i.e. on all levels) therapy.

Initiations are energetic and spiritual empowerments that we receive from a master (earthly or heavenly, human or celestial), from the universe, from our spirit, and our higher essence. Initiations harmonize us, attune us, energize us, awaken us, and lead us to higher stages of spiritual growth to the next phase of our personal journey. Initiations usually awaken and activate latent qualities and potential such as the power of healing ourselves and others.

Symbols and initiations manifest the power of energy, prayer, and invocation manifest the power of speech, meditation, and visualization manifest the power of the mind, channeling manifests the power of inspiration. All the spiritual practices together manifest the power of the heart, of the soul, of our core, and our essence.

By practicing all the methods with patience, persistence, consistency, faith, love, with a positive attitude, and joy, with serenity and wisdom, we become whole and complete, we manifest our light, our love, and our potential on all levels. We become like the angels, an embodiment of the highest energies and initiations, of the highest prayers and invocations, of the highest meditations and visualizations, of the highest symbols of spirit, of heaven, of the All That Is.

A Question for Thought, Meditation, and Further Study

Have you ever thought of your existence as a symbol? Or perhaps as energy? A prayer or an invocation? A meditation or a visualization?

Have you ever considered your physical body, in the here and now to be energy, a symbol, an invocation, a prayer, a visualization, a meditation?

By practicing energy and spiritual techniques, and methods of the highest level, purity, love, and awareness, you change the symbol, the invocation, the prayer, and the meditation that you are, that your physical body is. The purpose of your existence is to become the highest, supreme, final, absolute, and most perfect symbol, the highest and supreme, the final, absolute and most perfect meditation and visualization, the highest and supreme, the final, absolute and most perfect invocation and prayer!

How can I cleanse a space from negative energy? How can I charge and energize a space with higher positive energy?

To cleanse your space from negative energy and to charge it spiritually, follow the steps given below:

– First of all, clean thoroughly and tidy your space on a physical level.

– Make your space as clean, tidy, beautiful and harmonious as you can.

– Make sure that the colors in the room are luminous, beautiful, and positive. Create an atmosphere where you feel serene, relaxed, and joyful.

– Recycle or give away items that you don't like or don't use.

– Ask for advice from a Feng Shui consultant or study a Feng Shui book to make sure that the energy flows smoothly in your space.

– Energize and scent your space with pure essential oils. Use incense sticks, sage, or frankincense to purify the energy of the room and create a spiritually uplifted and clean atmosphere.

– Place crystals or beautiful healing energy objects. Make sure to cleanse and energize your crystals regularly.

– Place a big glass bowl filled with water and coarse salt (water and salt "attract" and transmute negative energy) in the middle of the room. Do the same at the corners of the room by placing smaller bowls or glasses filled with water and salt. After two to three days, discard the water. Repeat the process when you feel it is necessary.

– Use some soft and serene music like new age music, meditation music (or yoga, reiki, massage music, etc.), gong music, sounds of nature (birds, waves, etc.), mantras, prayers, classical music, etc.

– Light a few white candles. As you light the candles, dedicate them to the Divine Source, the Light, the Angels, and the Highest Good.

(Attention: the candles have to always be away from flammable objects and never be left unattended)

– Visualize White Light filling the entire room.

– Call upon the angels to illuminate your space. You may call upon your guardian angel and Archangel Michael. Ask them to purify and protect your space.

– Say a prayer or invocation (or a few of them).

– Draw Angelic Symbols on the walls or the furniture (choose intuitively). You can draw symbols energetically (with your palm/finger), visualize them, or draw them on pieces of paper and place them in the room.

– Dedicate with great faith, love, and gratitude your space to the Divine Source, the Light, the Angels, and the Highest Good.

You may also apply the technique "Creating Angelic Fields" given in this book (at the end of the "Guardian Angel" chapter). It is an extraordinary and prominent technique!

Finally, feel and see (both physically and mentally) that your space is 100% luminous and angelic – angelically luminous and luminously angelic! It is done and so it is! May you have the most pleasant stay in it!

I have a health issue. Which technique should I apply in order to help myself?

All the meditations and the techniques described in this book have multiple benefits on all levels. They relax deeply (mentally/spiritually) and revitalize profoundly (etherically /energetically); they reconstruct and positively charge our being with love, pure vital energy, and high spiritual light.

If I had to choose only three exercises (techniques, meditations, etc.) out of this book, I would suggest the study and daily practice of the following exercises:

– *Angelic Therapy (and Enhancing Angelic Therapy)*
– *Archangelic Techniques: Therapy of a certain spot, organ and/or system of the body*
– *White and Golden Light Meditation*

The exercises suggested below can also prove to be very useful:
– *Angelic Bath*
– *Spiritual Protection from Lower Energies*
– *Enhancing Spiritual Protection*
– *The Archangels in the Human Body*
– *Enhancing the Body with Archangelic Energies for Optimal Health*
– *Attunement to the Four Archangels of Light*
– *Facilitation and Empowerment of the Archangelic Attunement*
– *Archangelic Attunement: a 21-Day Plan*
– *Advanced Healing of the Subconscious*
– *Advanced Physical Healing: Materialization and Dematerialization*
– *Creating Angelic Fields*
– *Angelic and Archangelic Fields in the Body*
– *Violet Flame*
– *Archangelic Activation of the Energy Centers (Chakras)*
– *Archangelic Activation of Our Bodies*
– *Clearing Thought-Forms with Archangel Michael*
– *Archangelic Cleansing of the Negative Karma and Activation of the Positive Karma*
– *Removing Karmic Ties with the help of Archangel Michael*
– *Angelic and Divine DNA Activation*

(Note: to find the suggested exercises check the "Index of Exercises, Meditations and Techniques" at the beginning of the book.)

It is advisable to practice all of the above exercises, techniques, and meditations; they have the potential to help you profoundly as they supplement and enhance one another.

Don't neglect to follow the appropriate medical or psychological treatment and supervision. Remember: when you connect with your spirit and your soul, your true self and essence, the Supreme Source of All and its Angels, you are guided to the most appropriate means (doctors, treatment, etc.) for your wisest and most immediate Healing, your true and complete Healing. Remember that nothing is happening by chance and everything is for the Good! Go with the flow! Do it with awareness, trust, and love! Angels are always and constantly near you! Even at this moment!

Can I energize the water or the food with the vital and spiritual energy of angels and of the Source?

Yes! Place your hands (palms) above or around your food/water and ask the Divine Source and the Highest Angels of the Highest Light to energize and charge it positively. Take your time and keep your hands in this position for a while. Visualize pure and bright vital light surrounding, filling up, and charging the food or the water. Do it consciously, with Love, and here's to you!

I often read that after a meditation (or another spiritual practice) I need some grounding. What is grounding?

After every spiritual and energy practice it is necessary to return to the "here and now," to the physical reality, to our environment. We need to reconnect with Mother Earth, the matter, and our body in a more pure, creative, and harmonious way. We need "grounding": a better, more direct, powerful coordination with our physical body, Earth and matter; an empowerment of our physical (biological) self, our mind and our emotional wellbeing, so as to function with clarity, adaptability, effectiveness; to have health, balance, joy, and power.

You can ground yourself through:

– Physical activity and exercise
– Rest and sleep
– Body practices such as massage
– Taking a shower/ bath, washing hands, drinking plenty of water
– Proper, healthy and natural nutrition
– Being out in nature and/or having meaningful and loving contact with other people – Contact with the ground/earth, preferably soil, sand, or grass: walking barefoot and being aware of your feet touching the ground

– Contact and caring for animals and plants

– Having a strong intention and focusing on grounding yourself: visualize a white ray of light connecting your sitting point (first chakra, the base of your spine) to the center of the Earth. Alternatively, visualize an anchor, or tree roots spreading from the soles of your feet all the way down to the center of the Earth, like a strong and healthy tree.

– Affirmations: Affirm several times that you are 100% present in the here and now, in your physical body and on Earth; that you adapt fully, you function with clarity, easily, and effectively here on Earth, in matter, in your environment; you ground effectively your being, your spirit, your energy, and your power.

Why is grounding necessary after spiritual practice?

Grounding is necessary when a spiritual takeoff has taken place! The more we grow spiritually and energetically, experience insight, spiritual clarity and awareness, our auras and energies brighten, the harder it becomes to return to our physical body, to the "here and now." It becomes difficult to return to the material world, things seem heavier, negative, darker, tiring...

However, our goal is to spiritualize our entire life, to fill it with light, love, wisdom, and power, not to escape to another reality. We are here to become conscious of the Divine beauty, the Divine plan, the Divine perfection, our spiritual essence, our potential and talents, the unconditional love and profound wisdom we carry within us, now, in this lifetime! The entire universe contributed to our creation and the entire universe (and we, even more so!) wants us to be right here, right now (otherwise we wouldn't be here!). The process of transferring the knowledge, freedom, wisdom, love, light, vitality, positivity, completeness – that we experience in other planes of existence, in other dimensions and realms like the angelic realm – to our conscious mind, body and life, to the "here and now," to Earth is essentially our Grounding. Our Grounding is our Manifestation. By connecting to our Alpha (Beginning, Source, Divinity, Oneness, Wholeness) we illuminate, uplift, accept, love, heal fully, and substantially our Omega (personality, body, earthly/lower self). It is the definition of true bliss!

How can I protect myself from fallen angels?

It is actually quite simple. Just ignore them. Mentally affirm, "You don't exist!" Or send them away. Affirm, "away from here!" After you have negated their existence or sent them away, make sure to invoke the luminous/higher angels. Affirm, "Highest Angels of the Divine Light, I call upon you here!"

Is there a special technique to disengage from negative energy?

Yes! It is the invocation of Archangel Michael and the visualization of the Golden Light. Apply the technique described below.

ESOTERIC PRACTICE

Spiritual Protection from Lower Energies

Start by gradually breathing to your belly. Breathe in through the nose; breathe out through the mouth, slowly and gradually, without haste. Ask your body and your mind to relax and let go of any tension.

Visualize a bright golden fiery sphere of pure spiritual light and sheer vital energy surrounding you.

Visualize, feel, and imagine that you are inside the sphere of golden light.

The golden light – the highest vibration of the spirit – drives away all lower/harmful vibrations, energies, and influences. It is the absolute spiritual protection and the ultimate spiritual purification. The golden light is the energy/the Light of spirit, of logos, of consciousness, of the Divine Principle, Source, and Power.

As you continue to breathe deeply, use your intention to increase the golden light. It is as if you are inside a radiating golden sun... and you are indeed! You are inside a radiating golden sun!

Call upon Archangel Michael, the supreme angel of the Will and Power of God, the supreme angel of the Divine Guidance and Purification, the supreme angel that overcomes all harm and evil.

Bring Archangel Michael to your mind, or repeat his name a few times (silently or aloud): "Archangel Michael... Archangel Michael... Archangel Michael..."

Declare that by being in the presence of Archangel Michael, inside the Golden Light, you have 100% protection on all levels. Repeat the affirmation a few times: "Archangel Michael and the Golden Light, offer me 100% Protection, Divine Protection on all levels."

Wherever Archangel Michael (the power, will, protection, and guidance of God/the Divine) is present, there are no harmful energies around! Wherever there is Light, darkness is negated... "Archangel Michael!"

Take a few deep breaths and gently open your eyes. You are perfectly and fully protected!

You may combine the above meditation with the following techniques:

– Angelic Tratak Meditation (before the "Spiritual Protection from Lower Energies")

– Angelic Bath (after the "Spiritual Protection from Lower Energies")

See also "Clearing Thought-Forms with Archangel Michael."

ESOTERIC PRACTICE

Enhancing the Spiritual Protection

You can enhance and strengthen your protection on all levels through the Angelic Invocations and the Angelic Symbols.

The following Angelic Invocations are suggested:

– *Invocation to the Guardian Angel*
– *Invocation to Archangel Michael*
– *Invocation to the Powers (Authorities)*
– *Angelic Invocation for the Removal of Negative Energies*
– *Angelic Invocation for Protection*

The following Angelic Symbols are suggested:

– *Angelic Light*
– *Angelic Protection*
– *Angelic Power*
– *Angelic Clearing of Negative Influence*
– *Angelic Purification of Negative Energy*
– *Archangel Michael*
– *Guardian Angel*
– *Protection Angels*

It is not necessary that you use all the symbols or all the invocations that are suggested. You can use either symbols or invocations or both, before, during or after the above meditation. There are no rules or limitations. It doesn't matter if you use the symbols first and then the invocations or vice versa. Follow your inspiration and your intuition.

For all the Angelic Invocations and Angelic Symbols (plus detailed instructions on how to use them) refer to the respective books in the series Celestial Gifts.

I believe there is negative energy around or inside me. How can I eliminate it?

Apply the technique of "Spiritual Protection from Lower Energies" as described above: visualize, see and feel – as clearly and intensely as you can – bright golden spiritual light surrounding you and call upon Archangel Michael.

Ask from Archangel Michael to remove any negative energy from around, near, or inside you.

Carry out the process slowly and with intention. Repeat several times.

Additionally, you can use the Angelic Symbols and the Angelic Invocations mentioned earlier in "Enhancing Spiritual Protection."

Is there a way not to attract dark or negative energies? How can I avoid contact with fallen angels?

You can avoid contact with fallen angels by carrying out a deep and essential revisal, reorganization, rearrangement, and primarily an inner upgrade of your entire being and of what you emit. Throw out all the debris and garbage that you have been carrying for years (negative thoughts, beliefs, emotions or experiences). Begin to realize, observe, and focus on the positive things. Daily. See the beautiful, good, true, substantial things: yes, they do exist in overabundance – so much so that we take them for granted, and don't even realize them. Learn to think and feel positively, to forgive and experience joy, appreciation and gratitude. Practice unconditional, selfless love, a love beyond "egos," "shoulds" or "wants." Practice the true spiritual love that all the great masters taught. It is a commitment that takes great persistence, patience, everyday practice, soul-searching, self-observation, and self-improvement. It is a process that takes years, if not "forever!" By embracing such a way of being and living, you will not have any contact with dark energies and fallen angels. You will be way up higher than them! These lower energies will become a thing of the past!

How can I reach spiritual illumination and be utterly united with the Divine, the supreme, the absolute, the eternal? How can I fulfill my life's purpose? What is the way to experience true happiness?

Read the previous answer once more; study it carefully. It includes all the golden rules of life. Read also the answer to the last question of this chapter (the one regarding Angelic Advice).

Can the angels bring my soulmate and me together?

If you are ready to experience absolute and perfect love and romance, ultimate joy and bliss with another person – and not only in terms of romance and partnership but also in terms of friendship, family, and spirituality – then the entire universe and existence will make sure that it happens! Existence and the universe will have everything prepared and taken care of and the only thing you will have to do is simply to be present. As long as you are ready!

I wish to guide other people (e.g. my spouse, my children) on their spiritual path. To help them engage with spiritual, esoteric matters. I wish them to become awakened and aware of their potential, the wisdom, and the strength within them, I wish them to become whole and happy. What can I do to help them?

Each person – as dear as he/she is to us – has his/her own journey, his/her own path to travel, his/her own life lessons to learn in the school of Earth. Don't push or force situations even if it is for the person's own good – or rather, what you consider as "good." The only thing you can do is to become the best version of yourself, to become your higher self, the wise, conscious, spiritual self of love and freedom that you are. Become what you are in essence, on the spiritual dimension, on the utmost/divine level. Become what You Are. Express with love, wisdom, and power your spiritual truth; a truth full of genuineness, oneness, harmony, peace, offer, and benevolence.

As you come closer to this optimal state of being, this ideal experience, the world around you will transform, will change, will transmute with you. As you illuminate, liberate yourself and foster self-actualization, you create the potential for others to follow and do the same. Do everything that is necessary for your spiritual – whole and genuine – self, for your spiritual advancement and growth, do all the sacrifices, all the changes, and others will become awakened by your example.

What would angels advise us human beings to do?

Angels would give people – and you personally – the following advice:

1. Laugh! Laugh truly, spontaneously, deeply as often as you can. Laughter and joy increase the quality of your energy, your vibration, and they purify your thoughts and emotions. They are healing elements! Be happy; laugh lavishly and freely beyond the limitations of your mind. Laughter and joy emit and attract spiritual forces and naturally angels!

2. Find your inner child; begin each day by seeing the world in a fresh, playful, and innocent way!

3. Surround yourself with beauty: beautiful colors, plants, trees, and flowers. Remember that angels love flowers!

4. Choose a proper nutrition program that corresponds to your needs: observe which foods drain your energy and which increase your energy. Go for natural, aromatic, colorful, fresh, light and whole foods from Mother Earth. Avoid processed, heavy, refined, and dead foods.

5. Love nature and its elements: fire (light), wind, water, earth. All elements are sacred.

6. Accept and love yourself, others as yourself and the entire existence as yourself.

7. Forgive. Release.

8. Let go of fear.

9. Become love.

10. Live love experientially; do a good deed each day.

11. In your mind's eye, surround yourself with a radiant golden sphere of spiritual protection and guidance. Do it every morning and evening. See and feel the light, the love of the Spirit, of the Angels and of the Divine surrounding and filling you up.

12. Choose the good. Choose the good on all levels; choose the good everywhere and every time; choose the good in the "here and now;" choose the good, no matter what. Good is and will always be what You Are. All other choices are doomed to be smaller, lesser, inferior. Good will set you free.

ESOTERIC PRACTICE

Angelic Art

If you are an artist or you have art as hobby, call upon the angels of that art. Ask the angels to enhance and uplift your artistic work, to enrich it with their infinite light, their crystal clear energy, their creative force, and their beautiful celestial love! Ask them in every instance! Additionally, dedicate your art and your creativity to the highest good of all, the Divine Good. Ask from the Angels to awaken, activate, and enlighten all your superior, divine talents, all the splendid artistry of your spirit and your soul!

ESOTERIC PRACTICE

Angelic Painting

You don't need any special skill or talent to carry out this practice – though you already possess all the talents in the world, always, inside your infinite and divine spirit and soul!

Start by invoking, inviting, calling upon the Angels of Light, the highest angels of the highest light. Do it from your heart. Light a white candle and dedicate it to the Angels and the Divine Source of All Life, with much love. Relax, while you are peacefully looking at the golden candle flame. Immerse yourself in the flame; fill your being and your entire body with its warm glowing radiance.

Take a few pieces of white paper and several markers of various colors and shades.

In your mind's eye, ask the angels to guide you. Concentrate. Take a few deep breaths.

Begin to paint... playfully, freely, express yourself. Draw something or play with the colors. Release any fear, judgment, any thoughts, any inhibition, or expectation. Leave these elements outside your painting and express yourself cheerfully and freely.

Keep on painting. Use more sheets of paper; don't stop. Follow this process a few days in a row or whenever you feel the need to. Even though this exercise seems to be simple, it will relax and revitalize you, and furthermore it will help you find your expression and become a child again. It will prove to be an important aid on all levels of your being. Do not undervalue it; overvalue it! God/The Divine (the highest consciousness and creative principle of the universe) draws, paints, and colors the world and reality, every single moment, just as you can paint your world and your reality! Painting will bring you closer to the creative part of your being, the one that is your "most" Divine!

ESOTERIC PRACTICE

Angelic Prayer

Create your own personal prayer to God/the Divine and its Angels. Create a beautiful, positive prayer, full of love and light. Make it from your heart, spontaneously, genuinely, and truly. Use it with faith and respect, with humbleness and gratitude to communicate with the divine element so that you may receive power, wisdom, and guidance. Ask from the highest angels of pure spirit to help you in writing your prayer. If you feel like it, share your prayer with your loved ones. View your prayer as a celestial gift of heaven for that is what it is!

ESOTERIC PRACTICE

Angelic Invocation

In a similar way to the "Angelic Prayer," you can create an invocation to ask something specific from the angels.

For example:

"I call upon the Highest Angels of the Highest Light
to guide me to the perfect, most luminous and brilliant
Invocation of Love and Healing,
for the Highest Good of All!
Let it be so! And so it is! Thank You!"

ESOTERIC PRACTICE

Angelic Tratak Meditation

Tratak is a form of meditation with the eyes open. Usually it is carried out with a candle flame that enhances and uplifts your energy, aura, and spiritual consciousness. Tratak awakens and activates the ability of clairvoyance, all psychic abilities, as well as our spiritual potential. It is truly a wonderful and deep meditation, very effective and beneficial, a truly divine meditation. Fiery and luminous like the light and fire of the flame!

Here is the process of Tratak meditation, step by step:

Light a white candle.

Place it a meter away, in front of you, at eye level.

As you light the candle, you may dedicate it to your guardian angel, to Archangel Michael or other angels. Also to your Higher Self, the Divine Source, and the Highest Good of All.

Sit comfortably and relax.

Take some deep breaths.

Focus your eyes on the candle flame for a few minutes.

Keep gazing gently at the flame for as long as you can.

In the beginning gaze at the flame for three to five minutes. Later, after a few sessions of practice, reach up to 10 minutes.

Sense, feel the flame, the bright light, the warmth.

Feel that the light surrounds you and permeates your entire being, your whole body, feel the light filling you, flowing through you, illuminating you.

Bring your awareness to your beloved Guardian Angel, Archangel Michael, or another Archangel. Bring your awareness to the Spiritual Dimension, Spirit, the Highest Good, the Divine Light, God, the Absolute/Supreme/Infinite Reality, the Ultimate Source of Everything, of All-That-Is.

Close your eyes and see the "image" of the flame. You can keep your eyes closed for some more, visualizing the flame or open them and gaze at the candle flame once again. You may alternate between having your eyes open, gazing at the flame and having them closed, visualizing the flame. Alternate and stay some minutes in each state and repeat some times, relaxed, with no rush.

Remain in this fiery energy. Stay in this deep, intense, luminous, golden state; this deep, intense, luminous, golden experience.

The Angelic Tratak Meditation can be performed before any other meditation, exercise, or technique to complement and enhance it.

ESOTERIC PRACTICE

Angelic Crystal Healing

Do you know that you can combine the power and the spiritual qualities of angels with the power and the healing qualities of the Earth, its crystals, its minerals, and its gemstones? It is an extraordinary potential and an amazing process!

Angels, with their higher healing qualities energize and enhance the crystals and their field, while crystals ground, manifest and emit – like magnets, like transmitters, like gates – the higher healing energies of the angels. It is not a coincidence that people who own crystals, minerals, and gemstones often have sharp intuition, awakened spiritual and healing abilities; people who study and experience the angelic realm are drawn to the amazing mineral kingdom of Mother Earth!

Begin by studying a book about crystals and crystal therapy. There are several good books available. Then, you can buy crystals in a specialized shop that sells minerals and gemstones. Chose intuitively what you like and what draws your attention or follow the advice of a crystal therapist or a crystal therapy book, based on the properties of specific crystals. Cleanse your crystals from lower energies, purify and charge them, then place the crystals on you or near you. Crystals worn on the body or placed around you are used for meditation, invigoration, healing, and protection.

You can choose the three most known and important crystals:

– The clear quartz symbolizes and emits energy and light.

– The rose quartz symbolizes and emits love.

– The amethyst symbolizes and emits spiritual power, protection, and guidance.

Crystals can be either cut in various shapes and polished or in their natural state.

For example: Chose 10 small clear or rose quartz crystals. Having the intention of cleansing your crystals, hold them under cool tap water to release the lower energies. You can also purify crystals by burying them in sea salt inside a glass container. Leave the crystals for three to four hours and then rinse them under cool running water.

Now, you are ready to energize and charge your crystals with natural energies transmitted by the sun. Have this intention in your mind and place the crystals in the sunlight allowing them to absorb the powerful energies that the sun emits. After this process, hold the crystals in your hands, connect with them, feel them, give them more light and love! Hold them in your hands, mentally talk to them and dedicate them to the highest healing energies. Crystals are remarkably sensitive and wise – do you feel it?

There are several additional ways of cleansing, charging, and energizing the crystals in books about crystal therapy.

After you have cleansed and energized your crystals, place them on your body or around you with the intention of healing and activation. You can create a circle and sit or lie in its center. You can also place the crystals on your seven energy centers (chakras), on your palms or under the soles of your feet.

From your heart, call upon the Angels of Light to bless and charge with angelic qualities the crystals and you. You may call your guardian angel, the Angels of Healing, the archangels (Michael, Gabriel etc.).

Bring yourself to a state of receptiveness, in order to experience, to receive and stay in that energy for at least 10 minutes. Afterward, thank the Divine Beings for working with you, cleanse your crystals (with water, sea salt, sunlight, and focused intention). Take care of your crystals, give them extra energy, light, and love (use your mind and your hands) as they are exceptionally sensitive.

Repeat the process of crystal therapy in the following days and experiment! The angelic crystal therapy is truly amazing!

See also the answer to a relevant question in the chapter "The Archangels" in this book.

PART III

The Archangels

What are the Archangels? What is the difference between Archangels and Guardian Angels?

The Archangels are superior, higher angels of the light. Their purpose is to protect and guide all of humanity. They are universal, cosmic, and spiritual forces. Imagine the Archangels as the gravity, the attraction, the action, the motion, the creative energy in spiritual terms, in a spiritual cosmic level (of six dimensions). They are the forces of nature, the spiritual forces (remember that the spiritual essence and light is everywhere and is everything, in various frequencies). The spiritual powers are the same for everyone, just as forces of nature are – and they are both "objective."

The Archangels belong to the Divine and serve the Divine, and they move within the Divine but in a greater (higher, whole) spectrum of light, spirit, essence and consciousness. This is the reason why Archangels have infinite powers and potential. Attuning to the archangelic energies – the cosmic forces of the universe/of nature/of spirit – through meditation, prayer, invocation, visualization and symbols brings great vital energy and power to our body, our aura, our psyche, and our mind. Attunement to the archangelic realm purifies us deeply and uplifts us wholly. It is true spiritual bliss!

Guardian angels are more personal. Each Guardian Angel is connected directly to the soul and the personality of a person. Every soul has a Guardian Angel assigned to it for protection and guidance. A Guardian Angel is a divine blueprint, an angelic "duplicate" of a human being's soul. A Guardian Angel is our celestial "other half."

For more information regarding Guardian Angels, check the next chapter of this book.

Are the Archangels superior to angels?

In the spiritual realm there is no higher and lower. This is a human distinction, as in Spirit, everyone and everything has a righteous, perfect and eligible part. Nevertheless, from a human perspective, we can say that Archangels can be considered angels of a higher rank. They vibrate in a wider and higher spectrum of energy. The Angelic Hierarchy (the most well-known esoteric listing of the celestial hierarchy) has a total of nine distinct orders of celestial beings. Archangels are right above the rank of angels and they are both very close to humanity.

According to esoteric texts (and also experiences through higher spiritual attunement), angels are projections and extensions of the Archangels: angelic thoughts (children) of the Archangels. For example: the angels of healing belong to Archangel Raphael, the angels of serenity and regeneration to Archangel Gabriel, and the angels of divine will, spiritual guidance, cleansing, purification, and protection from evil belong to Archangel Michael.

Who are the most known Archangels?

Archangel Michael, Archangel Gabriel, and Archangel Raphael are the best known Archangels. They are the closest to humanity and they guide our overall healing and multidimensional development. Michael, Gabriel, and Raphael are the only Archangels mentioned in the Bible. The name of Raphael appears in the Book of Tobit that is part of the Roman Catholic and Orthodox Christian biblical canon, but it is not accepted by the Protestants (they regard it as part of the Apocrypha). Uriel is mentioned in the Apocryphal Book of Enoch. The Archangels Michael, Gabriel, and Raphael are celebrated by the Roman Catholic Church on the 29th of September and by the Christian Orthodox Church on the 8th of November.

Islam recognizes four Archangels: Michael (Angel of Mercy), Gabriel (the Angel that communicates with all the Prophets and the one that revealed the Qur'an), Raphael (the Angel that signals the coming of Judgment Day), and Azrael, who is the one who separates the soul from the body (the Angel of Death).

Are Archangels mentioned in texts prior to the three major monotheistic religions (Judaism, Christianity, Islam)? Is there something similar to Archangels in eastern philosophies and religions (Buddhism, Hinduism)?

Zoroastrianism (6th century BC) was among the primary and most important monotheistic religions (if not the very first monotheistic religion). It had a profound influence on the three largest monotheistic religions that followed: Judaism, Christianity, and Islam. Zoroastrianism passed on several parables, philosophical and moral principles, and various other elements to the three monotheistic religions – among others the distinction of good-evil and the battle between good and evil.

In Zoroastrianism, the Supreme Force is Ahura Mazda who created six Archangels called the "Amesha Spentas" (their name means "Bounteous Immortals"); they represent aspects of the Divine. Amesha Spentas are "Emanations" or "Divine Sparks" of the Divine. Those are perhaps the earliest references to Archangels. Zoroastrianism mentions Fravashi, Guardian Angels that all people have.

There are respective references to Archangels in eastern religions and philosophies: Buddhist tradition has Devas (celestial beings) and Dharmapalas (karma protectors), while Hinduism has Devas and Mahadevas.

So are the Archangels (Michael, Gabriel...) and Guardian Angels mentioned in other religions and traditions besides the three major monotheistic religions and Western esotericism?

Yes they are! If another religion, philosophical system, or tradition mentions a spiritual being that guides and protects us, then it refers to the Guardian Angel!

If you read or hear about great spirits or celestial beings of fire, light, protection, divine will, purification, or of the battle against evil, they refer to Archangel Michael (or the angels of his "order" and energy).

If you read or hear about celestial beings that heal, then it is a reference to Archangel Raphael (or his angels); if there are references to high spirits/incorporeal beings of water (water element) or of the psyche (and the emotions), of joy, serenity, or sleep, then it is related to Archangel Gabriel (or the angels of his order and energy).

This does not mean that they are referring to "our" Archangel Michael, Gabriel, Raphael and Guardian Angel; it is rather that we (all people, all religions and all spiritual traditions) refer to the same forces, qualities and states of nature, of the universe, of being. We refer to the same celestial, immaterial, spiritual, and transcendent beings!

Don't forget that Reality is supreme and infinite, and Truth is unspeakable. The human mind cannot fully perceive Reality and Truth and the human language cannot express them precisely. All philosophies – all human thoughts and ideas, all systems of knowledge – are just prisms on what Exists, perspectives of what Is.

How are the four Archangels related to human beings and nature's elements?

The four most known Archangels of the light represent the basic, primal, structural elements of nature: fire, water, air, and earth. The Archangels constitute the higher consciousness, the higher being and the higher self of nature's elements; they are its profound higher essence and source. Archangels (as the active forces of the Divine) have created the four sacred elements and thus all things in our universe (everything is a combination of the four elements) and beyond.

Here in our material universe, the earth element is dominant (matter), in the fourth dimension the element of water (feelings, emotions) prevails, in the fifth dimension it is the element of air (mind), and in the sixth dimension it is the element of fire (light, spirit) that dominates. There is a fifth sacred element, the mystical element of ether (bioenergy, life-force energy, etheric vitality) that is included in the element of air.

Each one of the Archangels is associated with one of the elements and the dimensions. The relationship between the Archangels, nature's elements, the dimensions, and human beings is summarized below. It is the fruit of studies of many great teachers and mystics (over the course of many years and many lifetimes). Study this information and meditate on it. It comprises the links between the various realms and therefore all the secrets, laws, and principles of the universe and of Life.

Archangel Michael:

Element: Fire (including Light)

Realm: Spiritual Realm (sixth dimension) and Mental Realm (fifth dimension)

Correspondence to the human physical body: blood, body warmth

Archangel Gabriel:

Element: Water

Realm: Emotional/Psychical Realm (fourth dimension)

Correspondence to the human physical body: body fluids

Archangel Raphael:

Element: Air (including etheric/life-force/vital energy)

Realm: Mental and Etheric Realm (fifth dimension and the aura-energy body-womb of the material realm)

Correspondence to the human physical body: breath, vitality

Archangel Uriel:

Element: Earth

Realm: Material Realm (world of the three dimensions)

Correspondence to the human physical body: dense matter (together with the angels of matter)

How many Archangels are there? Which ones do we know? What qualities, characteristics, and duties do they have and what do they represent? What sort of energies does each one emit?

The number of Archangels is countless. The most known Archangels are: Michael, Gabriel, Raphael, Uriel, Haniel, Jophiel, Zadkiel, Tzaphkiel, Chamuel, Raguel, Raziel, Ariel, Jeremiel, Samael, Azrael, Sandalphon, and Metatron.

Below you will find a list with the qualities and characteristics of each Archangel, including their resonance with colors and energies. Remember that the list is based upon the studies of esoteric teachers and mystics and on personal clairvoyant and meditative experiences and in no way is it fixed, absolute, or exclusive. Just like human beings, the Archangels – as Divine beings of great beauty, love, and wisdom – have all the potential, the qualities, and the characteristics of the Spirit within them.

The Main Qualities and Characteristics of the Archangels:

Michael: Protection, Guidance, Purification, Divine Will

Gabriel: Feelings, Serenity, Peace, Hope, Regeneration

Raphael: Healing

Uriel: Light, Grounding, Balance, Harmony

Sandalphon: Nature, Grounding, Balance, Harmony

Metatron: Enlightenment, Ascension

Haniel: Joy, Psychic Abilities, Emotional Communication

Chamuel: Love, Relationships

Raziel: Rites, Mysteries, Knowledge and Wisdom of the Universe

Ariel: Environment, Wild Nature, Water, Wind

Tzaphkiel: Maternal Energy and Love, Reflection, Angelic Realms

Zadkiel: Justice, Compassion, Forgiveness, Purification, Healing

Jophiel: Beauty, Art, Knowledge, Wisdom

Jeremiel: Mercy, Insight, Prophecy, Dreams

Samael: Transition, Change, Deep Healing, Materialization and Dematerialization

Azrael: Transition, Change, Healing of Subconscious/Shadow/Fears

Raguel: Friendship, Cooperation, Justice, Harmony

The Colors and Energies of the Archangels

Michael: Red (Fire, Purification, Protection) or Blue/Azure (Divine Will) or Gold (Divine Protection and Power)

Gabriel: Blue/Azure (Water, Feelings, Serenity) or Fuchsia (Divine Love, Care, Maternal Energy) or White (Purity)

Raphael: Green/Emerald Green (Body Healing) or Purple/Violet (Etheric Vitality, Life-Force Energy) or White (Light of Life)

Uriel: White or Silver

Sandalphon: Green, Stone/Earthly Colors

Metatron: Platinum

Haniel: Baby Blue, Turquoise

Chamuel: Pink

Raziel: Deep Blue

Ariel: Pale Green

Tzaphkiel: Turquoise

Zadkiel: Violet

Jophiel: Yellow

Jeremiel: Violet, Deep Blue

Samael: Deep Green

Azrael: Deep Red, Yellow, Green

Raguel: Orange, Yellow

Guardian Angel: All colors (rainbow) or White (purity) or Pink (selfless maternal love and care) or Azure (celestial serenity and protection)

A Question for Thought, Meditation, and Further Study:

Michael, Gabriel, Raphael, Uriel, Haniel, Jophiel, Zadkiel, Tzaphkiel, Chamuel, Raguel, Raziel, Ariel, Jeremiel, Samael, Azrael, Sandalphon, and Metatron:

Which archangelic name sounds special to you? Which name attracts you, which one ignites your imagination and which one you find strange or even repelling? It is most probable that you have something important to learn and receive from the respective Archangels! Study and meditate upon their energies and qualities.

Sometimes different books, teachers and spiritual systems attribute different qualities and colors to the same Archangels. Why is that? What are the "correct" colors?

There is not only one "correct" color. For example, Archangel Michael can be perceived as red energy and power (by virtue of fire that is his dominant element), azure (which symbolizes the sky, serenity, the infinite, Divine Will), gold (which symbolizes spiritual wisdom and power, pure consciousness), and so on. And vice versa, as we visualize specific colors, we attune to and receive the corresponding energies and qualities of each Archangel: e.g. if we visualize red flame within and all around us and we invoke Archangel Michael, we will strengthen our fire (power and our mental field) and get cleansed from negative energies, and evil (in all its forms) recedes. If we envision a golden flame within and around us while calling upon Archangel Michael, we will uplift our consciousness and reach greater spiritual wisdom and power while experiencing ecstasy and bliss. The same applies to all Archangels, their colors, and their qualities. The sky is the limit!

Is there only one Archangel Michael, Archangel Gabriel etc.? Or are there many of them?

This is one of the biggest secrets of all times! Every Archangel is not a single entity but a group of angelic beings. For example, Archangel Michael is not a single being but countless beings with the same qualities, characteristics, energies, and possibly common consciousness (super consciousness). When we say "human being," we mean all people and humanity, and we are not referring to a specific person. Similarly, when we speak of "Archangel Michael," we refer to the presences, the super-intelligences and the consciousnesses that belong to the order of Michael. What order is that? The order of Fire, of Divine Will, of Protection, of Guidance, of Purification and the Defeat of Evil: all the qualities that Archangel Michael represents, manifests and is! This applies to all the Archangels: there are countless Gabriels, Raphaels, and all the other Archangels that share the same quality and essence.

It is the first time I have heard about this multiplicity of the Archangels and it seems unbelievable!

Does it appear strange, paradoxical, or illogical? Is it contrary to what you have believed so far? Think about it for a moment: Who and what is man? Religions, philosophies ,and sciences (all of them: biology, medicine, psychology, sociology, anthropology, history), have only just begun to assemble the "puzzle" of our human existence. We know few things about what we are (and even less of why we exist!). We know so little about everything. How can we know about beings superior to us such as the incorporeal spiritual beings that the Archangels are? Let us keep our minds open, let us pray with our hearts, let us wish with our entire existence to receive and to keep receiving the blessings of knowledge! It is such an amazing journey to receive greater universal and substantial knowledge and wisdom!

Is there another spiritual secret that you have discovered and that has had a great impact on you?

Yes, there is! One of the most soul-stirring secrets that I was taught of and experienced personally! We know that the Archangels create the worlds, they are the forces of nature. The Archangels create (project) the elements: fire/light (Michael), water/liquid state of being (Gabriel), air (Raphael), and earth/solid state of being (Uriel and angels of matter).

What is incredible (for me, at least) is that Archangels do not only create and project the four states of existence (the four elements exist in both our universe and the immaterial superior planes in a different frequency and proportion), but they are the elements themselves. The Archangels are the elements and the elements are the Archangels! The elements have an archangelic nature. So sacred, so spiritual, and so ecstatic nature is. So sacred, so spiritual, and so ecstatic the universe, existence, and creation are. The All. So Divine!

So, when the wind blows on your face, it is Archangel Raphael, when the sun and the light warm you, it is Archangel Michael, when you swim in the sea, you are within Archangel Gabriel, and when you walk, you walk upon Archangel Uriel and the angels of matter and earth! And the same is true inside of you: Your breath is Raphael (air and ether), your blood and the warmth of your body are Michael, your body fluids are Gabriel (we are 70% water/liquid), and your bones are Uriel and the angels of gross solid matter. Isn't that amazing? Meditate upon this spiritual truth, upon this expanded and uplifted perspective of reality. Study it and dedicate 10 minutes every day to recognize such a spiritual reality and experience it.

MEDITATION

The Archangels in the Human Body

Sit comfortably and gently close your eyes...

Relax...

Bring your attention to your breathing...

Inhale deeply...

It is the energy and the power of Archangel Raphael...!

Keep this thought, meditate on your breathing, the energy of Raphael...

Continue to breathe deeply...

Bring your attention to the warmth of your body and your blood...

It is Archangel Michael...

Stay, observe, meditate on it...

Now, bring your awareness to the fluids of your body.

You are a 70% liquid being...

Archangel Gabriel...

See it, feel it, meditate on it...

Feel your bones, your mass, the dense matter you are made of...

Archangel Uriel and the angels of dense matter...

Feel and see, meditate on this...

Bless your elements: fire, air, water, earth.

See and feel them clearly.

See and feel they are clear.

They are healthy, bright, strong, beautiful, vivid, joyful, and balanced.

Thank the Archangels.

Ask for health, health in all your elements and on all levels of your existence.

Balance, cleanliness, and power, in all your elements, on all levels.

Open your eyes.

MEDITATION

Infusing the Body with Archangelic Energies for Optimal Health

A Continuation of the Previous Practice

As you practice the previous meditation upon the connection of the elements that you are made of (earth, water, air, fire), ask the Archangels to enhance their energy, vibration, and quality in the respective elements of your body. In doing so, your elements cleanse, strengthen, heal, and reach their higher potential. You experience spiritual illumination, bliss, vitality, and wellbeing on all levels of your being.

Carry out the previous exercise and in each element, declare the corresponding affirmation. See and feel the entire process clearly.

When you bring your awareness to the element of air and ether in your body, to your breath and to your etheric vitality, declare:

"Archangel Raphael, empower my breath... Enhance it with your pure light, infuse my breath with your divine energy..."

Simultaneously envision an intense white, gold, or golden-white light.

When you bring your attention to the element of fire in your body, to your blood and to the warmth of your body, declare:

"Archangel Michael, empower my fire... Enhance it with your pure light, infuse my blood with your divine energy..."

Again, envision an intense white, gold, or golden-white light.

Now bring your awareness to the element of water in your body, to your body fluids and declare:

"Archangel Gabriel, empower my water element... Enhance it with your pure light, infuse my body fluids with your divine energy..."

Visualize an intense white, gold, or golden-white light.

When you bring your attention to the element of matter in your body, to the dense mass of your body, declare:

"Archangel Uriel and angels of earth, empower my material body and my bones... Enhance it with your pure light, infuse the matter of my body with your divine energy..."

Envision an intense white, gold, or golden-white light.

Conclude the exercise by asking for health, strength, cleanliness, and balance in all your elements and on all levels of your existence.

Thank the Archangels and open your eyes.

Do the names of the Archangels have a specific meaning?

The archangelic names correspond to the vibration and energy frequency of each Archangel. Their names are their energy manifested in a form of sounds and words. The energetic, spiritual, meditative, and conscious use of the Archangels' names gives us the chance to manifest their properties. The sound and the expression of the archangelic names may even bestow a healing effect.

ESOTERIC PRACTICE

The Names of the Archangels

According to mystic Stylianos Atteshlis (known as Daskalos), the names of the four most celebrated Archangels have great esoteric value and power. This is their origin and interpretation:

Archangel Michael: Maha (means Great in Sanskrit) and El (God in Ancient Egyptian, Sanskrit, and Hebrew)

Archangel Gabriel: Ka (Soul, Sentiment in Ancient Egyptian), Vir (Element in Ancient Egyptian) and El (God)

Archangel Raphael: Ra (Sun in Ancient Egyptian), Fa (Vibration and Energy in Ancient Egyptian) and El (God)

Archangel Uriel: U (Space, Matter in Ancient Egyptian), Ra (Sun) and El (God)

The use of the primary sounds that constitute each name is related to the corresponding elements (fire, air, water, earth) and it can manifest the power, the energy, and the properties of the respective Archangels.

Exercise 1: Meditation upon the names of Archangels

Meditate upon the names of Archangels. Reflect on them, repeat them, see them in your mind's eye, feel them deep in your heart.

Archangel Michael: MICHAEL, MA-HA-EL

Archangel Gabriel: GABRIEL, KA-VIR-EL

Archangel Raphael: RAPHAEL, RA-FA-EL

Archangel Uriel: URIEL, U-RA-EL

Exercise 2: Manifesting the energies of Archangels with the use of sound

Experiment with the vibration, the power and the dynamic of sound. Repeat the archangelic names slowly and with intention, stressing the sounds, the letters, and the syllables: e.g. "MAAAA... HAAAA... EEEEL..." Repeat several times and then wait while observing what you are feeling.

Carry out the same process for each Archangel individually. Experiment with the common name ("Archangel Michael") as well as with the primary ("Maha-El"). In each case, feel that you are expressing the energy, the vibration, and the power of Archangels with sound, through your voice.

If I call on or attune to Archangels, what will happen?

You will receive a great amount of etheric, regenerating, and illuminating energy (ether, vital light). Temporarily, your consciousness will be uplifted and your perspective will be expanded. You may experience serenity, harmony, alignment with all existence or existential unity (All Is One). You may experience upliftment, transcendence, euphoria. You will receive and become Love: angelic, archangelic, Divine Love; unconditional and of infinite potential Love; creative power and Love. You awake the wisdom and the knowledge that lies in the most profound levels of your being. You will be empowered. You will experience liberation and purification, clarity and lucidity on all levels. Your body will benefit and your whole life will take on a golden hue! And this applies to resonance with any of the known great Archangels!

Do they have such powerful energy?

The presence, power, energy, and action of angels is indeed great! They are able to build whole universes and worlds! Everything that you see around you is Divine, spiritual, archangelic works! Archangels are the Divine Creativity in action, in manifestation and in motion. The Archangels' signatures (the four elements: fire, water, air, earth) are found all over the universe, the worlds, and the dimensions!

What does "attuning to the Archangels" mean?

It is an energetic connection with the Archangels, a communication, an alignment that occurs through the upliftment of consciousness to higher levels (superconsciousness, spiritual perception). It seems as if someone is changing the channel frequency in the receiver (mind, spirit) and it receives the signals of the archangelic "channels" of the higher realms. We raise our vibrational frequencies via intensive meditations, invocations, daily spiritual practice, spiritual upliftment, and euphoria; in doing so, we reach the vibrational level (frequency) of the archangelic vibrations. It is a (temporary) congruence of our consciousness with something else.

A human being and a consciousness are not restricted from matter, they have the potential to identify with anything that exists, with the all and with everything in it. A consciousness can identify with a leaf, a wave, a cloud, a ray of light, an animal, a plant, a rock. It is a spiritual practice of being at a higher level (although it is easier than it sounds), it is the transcendence of the "ego" and the limitations of the mind, it is an entrance to "beingness" that manifests in infinite forms and states. The highest attunement is oneness, the full union that is called "Theosis" – a state that all human beings are destined to experience one day!

How can I contact or be attuned to the Archangels?

You can contact the Archangels by using their names, meditations, invocations and/or symbols. You can also communicate with them by thinking of them, by calling upon them, by expressing pure and unconditional love and gratitude. The meditation that follows will assist you in reaching your goal.

MEDITATION

Archangelic Attunement

You can apply this specific meditation to attune to any one of the great Archangels and also any other angel you wish to resonate with.

Sit comfortably with your back reasonably straight, gently close your eyes. Your breathing gradually becomes slower and deeper, your belly expands with each inhale and shrinks with each exhale. Inhale energy, positivity and light, fill your body entirely. Discard anything that burdens you, anything negative and unnecessary.

Relax your body and mind. Be open and receptive... Take your time. Relax deeper, let go... Visualize a serene sphere of peace and harmony, of absolute protection and higher guidance, where you are at the center of the sphere... See it clearly and feel it...

Call upon the Archangel that you wish to resonate with... Visualize (see in your mind's eye and feel) the corresponding spiritual flame of the Archangel and his radiant energy shining all around you. See and feel the energy of the Archangel and the color corresponding to his spiritual flame – use the list with the colors given earlier in this chapter. Envision and feel the flame, the energy to be activated all around you, surrounding and permeating you.

The flame enfolds and permeates your body, your energy, your psyche, and your spirit. The flame illuminates you, on all levels. Gradually you become the flame... You are the flame...

You are fully and profoundly resonating with the Archangel... Say a prayer or an invocation to the Archangel that surrounds you with his magnificent energy and his radiating spiritual flame... Communicate... Ask... You shall receive! You are in full alignment with the Archangel!

Stay in this archangelic and luminous energy, enjoy the heavenly love and celestial wisdom of the Archangel. Whenever you feel ready, conclude the attunement by breathing slow and deep – inhale and exhale positivity, energy, and light. Thank the Archangel. Open your eyes.

How do you feel...? Write down your experience!

In the previous exercise, do I have to visualize the Archangels with specific colors?

Yes, you can use the list of the colors of the archangelic energies that was given in a preceding answer in this chapter. Thus, to resonate with Archangel Michael (perhaps the most important angel of light), follow the previous exercise and envision a red or azure or gold flame with respect to what you want to experience and receive: power and purification, protection and guidance, upliftment of consciousness and wisdom. Apply the same exercise of alignment with each Archangel. It is advised to practice consistently each day.

And what happens if I work too much with energies? Will I overload?

It is not a problem if you overwork with energies. You will assimilate them but it may take more time. You may experience some physical unease such as dizziness, tiredness, tipsiness, weakness, or some other purifying symptom (and it is good that it comes out!). Take care of yourself by drinking plenty of water (it detoxifies), taking baths and showers (they help in clearing and renewal), and walking (it grounds us and makes our body stronger). Get outdoors and connect with nature, breathe deeply, and rest. Make sure to eat pure and natural foods, and to get enough sleep. Whenever you need grounding and assimilation after your daily spiritual practice, just follow all of the above and it will be alright.

Which Archangels should I prefer to attune to?

Perhaps the most important and complete energetic and spiritual exercise is the archangelic attunement to the great Archangels of light and of the four elements: Archangel Michael, Archangel Gabriel, Archangel Raphael, and Archangel Uriel. They are the most recognized and celebrated Archangels (they are mentioned in many sacred texts and traditions), and also they are closer to human beings. The Archangels of the four elements work in support of the spiritual evolution of each person on Earth; they are the means, the path to optimal health, fulfillment, enlightenment, and happiness. Their presence and loving energies are vital for humanity.

Each Archangel corresponds to the various aspects of our being: Michael to the mental aspect, Gabriel to the emotional aspect, Raphael to the etheric aspect, Uriel to the material aspect, as well as the elements that constitute the physical body: Michael to fire (as blood and warmth), Gabriel to water (as the liquids of the body), Raphael to air and ether (as the breath), and Uriel to earth (as dense physical matter). By carrying out the archangelic attunement, we align with our Guardian Angel as well, the angel most personal and dear to us!

MEDITATION

Attunement to the Four Archangels of Light

It is a variation/adaptation of the very important meditative exercise that was taught by the great mystic Stylianos Atteshlis, known as Daskalos (meaning "Teacher" in Greek). In this exercise you will be using the colors that correspond to the elements of the Archangels and not the colors attributed to them in New Age books and the ones most commonly visualized in spiritual practices. Thus, envision the energy of Archangel Michael as red or golden red, which symbolizes the element of fire, instead of blue/azure (the color most often attributed to him in various meditative practices). Envision the energy of Raphael as purple/violet (etheric vitality) instead of green, and the energy of Gabriel as blue/azure (water) instead of fuchsia or other colors. By using this specific practice, we align with the Archangelic Elements. If you wish, you may carry out extra exercises with different colors in relation to what you wish to experience and receive.

The exercise:

Clean yourself and your space physically as well as energetically.

Make your space as clean, tidy, beautiful, and harmonious as you can. Energize and scent your space with pure essential oils.

Light a white candle and dedicate it to the Highest Good. Gaze at its flame (*caution: candles have to always be away from flammable objects and do not leave candles unattended*).

Sit comfortably with your back straight and close your eyes gently.

Take ten slow and deep breaths: inhale through the nose and exhale through the mouth. With each exhalation release tension and anything you no longer need, with each inhalation fill yourself with energy, positivity, and light. Carry out ten conscious, slow, deep, and energized breaths.

Relax. Ask your body and your mind to relax even more, to relax completely... Imagine being in serenity and harmony... Serenity and harmony surround you... Only serenity and harmony... Pure serenity and harmony...

Bring your intention to Archangel Michael and ask to tune into his energy, to resonate with him and receive the light, the energy, and the gifts he offers... Visualize a Divine Red Flame lighting up all around you. See and feel it... Intensify the flame by breathing deeper... Declare that you are fully within the energy of Archangel Michael... The red flame, the divine element of fire... It fills you, it is pure, and it purifies you... You experience protection, guidance, release from all the negative energies and influences, mental clarity and power, alignment with the Divine Will and the Divine Purpose... Observe how you feel... The Golden Red Flame of Archangel Michael shines within you and around you, illuminating you on all levels... You see it and you feel it...

Now, bring into your mind Archangel Gabriel and ask to be tuned into his energy, to resonate with him and receive the light, the energy, and the gifts he offers... Visualize a Divine Blue/Azure Flame lighting up all around you. See and feel it... Intensify the flame by breathing deeper... Declare that you are fully within the energy of Archangel Gabriel... The blue/azure flame, the divine element of water... It fills you, it is pure, and it purifies you... You experience upliftment, joy, serenity, love, emotional clarity, and balance... Observe how you feel... The Blue-Azure Flame of Archangel Gabriel shines within you and around you, illuminating you on all levels... You see it and you feel it...

Now, bring into your mind Archangel Raphael and ask to be tuned into his energy, to resonate with him and receive the light, the energy, and the gifts he offers... Visualize a Divine Purple/Violet Flame lighting up all around you. See and feel it... Intensify the flame by breathing deeper... Declare that you are fully within the energy of Archangel Raphael... The purple/violet flame, the divine element of ether... It fills you, it is pure, and it purifies you... You experience deep cleansing, transmutation, and healing on all levels of your being; deep cleansing, transmutation, and healing in your aura, energy channels, and energy centers; deep cleansing, transmutation, and healing in your body, your organs, and your cells... Observe how you feel... The Purple-Violet Flame of Archangel Raphael shines within you and around you, illuminating you on all levels... You see it and you feel it...

When you feel ready, bring into your mind Archangel Uriel and ask to be tuned into his energy, to resonate with him and receive the light, the energy, and the gifts he offers...Visualize a Divine White/Silver Flame lighting up all around you. See and feel it... Intensify the flame by breathing deeper... Declare that you are fully within the energy of Archangel Uriel... The white/silver flame, the divine element of earth... You experience harmonization, balance, rejuvenation, empowerment, and grounding... Observe how you feel... The White-Silver Flame of Archangel Uriel shines within you and around you, illuminating you on all levels... You see it and you feel it...

And now, envision the Divine Golden Flame lighting up all around you. See and feel it... Intensify the flame by breathing deeper... Declare that you are fully within the energy of your Higher Self, of your Spirit and Soul, of your Divine Consciousness and Essence... Ask to be attuned to the highest, sublime, divine element and to receive all its gifts... The golden flame, the Divine element of your spirit and soul... You experience higher consciousness, super consciousness... Observe how you feel... The Golden Flame of the Higher, of the Sublime, of the Divine shines within you and around you, illuminating you on all levels... You see it and you feel it...

To conclude, bring into your mind your Guardian Angel and ask to be tuned into his energy, to resonate with him and receive the light, the energy, and the gifts he offers... Visualize a Divine Pink Flame lighting up all around you. See and feel it... Intensify the flame by breathing deeper... Declare that you are fully within the energy of your Guardian Angel... The soft and gentle pink flame, the divine element of love... You experience profound care, personal protection, and gentle guidance... Observe how you feel... The Pink Flame of your Guardian Angel shines within you and around you, illuminating you on all levels... You see it and you feel it...

Thank all the Archangels and their loving energies for working with you. Gently come back to your body, feel it, move your body smoothly, and open your eyes. Rest.

For a deeper and more substantial experience and also a more intense and profound alignment with the Archangels, repeat the exercise for seven consecutive days.

For long-lasting results and continuous empowerment and upliftment, practice this specific meditation once a week.

This meditation can be combined with the meditations and exercises suggested below:

The Names of the Archangels
The Archangels in the Human Body
Infusing the Body with Archangelic Energies for Optimal Health

ESOTERIC PRACTICE

Facilitating and Empowering the Archangelic Attunement

You can facilitate and enhance even more the attunement to the Archangels by using Angelic Symbols and Angelic Invocations. Each method is sufficient. You can use only invocations or only symbols or both of them.

You can use the angelic symbols of the Guardian Angel and symbols of the Archangels Michael, Raphael, Gabriel, and Uriel (you can also use additional symbols that you choose intuitively).

You can use the Angelic invocations to the Guardian Angel and the four Archangels (Michael, Raphael, Gabriel, Uriel) and/or other invocations.

Apply the symbols and/or the invocations in respective moments while you practice the Attunement to the Four Archangels of Light.

ESOTERIC PRACTICE

Archangelic Attunement: a 21-day plan

Follow this plan whenever you feel like reconstructing, reorganizing, and illuminating essentially your being and your life, when you want to advance and take the steps on the path of spiritual self-improvement, self-awareness and evolution, steps towards the higher, divine wisdom, love and power: practice the archangelic attunement daily for 21 consecutive days. I recommend this 21-day plan of daily alignment with the four Archangels, your higher self, and your Guardian Angel to be carried out once every year.

Can I use crystals to invite angels and Archangels in my life? Can crystals help me see, hear, and communicate with them? To receive their protection, guidance, and their healing power?

Yes, crystals and gemstones are special and beautiful pieces of earth with various apocryphal and energetic healing properties. In essence crystals are energy in an ultra-condensed form and formations of ultra-condensed light. Crystals embody and emit higher vibrations; they – as luminous and colorful children of the earth – help us purify, transmute, and empower our energies and enrich our lives.

To invite into your home the higher energies, the light and love of the Angels and the Archangels, you may use the crystals and gemstones of the list given below. The list gives an overview of the various properties of crystals and gemstones.

Clear Quartz: "the king of all crystals," "the healer crystal," "the crystal of the light." Clear Quartz is the most important and useful crystal, it is easy to charge and program for a variety of purposes. It represents the light and etheric/vital energy. It offers energy, vitality, and light. Clear quartz charges, purifies, empowers, uplifts, balances, and boosts all levels of our being: the aura, the psyche, the mind, the spirit, and the body. It focuses, actualizes, and manifests our intention.

Rose Quartz: "the crystal of love." Rose Quartz emits and offers maternal energy, care, tenderness, love, warmth, emotional healing, balance, serenity, and tranquility. It opens the heart energy center (the heart chakra) to compassion, acceptance, forgiveness, gratitude, joy, and love.

Amethyst: the most "spiritual crystal," "the teacher of all crystals." Amethyst awakens consciousness, empowers intuition, and insight, opens the energy channels of the body, offers spiritual protection, guidance, and inspiration. It protects, cleans and energizes the aura, and also creates a pure spiritual atmosphere and peacefulness.

Smoky Quartz: Smoky Quartz helps to clear the subconscious, the negative aspects of self, it brings light in the darkness.

Citrine: Citrine offers power, joy, knowledge, releases negative thoughts and feelings, brings positivity, and illuminates.

Malachite: Malachite offers emotional healing, opening of the heart, good fortune, and abundance.

Agate: Agate creates good communication and protection.

Tiger's eye: Tiger's eye offers self-confidence, clarity in thinking, intuition, good luck, and invigoration.

Calcite: Calcite invigorates at all levels.

Amber: Amber offers abundance, knowledge, joy, power, positivity, and light.

Hematite: Hematite offers grounding, protection, and power.

Iron Pyrite: Iron Pyrite stabilizes, grounds, and manifests intention.

Aquamarine: Aquamarine enhances emotional communication, artistry, and serenity.

Tourmaline: Tourmaline assists us on grounding and protection.

Turquoise: Turquoise helps you connect with your inner child, enhances joy and playfulness, and it balances the male and female energies.

Carnelian: Carnelian stimulates self-confidence, sexual energy, and creativity.

Peridot: Peridot cleanses, releases, and rejuvenates.

Topaz: Topaz is excellent for any kind healing, especially physical healing.

Ruby: Ruby brings and increases passion and attraction.

Aventurine: Aventurine is a prosperity and abundance stone.

Emerald: Emerald increases prosperity, opening of the heart, and healing (especially physical).

Obsidian: Obsidian is the stone of protection and grounding of intention.

Morganite (Pink Beryl): Morganite is a love stone and it is associated with the heart chakra.

Lapis Lazuli: Lapis Lazuli enhances clarity and good communication.

Moonstone: Moonstone is a stone allowing female energy to flow; it increases attraction, passion, and beauty.

Diamond: Diamond heightens spirituality, purity, cleanness, and perfection.

Besides the well-known crystals of the above list, there are certain "special" crystals that connect us to angels, grounding and manifesting the light and the potential of our pure spirit. If by any "coincidence" these special stones come your way, adopt them and let them adopt you too!

Special "angel" crystals:

Angel Aura: Angel Aura helps us to discover our potential, our talents, and our charisma. It also enhances our connection with angels and especially our Guardian Angel.

Angelite (Anhydrite): Angelite facilitates resonance and clear contact with angels.

Azeztulite: Azeztulite offers illumination, mental boost, and healing.

Danburite: Danburite brings higher spiritual light.

Iolite: Iolite awakens knowledge and prophecy.

Ceraunite (Thunder-stone): Ceraunite grounds the power of the spirit.

Kunzite and Hiddenite (green Kunzite): Kunzite stones facilitate the opening of the heart to higher planes and the connection to Archangel Metatron and Shekinah (the Divine Source).

Moldavite: Moldavite facilitates the change of consciousness, the connection to celestial bodies, and the galaxy.

Blue Topaz: Blue Topaz is the crystal of truth and it connects to the spiritual laws.

Opal: Opal brings spiritual understanding and wisdom.

Selenite: Selenite enables the connection with the higher self, the higher consciousness, and perception.

Celestite: Celestite is a crystal for faith, higher vibration, transcendence of the ego and connecting with the angels of protection.

Seraphinite: Seraphinite advances us spiritually, empowers the spiritual body and enables connection to the Seraphim.

Sugilite: Sugilite empowers spiritual love.

Tanzanite: Tanzinite increases consciousness and perception of spiritual planes.

Rutile Quartz: Rutile Quartz offers spiritual energy.

Seriphos Green Quartz (Prasem): Seriphos Quartz assists in physical healing, heart initiation, and connection to the Seraphim.

Other crystals that are considered angelic are the ones that contain or present angelic forms (shapes, configurations, inclusions...) in their structure!

To connect and be attuned to specific Archangels choose a crystal that resonates with the angelic presence of your choice. Hold the crystal in your hands for ten minutes peacefully, gently, and meditatively. The list that follows will help you choose the appropriate crystal. It connects specific crystals and gemstones of Mother Earth to the angels and the Archangels of the celestial realm.

Michael: sugilite, kyanite, turquoise, lapis lazuli, tiger's eye, ruby

Gabriel: aquamarine, blue calcite, turquoise, lapis lazuli, danburite, citrine, clear quartz

Raphael: aventurine, emerald, malachite

Uriel: agate, onyx, galena, clear quartz, amber

Haniel: moonstone, angelite, celestite, red jasper, blue topaz

Jophiel: citrine, golden labradorite, pink tourmaline

Zadkiel: amethyst, tanzanite, lapis lazuli

Tzaphkiel: moldavite, green quartz, blue topaz, tanzanite

Chamuel: rose quartz, kunzite, green fluorite

Raguel: red jasper, carnelian, citrine, aquamarine, aqua aura

Raziel: petalite, lapis lazuli, blue agate, iolite, clear quartz

Ariel: rose quartz, pebbles, stones, green crystals

Jeremiel: amethyst, lapis lazuli

Sandalphon: malachite, aventurine, ceraunite, turquoise

Metatron: clear quartz, hematite, diamond, kunzite, hiddenite, watermelon tourmaline

Guardian Angel: clear quartz, rose quartz, any crystal that we are strongly drawn to

Angels of Protection: all red and black crystals

Angels of Abundance: all green, golden, and yellow crystals

Angels of Love and Romance: rose quartz, coral (it is not a gemstone but we do use it in crystal healing), all red, orange, coral, and pink crystals

Angels of Peace, Serenity, Communication: all blue and azure crystals

Angels of Emotional Healing, Angels of Arts, Angels of Inspiration, Angels of Joy, Angels of Children: all azure, green and turquoise crystals

Angels of Power, Balance, Will, Knowledge, Wisdom: all yellow and gold crystals

Angels of Meditation, Prayer, Channeling, Spiritual Advancement, Guidance, Illumination: amethyst and all violet and purple crystals

Angels of Healing: clear quartz, rose quartz, amethyst, all green crystals, crystals of a color that corresponds to the color of a blocked chakra

Attention: Remember to clean and charge the crystals before each use for meditation or healing.

See also the technique "Angelic Crystal Healing."

Can I use essential oils to fill the space around me with the positive higher energy and the protection of angels and Archangels?

Yes, essential oils are splendid, concentrated energies of mother nature, of the kingdom of plants, flowers, and herbs. Essential oils can influence positively and also empower each energy and spiritual work. They purify, protect, heal, balance, and uplift our aura, thoughts, feelings, mood, state of mind, and our perception.

We can use essential oils while taking a bath: add 10–15 drops of your favorite essential oil to the warm water and circulate it throughout; get in, relax, and enjoy the wonderful aroma while you soak.

We can use essential oils in massage to maximize the healing power of massage itself: before using essential oils for massage they must be diluted in carrier oil. Add 10–15 drops essential oil to 100 ml pure carrier oil (for example, almond or jojoba oil) and then massage the body with it by using light, gentle movements and strokes.

Another option is to use an aromatherapy diffuser or an oil burner to release the scent and energy of the essential oils in the entire room. You can read a book about aromatherapy or consult an aromatherapist to learn which essentials oils correspond to your needs.

The list given below gives valuable information about which essential oils invoke a specific angel or quality that we wish to invite into our space, energy field, and our lives.

Angels, Archangels, and Essential Oils (that Manifest Their Energy)

Michael: thyme, clove, lavender, myrrh, pine, frankincense, sage

Gabriel: basil, spearmint, melissa, peppermint, rose

Raphael: sandalwood, mandarin, hyacinth

Uriel: mandarin, melissa, chamomile

Haniel: clove, lemon, rose, mandarin, myrrh

Jophiel: lemon, narcissus, bergamot

Zadkiel: basil, rosemary, cedar, sage

Tzaphkiel: clove, thyme, pine, sandalwood, rose

Chamuel: lavender, frankincense, rose, chamomile

Raguel: eucalyptus, peppermint

Raziel: laurel, cinnamon, sage

Ariel: all nature's aromas

Jeremiel: myrrh, jasmine, frankincense, lavender

Sandalphon: peppermint, spearmint

Metatron: geranium, jasmine, cedar, cypress, sandalwood

Guardian Angel: any essential oil we really like!

Angels of Protection: lily, lilac, lotus, bergamot, heliotrope, clove, fennel, cumin

Angels of Abundance: pine, cedar, patchouli, ginger, nutmeg, benzoin, basil

Angels of Love and Romance: rose, vanilla, gardenia, orange, cinnamon, coriander

Angels of Peace, Serenity, Communication: pine, lavender, chamomile, melissa, peppermint

Angels of Emotional Healing, Angels of Arts, Angels of Inspiration, Angels of Joy, Angels of Children: mandarin, ylang ylang, rose, myrrh, lavender

Angels of Power, Balance, Will, Knowledge, Wisdom: heliotrope, lemon, narcissus, bergamot, laurel

Angels of Meditation, Prayer, Channeling, Spiritual Advancement, Guidance, Illumination: myrrh, frankincense, ylang ylang, patchouli, sage, sandalwood, cypress, lavender, melissa

Angels of Healing: eucalyptus, lavender, mandarin, hyacinth, geranium, rosemary

Don't wait! Scent your aura and your space with the ethereal aromas of nature and invite the angelic energies into your life!

I have read that Archangels Azrael and Samael are angels of death and therefore dark angels. Is it right to call upon them (with meditations, invocations, symbols) or to even mention their names?

Spiritual study, esoteric work, symbols, meditations, and invocations to celestial beings enable us to connect with them. All spiritual practice facilitates our attunement to cosmic energies and forces. Azrael and Samael are Archangels of the Law of Duality and therefore of the lower dimensions as well as of the physical one. They represent the lower or negative pole or what is considered by human beings as such.

They symbolize and manifest negativity and darkness, but also the understanding and the healing of these elements; human fear but also its clearing and overcoming; negative/unpleasant feelings and thoughts, but also their acceptance and transmutation; the lower, limited, egoic, selfish, shadow self of man, the subconscious mind and all the negative habits and vices, but also their recognition and transcendence.

Azrael and Samael represent, manifest and are all these elements but at the same time they are the Meaning, the Value, and the Purpose behind these elements. And these elements have supreme and absolute meaning, value, and purpose. They are infinitely precious and an integral and essential part of Life, of the Whole, of the Divine. Earthly life, human life, without these specific elements would lose its sacred value, meaning, and purpose. An Earthly life, a human life, is the process of bringing these elements to their purification, transmutation and healing; grounding the higher and uplifting the lower; creating and realizing oneness on all levels, divinity on all levels.

Archangels Azrael and Samael are associated with matter in its dense form, with life in the physical world of the third dimension but also with death as the completion of physical/material life. Death as the transition, the bridge, the entrance to something new. Death is a part of life and a natural consequence of it; death is the completion, the culmination of life in the material world of the third dimension. Death is not something dark and negative; it is universal and natural, completely and totally interconnected with Life. We see it in our feelings, thoughts, breaths and cells; one replaces the other all the time, living and dying and rebirthing. Every day we die and we are reborn. We need to die (let go of the old) in order to be reborn (receive the new). All of our past thoughts, feelings, breaths, and cells have "died" and new ones are living and they are experienced at every moment! We need to "die" in order to live! Life and death are one, and in the end, there is no real death, there is only life: one continuous, ever-flowing life.

By doing esoteric work, using symbols, invocations, and meditations about these two Archangels in conjunction with the higher Archangels like Archangel Michael (the Light and Fire, the Purification, the Divine Will and the Divine Power), we clear the lowest aspects of ourselves. We work on how we perceive the physical realm, our flaws and vices, the unknown, fear, and death; the lower and unpleasant aspect of life; negativity, darkness, and evil. To face and transcend the negative pole, we need to look right in the eyes of it and understand it. How can you transcend something that you do not perceive or that you are not aware of?

Esoteric study and spiritual practice in the form of meditations and invocations do not have negative effect. Their essence, qualities, and intention are purely positive and their purpose is healing. All esoteric practice is spiritual "technology" of light: it purifies and transcends the negative. Archangels Azrael and Samael are part of the Divine Plan. The collaboration between the great mystics of humanity and the two Archangels is necessary since mystics work in the area of helping each human being to reach fulfillment, enlightenment, and the ultimate union with the Divine All. This collaboration is done from a higher level of consciousness and with the help and support of the higher Archangels, like Michael and the others. The key that makes all the difference is intention and that is deep, total, and complete healing; to heal of even the lowest/darkest/most negative aspects of ourselves.

A well-kept secret of esotericism is that working with Archangels Azrael and Samael and at the same time with the Higher Archangels is something that can bring about the most miraculous healing in the physical body. Azrael and Samael are not only responsible for death, duality, and the lower/negative pole, they are responsible for providing the dense matter to the physical body. That is the reason why taking them into account, in alignment with the Higher Archangels of the Light, can produce the most remarkable results.

And what about Lucifer?

It is highly intriguing from a philosophical and metaphysical point of view that Lucifer – whose name means "light bearer," also known as "Satan" (meaning "the opposer, the adversary" in Hebrew) – was initially an Archangel! Lucifer was the most beautiful and luminous Archangel. Then he exalted himself against God and he fell from grace. Archangel Michael was the one that led the battle against Lucifer and succeeded in casting him out of heaven along with the angels who had chosen to follow him.

This parable has many layers, one can reflect upon the meaning and correspondence of this parable to the course of man on Earth and his life in the material world. Metaphysically, it is considered that human beings have fallen (from spirit to matter) and now we are finally awakened to return: from matter to Spirit, from separation to wholeness, from semiconsciousness to superconsciousness, from the small limited "ego" to the great infinite All!

Who are the most peculiar angels that have been ever mentioned?

In a way, all angels are considered weird creatures by human beings because angels do not have a material form but a purely spiritual one (they consist of energy and light).

From the celestial orders of the most known and accepted angelic hierarchy, perhaps the most peculiar group of angels is the one of Thrones. Thrones are described in the scriptures as great fiery wheels covered with hundreds of eyes that carry the throne of God (hence the name). Other peculiar classes of the first sphere are the Seraphim and the Cherubim. Seraphim are described either as "burning serpents" or creatures with six wings that praise God constantly. Cherubim mentioned in scriptures are often depicted with the faces of a man, an ox, a lion, and an eagle. Cherubim have four wings and they guard the throne of God.

Most likely the description of these specific classes of angels is not to be taken literally, as it is a symbolic description (there is a spiritual meaning in each characteristic of the description). How man views angels has to do with his perception as well as with what he needs to experience at any particular time. Angels may take any form they wish. The descriptions of these highest angelic beings (as depicted in the Bible and other texts) are truly interesting and arouse the spiritual "curiosity" and spiritual nature of human beings.

In the various encyclopedias of angels, we find several other peculiar angels such as the ephemeral angels: God creates them each morning, they chant His Glory all day, and when they return in the evening, they are reabsorbed by the Divine Light!

The fallen angels may also be considered odd. According to esoteric traditions, 1/3 of the angels followed Lucifer when he, out of pride and selfishness, was thrown out of heaven. Lucifer disconnected from the Perfection, Wholeness, and Oneness of the Divine; instead Lucifer created opposition, conflict, darkness, and hell (a negative dimension of low vibrations, without light or love). Lucifer became proud of his own glory and wisdom; he refused to show appreciation, love and respect to the divine creation of man as the rest of the angels did. Lucifer chose to rebel against God and he was exiled from heaven (from oneness/wholeness and the highest dimension).

It is hard to conceive why Lucifer would do that or what the purpose of his action was. It represents the first (and the ultimate) separation from the whole/source and the descent into matter. It is a question that has occupied human intellect for eons and it comprises the unanswered riddle of the existence of evil. If such a separation didn't take place, the journey of man into matter would not have happened (the exit from Eden)... Thus, did it have to happen like this? Was it a divine plan? Was it a plan of our higher self and our soul? Isn't it incredibly paradoxical? It is impossible to find the answers when we live in the third dimension, the world of matter! But one day we will know! The fallen angels have intrigued humanity for a long time and they have become a popular subject of myths, stories, books, and even movies!

What is the Angelic Hierarchy?

The Angelic Hierarchy is a human classification of the ranks of angels.

The most universally accepted classification of the ranks of Angels is that of Pseudo-Dionysius the Areopagite, a philosopher of the fifth to sixth centuries AD; it was later adopted by Thomas Aquinas, whose life spanned from 1225–1274 AD. According to this angelic classification, celestial incorporeal spiritual beings are divided into definite Orders, each with different duties and separate frequencies and vibrations of energy. The Angelic Realm is divided into nine distinct Choirs or Orders of Angels within three major groups, known as Heavenly Spheres.

The nine Angelic Choirs or Orders are:

Seraphim
Cherubim
Thrones or Ophanim
Dominions
Virtues
Powers or Authorities
Principalities or Rulers
Archangels
Angels

Each Sphere contains three Orders or Choirs:

First Sphere (closest to the Divine): Seraphim, Cherubim, Thrones or Ophanim

Second Sphere: Dominions, Virtues, Powers or Authorities
Third Sphere (closest to earth and humanity): Principalities or Rulers, Archangels, Angels

You will find detailed information about the nine angelic orders and about all the angels and Archangels in the Index section of this book.

MEDITATION

Attunement to the Heavenly Spheres

Clean yourself and your space physically as well as energetically.

Make your space as clean, tidy, beautiful, and harmonious as you can. Energize and scent your space with pure essential oils.

Light a few white candles. As you light the candles, dedicate them to the Divine Source, the Light, the Angels, and the Highest Good.

Caution: candles have to always be away from flammable objects and do not leave candles unattended.

Sit comfortably with your back reasonably straight and close your eyes gently.

Take ten slow and deep breaths: inhale through the nose and exhale through the mouth. With each exhalation release tension and any negative emotions you might be feeling; with each inhalation fill yourself with energy, positivity, and light. Carry out ten conscious, slow, deep, and energized breaths.

Relax. Ask your body and your mind to relax even more, to let go of the tensions, to relax completely... Imagine being in serenity and harmony... Serenity and harmony surround you... Only serenity and harmony... Perfect serenity and perfect harmony...

Visualize you are inside a bright golden sphere of absolute protection and of the highest guidance. Golden love, wisdom, and power surround you, they fill your being, they illuminate you with the golden light of your spirit and your soul. You are within the golden sphere of the absolute protection and of the highest guidance, of the golden love, wisdom, and power. Your Guardian Angel is right there with you; he protects you, he guides you, he accompanies you... Take a deep breath...

Envision that you are flying high... You are ascending... You arise to a higher dimension of existence... A plane of infinite pure energy and radiant light... High above, you see a celestial spiritual sphere. You keep on rising (energetically and consciously) and you enter this celestial spiritual sphere... You now find yourself in this high spiritual level... You see celestial beings of supreme light and love... Amazing transcendental beings of pure spirit, brilliant light, and fiery love... They are the Angels, the Archangels and the Principalities! Your intention is positive, luminous, clear, and strong... Gradually you connect to them, you are attuned to their divine energies... Angels... Archangels... Principalities... You receive energy, light and love of a divine quality and essence... You are energized, illuminated, you become light, you become love... Angels... Archangels... Principalities... Warmly and wholeheartedly thank the heavenly beings and keep this sacred connection and heavenly energy... Take a deep energetic breath...

You keep on flying higher and higher... You are ascending... There is a second celestial sphere, an even higher divine sphere... You rise more (energetically and consciously) and you enter this celestial sphere... You find yourself in this even higher plane of existence... You meet more transcendental beings of pure spirit, radiant light, and fiery love. They are the Powers, the Virtues, and the Dominions... Gradually you connect to them, you are attuned to their divine energies... Powers... Virtues... Dominions... You receive energy, light and love of a divine quality and essence... You are energized, illuminated, you become light, you become love... Powers... Virtues... Dominions... Warmly and wholeheartedly thank the spiritual beings and keep this sacred connection and spiritual energy... Take a deep spiritual breath...

You continue to fly even higher, ascending... Even higher, to the greatest possible height that exists... There is a third celestial sphere, the ultimate supreme divine sphere... You rise fully (energetically and consciously) and you enter this sphere... You find yourself in the ultimate supreme plane of existence... You meet the highest transcendental beings of the pure spirit, radiant light, and fiery love. They are the Thrones, the Cherubim and the Seraphim... Gradually you connect to them, you are attuned to their divine energies... Thrones... Cherubim... Seraphim... You receive energy, light and love of the highest divine quality and essence...You are energized, illuminated, you become light, you become love... Thrones... Cherubim... Seraphim... Warmly and wholeheartedly thank the divine beings, keep this sacred connection and divine energy... Take a deep divine breath...

Gently you start to come back... You are coming back to earth... More and more... You are grounding... Grounding and returning back... Fully and perfectly, harmoniously and serenely. All is good, all is beautiful, and all is perfect!

You feel amazing, splendid, sublime, you feel incredible purity, luminosity, and joy on all levels! Your soul is smiling, laughing, and rejoicing! And so does your body!

With Love, you are always inside the heavenly spheres, you are one with the Angels, the Archangels, the Principalities, the Powers, the Virtues, the Dominions, the Thrones, the Cherubim, and the Seraphim...

With Love, the heavenly spheres are always within you, you are one with the Angels, the Archangels, the Principalities, the Powers, the Virtues, the Dominions, the Thrones, the Cherubim, and the Seraphim...

Gently open your eyes!

Secret of Empowerment: Combine this exercise with the Angelic Invocations or with the Angelic Symbols (or both) of the nine angelic orders (Seraphim, Cherubim, Thrones, etc).

ESOTERIC PRACTICE

Archangelic Techniques

Archangelic Techniques are similar to Archangelic Attunements: they are attunements to Archangels combined with archangelic invocations. Archangelic Techniques offer us help, healing, and support to life areas that are connected spiritually with the respective Archangels.

There is a basic archangelic technique that can be applied and adjusted for all Archangels and all energies and conditions related to them, the various matters that we human beings are called to resolve, heal, and enlighten. Archangels – as the purest and highest forces of light – are always near us. Archangelic Techniques are our own way to recognize, receive, and accept the pure and luminous energy, together with the infinite and benevolent support that the Archangels wish to offer us.

The Basic Archangelic Technique is given below; each time, we use the name of the Archangel and the Divine Quality that we wish to receive and experience respectively to the area we wish to heal and illuminate. Following the Basic Archangelic Technique is a list of Specific Archangelic Techniques with the areas that we wish to heal and illuminate and also the corresponding Archangels and their Divine Qualities.

The Basic Archangelic Technique

Sit comfortably with your back straight and close your eyes gently. Bring your hands together, palms touching, in front of your chest in a prayer position.

Take some slow and deep breaths; inhale through the nose and exhale through the mouth. Feel serenity on all levels, harmony on all levels, purity on all levels, and illumination on all levels.

Feel that you are in a higher state of consciousness, you think, you feel, you perceive, you function and you resonate at a plane of higher consciousness. You shine like the sun, you radiate the highest and purest energy, golden luminosity, and power...

Invoke the Archangel .... (the Archangel you wish to resonate with) from your heart by repeating his name silently three times.

Envision the Infinite Divine Energy, the Highest Spiritual Flame of the Archangel ...., envision it as a Golden Flame or the Color that corresponds to the Energy of the respective Archangel you are invoking.

The flame of the Archangel is fully activated. It is within you and all around you, it permeates you, it fills you up and it surrounds you. You see and feel it clearly.

Repeat silently the name of the Archangel four times more.

Visualize (see and feel) yourself within the high energy of the Archangel .... The flame, the energy and the light of the Archangel are growing stronger and stronger... You see it and you feel it clearly.

Declare silently or aloud three times:

"Infinite Light, Infinite Love, Infinite Wisdom, Infinite Power!

The Archangel .... and the Angels of the Divine .... (quality), of .... (quality) on all levels and all the Highest Angels of the Highest Light, offer me Divine .... (quality), ... (quality) on all levels.

Infinite Power, Infinite Wisdom, Infinite Love, Infinite Light!"

Visualize a golden sphere of light around you, a perfect golden luminous sphere. You are in its center, energetically, spiritually and physically. You see and feel it clearly. Take some deep breaths.

Feel thankfulness from your heart. Light a white candle in the name of Archangel ...., of the Angels of the Divine .... (quality), and the Ultimate and Supreme Divine Source.

You feel infinite joy and gratitude, completeness and freedom, universal grace and spiritual bliss!

Repeat the technique two times more, the same day or over the following days.

It is also of great importance to mobilize yourself and become more active, to make choices and take practical steps that are related to what you have asked for. What you receive with this technique on an energetic and spiritual level, manifest it externally with practical steps and actions.

Instructions: Apply the Basic Archangelic Technique for any of the matters or areas described below. Each time use the name of the Archangel and the respective quality you wish to experience and receive (e.g. protection, purification, love... etc.). Notice that in certain areas and matters there are two Archangels corresponding to them. Call upon both of them and envision their energies (colors) simultaneously or one after the other. Ask for the Divine Quality of the respective matter or area (Divine Protection, Divine Purification, Divine Love... etc). As always, practice the Archangelic Techniques with the deepest and the highest love! Have a blessed practice!

Specific Archangelic Techniques:

Energetic and Spiritual Protection (Archangel Michael)

Apply this technique whenever you need energetic and spiritual protection. Call upon Archangel Michael and envision his flame to surround you, permeate, and fill you. The flame is blue (protection). Ask the Archangel Michael and the Angels of Protection to offer you Divine Protection, Protection on all levels. Continue and complete the technique.

See also the technique "Spiritual Protection from Lower Energies" described in the previous chapter.

Guidance and Connection to the Divine Will (Archangel Michael)

Apply this technique whenever you need spiritual guidance and attunement to the Divine Will and the Divine Plan. Call upon Archangel Michael and envision his flame to surround you, permeate, and fill you. The flame is golden (Divine Will). Ask the Archangel Michael and the Angels of Divine Guidance to offer you Divine Guidance, Guidance on all levels as they attune you to the Divine Will and the Divine Plan. Proceed forward and complete the technique.

Purification, Cleansing from Lower Energies, Influences, and Thought-Forms (Archangel Michael)

Apply this technique whenever you need cleansing from anything negative. Call upon Archangel Michael and envision his flame to surround you, permeate, and fill you. The flame is red (fire, purification). Ask the Archangel Michael and the Angels of Divine Purification to offer you Divine Purification and Cleansing, Purification and Cleansing on all levels. Proceed further and complete the technique.

See also the technique "Clearing Thought-Forms with Archangel Michael" described in Chapter V of this book.

Emotional Healing, Serenity, and Joy (Archangel Gabriel)

Apply this technique whenever you need emotional healing and an emotional upliftment. Call upon Archangel Gabriel and visualize his flame to surround you, permeate, and fill you. The flame is blue/azure (emotion, serenity, joy). Ask the Archangel Gabriel and the Angels of Divine Serenity and Joy to offer you Divine Serenity and Joy, Serenity and Joy on all levels. Proceed as usual and complete the technique.

Deep, Calm and Restful Sleep (Archangel Gabriel)

Apply this technique when you want to sleep peacefully and rest deeply. Call upon Archangel Gabriel and envision his flame to surround you, permeate, and fill you. The flame is blue/azure (serenity). Ask the Archangel Gabriel and the Angels of Divine Sleep, of Divine Serenity, and of Divine Rest to offer you Divine Sleep, Divine Serenity, and Divine Rest; Sleep, Serenity, and Rest on all levels. Continue further and complete the technique.

Good Dreams (Archangel Gabriel)

Apply this technique to see higher, pleasant, bright dreams. Call upon Archangel Gabriel and envision his flame to surround you, permeate, and fill you. The flame is blue/azure (serenity). Ask the Archangel Gabriel and the Angels of Divine Dreams to offer you Divine Dreams, Divine Dreams on all levels. Proceed as usual and complete the technique.

Conscious Dreams and Remembering Your Dreams (Archangel Gabriel)

Apply this technique to be conscious in your dreams and to be able to remember your dreams. Call upon Archangel Gabriel and envision his flame to surround you, permeate, and fill you. The flame is blue/azure (serenity). Ask the Archangel Gabriel and the Angels of Divine Dreams, of Divine Consciousness, and Remembrance to offer you Divine Consciousness in your Dreams and Remembrance of your Dreams, Consciousness and Remembrance on all levels. Continue as usual and complete the technique.

Conceiving a Baby, Having a Healthy Pregnancy and an Easy Labor (Archangel Gabriel and Tzaphkiel)

This technique is used for conceiving a child, having a smooth pregnancy, and ensuring that mother and baby will both experience a smooth delivery. Call upon Archangels Gabriel and Tzaphkiel and envision their flame to surround you, permeate, and fill you. Their colors are fuchsia, pink, blue/azure, and turquoise. Ask the Archangels Gabriel and Tzaphkiel and the Angels of Divine Conception, Pregnancy, and Labor to offer to you the best possible conception, pregnancy, and labor. Proceed as usual and complete the technique.

Child Matters, Upbringing Children (Archangel Gabriel and Tzaphkiel)

This technique is for any matters concerning the upbringing and caring of children as well as the guidance and protection of children. Call upon Archangels Gabriel and Tzaphkiel and envision their flame to surround you, permeate, and fill you. Their colors are fuchsia, pink, blue/azure, and turquoise. Envision their energy surrounding, permeating, and filling your child as well. Ask the Archangels Gabriel and Tzaphkiel and the Angels of Divine Children Care to offer to your child Divine Care, Protection, and Guidance. Proceed as usual and complete the technique.

Healing (Archangel Raphael)

Apply this technique whenever you need healing, empowerment and revitalization. Call upon Archangel Raphael and visualize his flame to surround you, permeate, and fill you. The flame is green/emerald green (physical healing and harmony). Ask the Archangel Raphael and the Angels of Divine Health to offer you Divine Health, Health on all levels. Continue further and complete the technique.

See also the technique "Angelic Healing" in the previous chapter.

Healing a Specific Part, Organ and/or System of the Body (Archangel Raphael)

Apply this technique to heal a specific part of the body (or organ, system, etc.). Call upon Archangel Raphael and visualize his flame to surround you, permeate, and fill you. The flame is green/emerald green (physical healing and harmony). Do the same visualization for the part/organ/system you wish to heal. Ask the Archangel Raphael, the Angels of Divine Health, and the Angels of the Divine Function of the Specific Part (organ, system) to offer you Divine Health on the specific part/organ/system, Health on all levels. Continue further and complete the technique.

See also the technique "Angelic Healing" in the previous chapter.

Healing Another Person (Archangel Raphael)

Apply this technique to help another person who wishes to receive healing. Call upon Archangel Raphael and visualize his flame to surround you, permeate, and fill you. The flame is green/emerald green (physical healing and harmony). Visualize the flame surrounding, permeating, and filling the other person as well. Ask the Archangel Raphael and the Angels of Divine Health to offer to the person Divine Health, Health on all levels. Proceed further and complete the technique.

This technique can be also applied for healing animals and plants or for planetary healing.

See also the technique "Angelic Healing" in the previous chapter.

Grounding, Balance, Harmony (Archangels Uriel and Sandalphon)

Apply this technique whenever you need grounding, connection to matter and earth, being in the "here and now," whenever you need balance and harmony. Call upon Archangels Uriel and Sandalphon and envision their flame to surround you, permeate, and fill you. Their colors are white/silver and stone/earthly colors. Ask the Archangels Uriel and Sandalphon and the Angels of Divine Balance, Grounding and Harmony to offer you Divine Balance, Grounding and Harmony on all levels. Proceed as usual and complete the technique.

Love, Romance, Relationship Healing, Twin Flame Attunement (Archangel Chamuel)

Apply this technique if you wish to heal, illuminate and improve your intimate life. Call upon Archangel Chamuel and visualize his flame to surround you, permeate, and fill you. The flame is pink. Ask the Archangel Chamuel and the Angels of Divine Love, of Divine Romance and of Divine Relationships to offer you Divine Love, Divine Romance, and Divine Relationships on all levels. Continue as usual and complete the technique.

Friendship, Communication, Collaboration (Archangels Raguel and Haniel)

Apply this particular technique to facilitate better communication, collaboration, friendship and bring joy and harmony to all your relationships. Call upon Archangels Raguel and Haniel and visualize their flame to surround you, permeate, and fill you. Their colors are orange/yellow and azure/turquoise. Ask the Archangels Raguel and Haniel and the Angels of the Divine Friendship, Communication, Joy, Unity, and Collaboration to offer you Divine Friendship, Communication, Joy, Unity, and Collaboration on all levels. Continue as usual and complete the technique.

Insight and Psychic Abilities (Archangels Jeremiel and Raziel)

Apply this technique if you wish to empower your spiritual perception. Call upon Archangels Jeremiel and Raziel and visualize their flame to surround you, permeate, and fill you. The flame is deep blue. Ask the Archangels Jeremiel and Raziel and the Angels of Divine Perception and Insight to offer you Divine Perception and Insight, Clear Perception and Insight on all levels. Continue as usual and complete the technique.

Transmutation, Spiritual Healing (Archangel Zadkiel)

Apply this technique whenever you need spiritual healing and empowerment and also for the transmutation (transforming a lower element into a higher element) of negative energy, feelings, thoughts and situations. Call upon Archangel Zadkiel and visualize his flame to surround you, permeate, and fill you. The flame is violet. Ask the Archangel Zadkiel and the Angels of Divine Transmutation to offer you Divine Transmutation, Transmutation on all levels. Proceed further and complete the technique.

See also the "Violet Flame Meditation" in Chapter V of this book.

Spiritual Evolution, Enlightenment and Ascension (Archangel Metatron)

Apply this technique to empower yourself to move forwards on your spiritual path towards ascension and enlightenment. Call upon Archangel Metatron and visualize his flame to surround you, permeate, and fill you. The flame is platinum. Ask the Archangel Metatron and the Angels of Divine Illumination and Ascension to offer you Divine Illumination, Illumination on all levels. Proceed as usual and complete the technique.

Justice (Archangels Raguel and Zadkiel)

Apply this technique to facilitate justice or judicial matters. Call upon Archangels Raguel and Zadkiel and visualize their flame to surround you, permeate, and fill you. Their colors are orange/yellow and violet. Ask the Archangels Raguel and Zadkiel and the Angels of Divine Justice to offer you Divine Justice, Justice on all levels. Proceed further and complete the technique.

Beauty, Youth and Healthy Body Weight (Archangels Jophiel and Uriel)

This technique is helpful for obtaining optimal/healthy body weight and manifesting the harmony, beauty, and youthfulness of your true self and your perfect spirit. Call upon Archangels Jophiel and Uriel and visualize their flame to surround you, permeate, and fill you. Their colors are yellow and white/silvery. Ask the Archangels Jophiel and Uriel and the Angels of Divine Beauty to offer you Divine Beauty, Beauty on all levels. Continue as usual and complete the technique.

Note: While applying this technique, instead of beauty, you can ask for youthfulness or optimal/healthy body weight.

Creativity, Artistic Matters (Archangels Jophiel and Gabriel)

Apply this technique to stimulate inspiration and creativity but also for any matters concerning arts. Call upon Archangels Jophiel and Gabriel and visualize their flame to surround you, permeate, and fill you. The colors are yellow and fuchsia. Ask the Archangels Jophiel and Gabriel and the Angels of Divine Inspiration and Creativity to offer you Divine Inspiration and Creativity on all levels. Continue further and complete the technique.

Forgiveness (Archangels Zadkiel, Chamuel and Gabriel)

Apply this technique to forgive people that have hurt you and let go of painful situations; to release anger, bitterness, and resentment; to overcome guilt and forgive yourself. Call upon Archangels Zadkiel, Chamuel, and Gabriel and visualize their flame to surround you, permeate, and fill you. Their colors are violet, pink, and azure. Ask the Archangels Zadkiel, Chamuel, and Gabriel and the Angels of Divine Forgiveness to offer you Divine Forgiveness and Release, Forgiveness and Release on all levels. Proceed further and complete the technique.

Death, Grief (Archangels Azrael, Samael, Michael and Gabriel)

Apply this technique whenever you need comfort and support in periods of shock, loss or grief. Call upon the Highest Spiritual Power and Archangels Azrael, Samael, Michael, and Gabriel (all four Archangels are participating in the sacred transition) and visualize their flame to surround you, permeate, and fill you. Their energies are intense red, intense green, pure white, and pure golden. Ask the Archangels Azrael, Samael, Michael, and Gabriel and the Angels of Divine Support and Release to offer you Divine Support and Release, Support and Release on all levels. Continue as usual and complete the technique.

Death, Transition (Archangels Azrael, Samael, Michael, and Gabriel)

Apply this technique when you want to assist a person who has left his/her physical body to pass gracefully into the spirit world and ascend into higher planes of existence; to facilitate his/her consciousness to experience greater guidance, protection, freedom, serenity, and bliss. Call upon the Highest Spiritual Power and Archangels Azrael, Samael, Michael, and Gabriel (all four Archangels are participating in the sacred transition) and ask them to surround the deceased person with their divine energy, their divine light and divine flame. Envision their light and energy as white/golden. Ask the Highest Spiritual Power, the Archangels Azrael, Samael, Michael, Gabriel, the Angels of Divine Transition to Higher Planes, the Angels of Heaven and the Angels of Divine Peace to protect, guide and assist the person in his/her Divine Transition. Ask for Divine Support, Guidance, Liberation, Peace, and Bliss on all levels. Ask it wholeheartedly with great faith and love. Envision a perfect golden sphere of light surrounding the person and proceed as usual until you complete the technique.

Healing of the Environment, of Plants, and of Animals (Archangel Ariel)

Apply this technique for healing of the Earth, nature, plants, and animals. Call upon Archangel Ariel and visualize his flame to surround you, permeate, and fill you. The flame is light green. Visualize the flame surrounding and enfolding the planet as well. Ask the Archangel Ariel and the Angels of Earth to heal the environment, the animals, the plants and the Earth on all levels. Proceed further and complete the technique.

Learning, Knowledge, Wisdom (Archangels Jophiel and Raziel)

Apply this technique for facilitating matters of learning and education, and to resonate with the universal knowledge and wisdom. Call upon Archangels Jophiel and Raziel and visualize their flame to surround you, permeate, and fill you. Their colors are yellow and deep blue.

Ask the Archangels Jophiel and Raziel and the Angels of Divine Learning, Divine Knowledge, and Divine Wisdom to offer you Divine Learning, Divine Knowledge, and Divine Wisdom, Learning, Knowledge and Wisdom on all levels. Continue further and complete the technique.

ESOTERIC PRACTICE

Two Advanced Archangelic Techniques

The Archangelic Techniques that will be described below expand beyond the structure and frame of the Basic Archangelic Technique that we have used so far. These two particular techniques are highly advanced in their nature. They follow a technique of great importance described earlier in this chapter called "Attunement to the Four Archangels of Light." The two advanced archangelic techniques have been a privilege of the great mystics and teachers and have remained hidden until now. It has been decided recently that due to collective spiritual maturation, overcoming and completion of karmic elements and lessons, but also due to the emergence of new needs, that more advanced techniques will be given to human beings with absolute love and respect for the benefit of humanity and for the highest common good.

Note: Before you proceed further with the two advanced techniques, you may want to check again the question about the nature and the purpose of Archangels Samael and Azrael that was answered earlier in this chapter. Proceed with the two advanced techniques only after practicing sufficiently the "Attunement to the Four Archangels of Light," after studying and meditating upon all the exercises given in this book. If for any reason the elements of fear or doubt are present, then the two techniques are practiced by your limited/lower consciousness. These techniques were designed to be practiced by your higher spiritual consciousness; only then the techniques can have the higher, profound, amazing, wondrous, and immediate healing effect for which they were given.

Instructions: Practice the following techniques (just as all the techniques and exercises of this book) with higher consciousness and perception, with a pure and focused intention, full of Light and Love. From Light and Love, to Light and Love, through Light and Love. Have Light and Love as your starting point, as your intention and as your goal.

Apply the techniques from a higher point of power and confidence, from a higher level of wholeness and abundance instead of deficiency and shortcoming; a spiritual point of faith, certainty, knowledge, wisdom, mastery, and unity instead of fear and separation.

Proceed in these techniques as if you are your higher self (and you are indeed, if you choose it so), as if you are an Angel of the Light and not a mix of light and darkness, of good and evil, of higher and lower, the mix that you frequently believe you are. Bring 100% of your intention, your mind, your consciousness and your beingness into this true, substantial, essential, angelic, and divine state; the all-luminous, all-loving, all-powerful, and all-wise state. Then, not only you believe and expect, but you experience and co-create True Miracles!

The Advanced Archangelic Techniques are a gift of the Divine Source, of the Spirit, and of its Archangels. Approach them, study and practice them with ultimate and absolute love, ultimate and absolute humbleness, ultimate and absolute respect, and ultimate and absolute gratitude.

ESOTERIC PRACTICE

Advanced Healing of the Subconscious
(The Four Archangels of Light and Azrael)

It is a prominent advanced technique of higher energy and dynamics, and of absolute spiritual consciousness and awareness. You can use this technique for deep healing and transmutation of the subconscious mind; healing and transmutation of subconscious negative programs but also of the limiting thoughts, shocks, and traumas that are recorded in the subconscious. This technique can also be applied to dependency issues of any kind. Even though it is an intense, powerful, and advanced technique, it is also a totally safe technique that brings only good, the higher good. The benefits of the technique are multiple and precious.

Begin by doing the "Attunement to the Four Archangels of Light" that was described earlier in this chapter.

When concluding the attunement, after the pink/fuchsia flame of the Guardian Angel, invoke again the Archangels Michael, Gabriel, Raphael, and Uriel (just think of their names and call them close you). Also call forth Azrael.

Visualize the intense deep red flame of Archangel Azrael to surround you, permeate, and fill you.

Ask the Archangels Michael, Gabriel, Raphael, Uriel, and Azrael and the Angels of Healing of the Subconscious to offer you deep, true, and complete Healing of the Subconscious.

Ask for the exact things you wish to happen: release from negative thoughts, healing of traumas and psychological/emotional shocks, healing of fears, healing of dependencies or addictions, transmutation of negativity and negative programming etc.

Ask your Higher Self, your Guardian Angel, and the Archangels to be transferred into your subconscious (it is absolutely safe).

Now you are energetically and consciously in your Subconscious Mind.

By centering your intention, visualize (imagine, see, and feel) the flames of the four Archangels lighting up one after the other and burning bright, right here, in your subconscious. For the flames use the colors of the specific attunement and of the elements representing four Archangels: red, blue, purple, silver. Wait a little. Then, see the flame of Azrael lighting up in intense deep red color. Wait again. Now, envision the Divine Golden Flame of Spirit lighting up in your subconscious. Imagine it, see it with your inner vision, feel it, as clearly and intensely you can.

See the Golden Flame of Spirit, of your Higher Self, and of your Soul radiating in your subconscious, emitting its Light, the Golden Light of Infinite Love, Wisdom and Power, transmitting Divine Light, Divine Love, Divine Wisdom, and Divine Power. Give yourself plenty of time to experience this energy, illumination, and change.

Once more, declare that you wish to receive Healing in your Subconscious Mind and what precisely you want to change: release from negative thoughts, healing of traumas and psychological/emotional shocks, healing of fears, healing of dependencies or addictions, transmutation of negativity and negative programming etc.

See and feel it truly happening. Affirm that you have received the healing and the transmutation. Affirm silently or aloud three times the following:

"Infinite Light, Infinite Love, Infinite Wisdom, Infinite Power!

Archangels Michael, Gabriel, Raphael, Uriel, Azrael, and the Angels of Healing of the Subconscious, and all the Highest Angels of the Highest Light, offer me Divine Purity, Brightness, Freedom, and the Positivity of Life in my Subconscious Mind and on all levels.

Infinite Power, Infinite Wisdom, Infinite Love, Infinite Light!"

Afterwards, visualize a spiritual sphere of light surrounding you, a perfect golden and radiant sphere: you are in the center of the sphere, physically, spiritually, and energetically. You see it and you feel it clearly. Take some deep breaths.

You feel abundant joy and gratitude, wholeness and freedom, universal grace and bliss!

Complete the Archangelic Technique by thanking all the Archangels and their loving energies.

Gently come back to your body, move your body smoothly and open your eyes. You may want to take a bath, drink plenty of water, and rest.

Similarly to the other Archangelic Techniques, repeat the technique two times more – not the same day, but over the following two days. Repeat it, whenever and as many times you are guided to do so by your intuition and insight (e.g. once a week for a period of time).

Become active and mobilized, make choices and actions that are related to what you have asked and experienced by practicing this technique. Manifest with your actions what you have received through this technique on a spiritual and energetic level.

ESOTERIC PRACTICE

Advanced Physical Healing:
Materialization and Dematerialization
(The Four Archangels of Light and Samael)

The second advanced and important technique is about healing dense matter: the more condensed energies of the body. This technique can be used to facilitate change in a cellular level, to the DNA, to the bones etc. It can also achieve dematerialization of energies and materials that we no longer need, and materialization of energies and materials we do need. Apply this technique whenever there is need for a profound and immediate healing of the physical body.

Similarly to the previous advanced technique, this technique is also advanced, intense, and powerful, with many significant and precious benefits. It is completely safe and it brings only higher good.

Begin by doing the "Attunement to the Four Archangels of Light" that was described earlier in this chapter.

When concluding the attunement, after the pink/fuchsia flame of the Guardian Angel, invoke again the Archangels Michael, Gabriel, Raphael, and Uriel (just think of their names and call them close you). Also call forth Samael.

Visualize the deep green flame of Archangel Samael to surround you, permeate, and fill you.

Ask Archangels Michael, Gabriel, Raphael, Uriel, and Samael and the Angels of Healing of the Matter, of Materialization, and of Dematerialization to offer you deep, true, and complete Physical Healing. Ask for the exact things you wish to happen: materialization of energies, elements, and materials that your body needs; or dematerialization of energies, elements, and materials that your body needs to discard.

Ask your Higher Self, your Guardian Angel, and the Archangels to be transferred to the physical spot that needs healing (it is absolutely safe).

Now you are energetically and consciously in the material/physical spot that needs healing.

By centering your intention and your mind, visualize (imagine, see and feel) the flames of the four Archangels coming into life and lighting up in this particular spot with the colors of the specific attunement and of the elements representing the four Archangels: red, blue, violet, silver. Wait a little. Then, see the flame of Samael rising (deep green). Wait again. Now, envision the Divine Golden Flame of Spirit lighting up in the same physical spot. Imagine it, see it with your inner vision, feel it, as clearly and intensely as you can.

See the Golden Flame of Spirit, of the Higher Self, and of your Soul radiating in that physical spot, emitting its Light, the Golden Light of Infinite Love, Wisdom and Power, transmitting Divine Light, Divine Love, Divine Wisdom and Divine Power. Give yourself plenty of time to experience this energy, illumination, and change.

Once more, declare that you wish to receive Physical Healing and what precisely you want to change: materialization of energies, elements, and materials that your body needs; or dematerialization of energies, elements, and materials that your body needs to discard. See and feel it truly happening. Affirm that you have received the healing.

Affirm silently or aloud three times the following:

"Infinite Light, Infinite Love, Infinite Wisdom, Infinite Power!

Archangels Michael, Gabriel, Raphael, Uriel, Samael and the Angels of Physical Matter and all the Highest Angels of the Highest Light, offer me Divine Purity, Brightness, Power, and the Positivity of Life in my Physical Matter and on all levels.

Infinite Power, Infinite Wisdom, Infinite Love, Infinite Light!"

Afterwards, visualize a spiritual sphere of light surrounding you, a perfect golden and radiant sphere: you are in the center of the sphere, physically, spiritually, and energetically. You are illuminated on all levels. You see the flame and you feel it and so it is. Take a few deep breaths.

You feel abundant joy and gratitude, wholeness and freedom, universal grace and bliss!

You feel abundant joy and gratitude, wholeness and freedom, universal grace and bliss!

Complete the Archangelic Technique by thanking all the Archangels and their loving energies.

Gently come back to your body, move your body smoothly, and open your eyes. You may want to take a bath, drink plenty of water, and rest.

Similarly to the other Archangelic Techniques, repeat the technique two times more – not the same day, but over the following two days. Repeat it, whenever and as many times you are guided to do so by your intuition and insight (e.g. once a week for a period of time).

Become active and mobilized, make choices and actions that are related to what you have asked and experienced by practicing this technique. Manifest with your actions what you have received through this technique on a spiritual and energetic level.

Attention: these two advanced techniques, just as all the exercises, the techniques, the meditations, and all information given in this book, should not be considered a replacement for formal medical or mental treatment. For any physical or mental health problems, please seek professional consultation. The exercises and techniques given in this book are meant for preventive as well as empowering and supplementary use.

ESOTERIC PRACTICE

Enhancing the Archangelic Techniques:
Seraphim, Cherubim, Thrones, and Elohim

There is an advanced method to enhance and empower all the archangelic techniques with the help of the highest orders of angelic beings: the Seraphim, the Cherubim, the Thrones, and the Elohim.

The Seraphim, the Cherubim, and the Thrones belong to the first and highest heavenly sphere, vibrating at the frequency of divine perfection. They are the ultimate divine energies and powers of infinite love, supreme wisdom, and brilliant light; their consciousness is divine and oceanic.

The Elohim are not part of the known Angelic Hierarchy, but they are viewed by esoteric traditions and sources as supreme spiritual entities of divine consciousness and infinite light. Elohim are seven or twelve divine beings and they are the primary emanations of the Divine Source; they are creators of dimensions, universes, and worlds. Elohim are the hands and the creative power of God.

To enhance all the archangelic techniques we call upon the Seraphim, the Cherubim, the Thrones, and the Elohim. We invoke them at the beginning and at the end of the process.

We simply declare:

"Beloved Seraphim, Cherubim, Thrones, and Elohim,

bless, seal, and manifest fully and perfectly this process."

We can also write the names, Seraphim, Cherubim, Thrones, and Elohim, on a piece of paper, with capital letters, one name under the other as in a list, using a golden pen:

SERAPHIM

CHERUBIM

THRONES

ELOHIM

We read this in the beginning and in the end of each technique in order to enhance it. If we wish, we may also light four candles, dedicating each candle to each order of divine beings.

PART IV.

The Guardian Angel

Do I have a Guardian Angel?

Each human being has a personal Guardian Angel, a guide, protector, and guardian of our personality, of our earthly self. It is a precious gift from our soul, our higher self. Our earthly self (our current personality), our higher self (our eternal beingness), and our Guardian Angel actually comprise a single and perfect unity. We are one, the One manifested in a triad: eternally (our higher self), angelically (our Guardian Angel) and temporarily, earthly, in the physical "here and now" (our personality). That is how close, how connected we are! It is the supreme spiritual wonder, infinitely wondrous!

Our Guardian Angel is as close, intimate, dear, and egofied (united with our beingness) as one can be. The Guardian Angel is our faithful and silent companion, our connection to our true nature: we are eternal and perfect souls within the bliss and completeness of the Divine Source. The Guardian Angel guides and protects us always accordingly to the wishes of our higher self, the intention, the choices, and the plans of our soul.

The Guardian Angel is the Love, the Protection, and the Guidance of the Divine for each one of us individually and personally – the always present Love, Protection, and Guidance of the Divine in Angelic Form! Present at all times and in all places! It was and it is always so, despite the seeming adversities and struggles, the problems and the challenges of life (they are only a moment in eternity). Spiritually, this is the only "logical" truth and reality – the absolutely "logical."

If a Guardian Angel watches over me, how come so many bad things have happened to me? If everyone has a Guardian Angel, why is there pain and suffering in the world? Why Guardian Angels leave people to suffer, starve, become ill, or die? Especially children.

Everything that happened and happens in our lives is a result of our free will and choice, as paradoxical as it may sound (appearances are deceiving). Life is the aftermath, the process and unfolding of our own consciousness, our own projection, energy, and action. Life is the result of our individual and collective choice and will; subconsciously, consciously, and super-consciously; a choice that stems from a higher plane of energy, essence and consciousness, a level that transcends the current limiting perception of personality.

Everything we experience results from the choices we make (once more, individually and collectively, subconsciously, consciously, and super-consciously) in accordance with what we know, what we want and the karmic debt we have undertaken to balance so we can grow and advance on all levels. Karma is the Great Teacher. It is as if we engage in reading a huge volume on a knowledge area that we crave to learn, understand, and experience. The weight seems great (even burdensome) but we want to lift it strenuously. And indeed, it is worth to lift it. It is the great value of life, the supreme value.

The Guardian Angel cannot bypass our free will to experience greater maturation and self-discovery through the various separations, conflicts, and sorrows we experience in our lives. We "desire" to experience duality, contrast, conflict, evil, pain, fear, sorrow, darkness, loss, limitations. Only then, we can return to the wholeness of light and the perfection of spirit, more wealthy and conscious than ever. We have experienced the most peculiar and distant states: darkness, pain and negativity, duality and contrast.

As soon as we start to come back to the sheer wholeness of light and the perfection of spirit, we cease to "desire" these states. We desire only the higher, the substantial, the luminous, the boundless, the good, the Highest Good. We desire the good, the Highest Good, no matter what. The expansion, the transmutation, the ascension has begun; finally, the path to enlightenment is open. We ourselves have opened this path by being awakened from the lethargy of materialism and of mass consciousness. We have hit rock bottom and now we start to rise. We have experienced too much disconnection and sorrow, too much opposition and conflict, too much anger and fear, too much suffering.

This entire process is paradoxical, dense, heavy, and dark as matter itself. At the same time, the journey of life is so extraordinary and sacred that nothing in the universe can stop it, block it, or negate it. As we grow and expand, as we purify ourselves mentally and emotionally, as we become spiritually awakened and energetically empowered, we allow our self to transcend the past, the mistakes, and the limitations of our duality. We become able to receive the infinite joy, guidance, and support of the universe and of existence. Only then, we are ready to consciously attune to and follow our Essence, our Soul, our True/Inner/Higher Self; and our Guardian Angel. We experience freedom, wholeness, the joy of spirit and heaven, here in our everyday earthly physical life. The circumstances may remain the same, but the perspective and the viewpoint have changed. It is we, our mind, and our consciousness, that form the perspective.

The answer to the question "Why there is so much evil and suffering in the world?" is beyond the capability of the human mind and understanding. Why is there so much sorrow, injustice, poverty, illness, war, pain? Why is there suffering in the world? This is the great philosophical and metaphysical mystery of all times: why is there evil?

On a spiritual level, we may aim to understand that evil exists to serve as the counterpart of good, so good can choose to realize and consciously choose itself on all levels. Evil gives an opportunity for good (the light, the spirit) to experience itself directly and personally. Evil on Earth (in any form) is a choice, and the aftermath of man's selfish limited thought (in a collective and individual level) and his low level of emotional, mental, and spiritual growth.

According to the Law of Karma, we have chosen our experiences (good and bad), we have caused and created them. The Karma includes also our poor choices, choices we made consciously or unconsciously, on a collective or individual level. Suffering and pain are not only results of karma and human limited perception and consciousness, but they are also lessons for the soul to learn in the material plane; Lessons for the advancement of the Soul, Lessons from the School of Life, Lessons from the School of Earth.

However, our earthly personality – our current earthly self – when faced with evil and negativity on Earth (in any form) is not able to fully understand the purpose of evil. Surely there is an explanation about everything and everything has a cause, a reason and a purpose. Words fall short to describe this purpose. When we reach ascension, enlightenment and theosis, once we return to the All and to the Diving Beingness (return to Eden, "return of the prodigal son"), we probably not only understand but also experience these inconceivable truths that in the present (where "appearances can be deceiving") appear as absurd, conflicting, and paradoxical.

Check also the answer related to this topic in Chapter II "Contact with Angels."

Is there a chance that I have more than one Guardian Angel?

Our personal Guardian Angel who is united with us ("egofied," from the third chakra) is only one. As we evolve energetically, consciously, and spiritually, we may connect to more angels that serve as protectors and guides. We are able to perceive them through our awakened psychic abilities (intuition, clairvoyance, clairaudience). The angel of our soul, just like our inner self, is always one.

If not, what are the other ethereal presences I feel often around me?

Perhaps they are angels that you have drawn to you with your thoughts, feelings, and actions. They can also be your spirit guides, people that no longer have a physical form and function as teachers/guides from higher realms. Sometimes people that have passed away may serve as spirit guides, and often they could be our relatives or people with whom we shared a special connection; now they have advanced spiritually and developed higher consciousness, power, and wisdom to guide human beings.

Do Guardian Angels evolve?

It is possible that Guardian Angels follow some kind of evolution journey, a celestial advancement.

Are the powers of a Guardian Angel enhanced when we are more awakened and we expand spiritually and energetically therefore functioning from a higher level of consciousness? Is there an effect on our Guardian Angel or in our relationship with him?

There are two viewpoints on this matter:

The first is that when we awaken and advance spiritually, our Guardian Angel advances as well. He is empowered, he "comes to life," he manifests himself, he actualizes his full angel strength and duties. We energize our Guardian Angel and he energizes us. It is at that point that we connect to him and receive abundantly his loving energy, protection, and guidance.

The second viewpoint is that our Guardian Angel is already complete and perfect; he is already in the highest energetic and spiritual spot. By our awakening, spiritual growth, and self-improvement, we can connect to our Guardian Angel, we can finally acknowledge his blessed angelic energy and presence, his protection and guidance.

In both cases, the point is that it is absolutely necessary and desirable for us to awaken spiritually, to uplift energetically, to improve and expand emotionally, mentally, and consciously.

Does our Guardian Angel remain the same throughout all our lifetimes?

Yes, our Guardian Angel remains the same since our first incarnation. Our Guardian Angel accompanies us from the time our Divine Monad (the divine aspect of our beingness) created the Higher Self (the spiritual aspect that was individualized) who in turn created our four bodies (mind, emotions, ether, physical matter), giving us the possibility to take a material form on the physical level.

Do we finally meet our Guardian Angel when we complete our life on Earth and leave our physical body?

Yes, we meet our Guardian Angel at the end of each one of our lives! It is a déjà vu experience! It is as if we exclaim, "Oh it is you! I remember you my dearest celestial love! You were always there for me, always next to me!"

Our Guardian Angel assists us in summarizing what we have learned in this life before we move further; he is our personal divine helper, guide, and companion. At the end of each life, we recall fully as we cross over the veil, as we pass from what is false to what is true, from the darkness to the light, from the disconnection and the conflicts of our material life to the unity, the absolute freedom and the blissful serenity of the spirit and of our soul.

Does our Guardian Angel need something from us?

Our Guardian Angel "needs" our recognition, our becoming conscious, our perception and awareness of his existence. He needs the innocence and kindness of our heart, and also our spiritual maturity and responsibility: to take the responsibility for everything we are, everything we do and everything that happens to us so we can heal (we are able to heal something that we have responsibility for, and influence and power over). Our Guardian Angel needs our openness and receptiveness, as if we are children; he needs our love, our unconditional love and our trust, our perfect trust. Above all, he wants us to communicate with him openly, freely, wholeheartedly, innocently, fearlessly, personally, heavenly. To really experience our unbreakable bond of friendship and companionship!

Is there a chance that my Guardian Angel is Archangel Michael, Gabriel, Raphael, or another known archangel?

Several people have the feeling that Archangel Michael or Gabriel or Raphael (or another known archangel) is their Guardian Angel. They sense it, hear it, see it during a meditation, or they receive it as a piece of information through channeling. The Archangels are close to all human beings without exceptions (they are cosmic energies and forces of the Divine Beingness). However, our Guardian Angel is special, specific, and unique for every person. The vibration, the quality, and the energy of the Guardian Angel may resemble the ones of a famous Archangel (or how we perceive the Archangels) and maybe even the Guardian Angel's name is similar to an archangel's name. Nevertheless, the energy, the presence, the vibration, and the name of a Guardian Angel will be unique and slightly different to those of the Archangels.

Can I call upon my Guardian Angel? Can I talk to him and ask for protection and guidance?

It is the best thing you can do in your earthly life!

What is the name of my Guardian Angel? Can I find out the name from

a teacher or a medium (that channels spiritual information from other realms)? Can I find out the name myself? What happens when an expert of spiritual matters tells me a different name for my Guardian Angel than the one I feel or hear? What happens if I hear or see/feel different names during my meditation in various periods of my life? Does this mean that the name of my Guardian Angel changes?

This topic is more complicated than it sounds... Our Guardian Angel has a name that expresses his energy and essence; his name corresponds to his vibration. The use of his name manifests his energy and it is a means of connection and communication, a way to relate to him – just as we relate to a person when we use his name.

We may "sense," or hear (internally) or see (with our mind's eye) the name of our Guardian Angel in a meditation. We can also receive the name of our Guardian Angel from a person with advanced psychic and spiritual abilities (intuition, clairaudience, clairvoyance, clairsentience, channeling).

We use the name of our Guardian Angel to invoke him, invite him, thank him, and to connect to his loving presence; to ground and manifest the angelic energies, the personal protection, care, and guidance our Guardian Angel offers us. It is necessary to know our Guardian Angel's name and indeed, we learn it and we receive it during our spiritual awakening. It is a part of our path to enlightenment and the union with the Divine Beingness/Divine All. It is a part of our journey to the Ultimate Awareness of the Self: our Guardian Angel is an essential part of our self, our beingness; he is the most luminous and spiritual, beloved and sacred, selfless, and angelic part! He is the guard, the companion, and the guide of our self on all levels.

However, it is important that we realize that no name (or word) fully represents our Guardian Angel, just like no name fully represents us. For example, a candle (or any other object) is named "candle" for communication purposes. We can use different words in various languages, or even the same words with different pronunciation. We can write the word in order to communicate it. An object doesn't have its own innate name; a name that substantially corresponds 100% to the particular object; a name that is truly, essentially and objectively the object itself. We human beings call candles a "candle" (or use any other spoken or written word) for the sake of agreement and communication.

Similarly, let's imagine that the name of our Guardian Angel is "A." In this particular lifetime and period of our life, we call upon "A" and truly he is "A" to us! "A" manifests his presence and energy; Our Guardian Angels is "A" and "A" is our Guardian Angel. Years later, we might feel/see/hear that the name of our Guardian Angel is "Z" and "Z" may seem more correct as our Guardian Angel's name. "Z" may be a name phonetically close to "Z," or slightly different (another pronunciation or accent) or completely different than "Z" (a completely different name).

Again, "Z" represents the name of our Guardian Angel to enable us to communicate and connect to him at that point of time. It will probably be a more "true," a more "accurate" name. There is no name or word that absolutely corresponds to our Guardian Angel – words are human inventions and celestial beings are transcendental.

This does not mean that we reject the human names of angels, for they still have value and a higher frequency. They can express and manifest angelic, loving, healing, and protecting vibrations. The name truly represents our Guardian Angel in our mind and heart, invoking and manifesting him. It is the word by which we identify our Guardian Angel, a word that connects his image, energy and presence to us, mentally and energetically.

The name of the Guardian Angel may be similar to an archangel's name; however the Guardian Angel is not an Archangel. The name of a Guardian Angel is a name we understand, attune, and feel close to; a name of higher energy that offers us angelic love and care, protection, and guidance. It is the name through which the Guardian Angel communicates, listens, receives, responds, emits, and attunes to us.

The discovery and use of our Guardian Angel's name promotes and advances our personal and spiritual growth. Alongside with regarding as valid, true, and of higher vibrational frequencies the name of our Guardian Angel (and it is!), it is wise to be open and receptive to future changes (small or complete modifications). Remember that no name or word is absolute. Words are human and can be limiting when it comes to describe celestial beings. Being receptive and open to future changes of our Guardian Angel's name means we are open to a more high and lucid connection with him.

We need to trust, love and respect our agreement with our Guardian Angel; we need to perceive and use the name of the Guardian Angel as true, substantial, and accurate. We use and treat the name of the Guardian Angel just as we received it (ourselves or from a teacher/medium): with love, respect, and faith.

A similar approach is valid for our own name. We may feel that our name doesn't express us in the present or that it didn't represent us at our birth. The name that we were given has a high value and importance – however, we can adopt another name that expresses us more, or be given a name through a spiritual teacher. We may even receive the name through personal spiritual practice and meditation. Our new name corresponds to a higher vibrational frequency and it has an uplifting function, it is closer to our essence. Yet again, another paradox: our essence doesn't have a name. Even the highest energetic and spiritual name cannot reach our essence. We perceive and employ names that are closer to it and more substantial, they function as a ladder to our essence. When we reach our essence, we will discard the ladder. We will no longer need the ladder, we are where we are supposed to be... After all, who will call whom? We are what we are; we are what it is!

ESOTERIC PRACTICE

Your Guardian Angel's Name

Read carefully the answer of the next question and actualize all its points.

In addition to that, you can apply the following technique to receive the name of your Guardian Angel:

Prepare yourself by clearing your space and your self, both physically and energetically.

Take a white piece of paper and a pen/marker.

Start by taking deep breaths and concentrate. Visualize a perfect golden sphere of energy, light, and love surrounding you. See and feel it clearly.

Ask your Guardian Angel to reveal his name in verbal or written form.

"Beloved Guardian Angel, what is your name? Please tell me, help me hear it, see it, or write it. I absolutely love you and I thank you supremely!"

Relax, be open and receptive. Let your mind completely free.

What name do you "hear" or what name do you "see"? Wait...

And again, what name do you "hear" or "see"?

To put it in a different way: If your Guardian Angel told you his name, what name would that be? If he wrote his name on a piece of paper, what would he write? Can you envision it? Can you see or hear it?

Relax completely once again and be open and receptive for a few moments. Imagine your angel telling you his name or writing it down for you.

Open your eyes, take the pen and the paper, and write down the name that your angel told you or showed you.

Repeat this exercise for seven days.

Have patience, trust, and be persistent! Greater patience, greater trust, and greater persistence!

Yes, you can receive and you shall receive!

I want so much to connect with my Guardian Angel! How do I do that?

You are already in full connection, attunement, and unity with your Guardian Angel, in a subconscious and super-conscious level (from the level of your higher self). What remains is for you to reflect and meditate upon this fact, to feel it and experience it in your daily life. If you wish to connect and attune to your Guardian Angel on a conscious level (manifesting the connection in your life), or to be precise, if you wish to become conscious of the connection and the attunement to your Guardian Angel that already exists and existed always, follow the advice given below:

1. Candle: Light a white candle everyday (it symbolizes purity, light, and spirit) and dedicate it to your Guardian Angel. Look at the warm flame of the candle for a few minutes and relax. Think of your angel, talk to him, and invoke him. Feel his presence and his energy. Feel, experience, and send him your love; receive, feel, and experience his Love. Make the lighting of the candle an everyday practice.

2. Dedication: Dedicate your day to your Guardian Angel. Dedicate a space in your house or an object (e.g. a crystal). Do it with all the intention, the power of thought, and the power of love that you possess.

3. Waking up and going to sleep: When you lie down on your bed to sleep, bring into your mind your Guardian Angel. Do the same in the morning when you wake up. Think of your Guardian Angel for a few moments, and feel his vibration and energy lovingly surrounding you. Repeat this practice every day.

4. Calling: Call upon your Guardian Angel as frequently as possible. Simply, ask him to be near you, to grant you his presence.

5. Meditation: Close your eyes, take some slow and deep breaths, and relax. Visualize that you are surrounded by a luminous white light of life and love. Ask your Guardian Angel to be there with you. Call upon him, welcome him. Stay in this state of silence, serenity, and harmony for ten minutes or more. Practice this meditation daily or as frequently as you can.

6. Thoughts: Think of your Guardian Angel throughout the day. Talk to him. He is the most dear spiritual companion and friend that you have ever had! He will not abandon you ever. He is the Celestial, Spiritual Love in its Angelic Form!

7. Senses: Be attentive, be sensitive! Do you feel chills, tingles, waves, pulsations, vibrations, flow, electricity, warmth, cold, air... when there are no changes in the environment around you? You have angelic visitations!

8. Thankfulness: Take a minute to thank from the depths of your heart with absolute love and gratitude, the Guard of your Soul, your Guardian Angel!

9. Writing: Keep pieces of paper near you so you can write down thoughts, feelings, sensations, visions, and experiences. Write down questions and answers, "coincidences," synchronic events, and dreams. Draw, paint, write poetry, quotes, and sayings. Also, draw symbols.

10. Diary: Ideally, keep a diary (not just random pieces of paper) where you regularly write down about your spiritual development and your angelic experiences! Dedicate the diary to your Guardian Angel and ask for his support, assistance, and inspiration.

Remember and keep reminding yourself:

"All is Love and Love is All!"

Blessings and angels, the world is full of them!

Have an angelic practice,

With Love!

ESOTERIC PRACTICE

Angels and Gratitude

Angels love gratitude! Gratitude calls them, attracts them, magnetizes them like divine nectar! And we humans feel gratitude as heaven, as paradise, as divine nectar in our hearts! Gratitude heals wounds. Gratitude restores. Gratitude liberates. Gratitude is consciousness, recognition, awareness, connection, return, and fullness and it emanates from these states.

Do the following exercise to cultivate more gratitude:

First, make a list of everything you are grateful for. A list of all the good and beautiful things that exist, that you have in your life, all the good and beautiful things that you experience. Events, conditions, people, relationships, moments, things, pleasures, joys, strengths, abilities, talents. A list of all the good and beautiful, complex and simple, spiritual and material, past and present, large and small elements of life that you are thankful for!

Next, make a second list of negative things you have experienced. All the difficulties, problems, blockages, and obstacles in your life. Everything that is a source of stress, pain, or sorrow. Think that everything in life has a meaning and a value, a purpose. The same is true for all negative and unpleasant elements. See how through these elements you have become what you are. All of them help you focus more on what you desire, on the good and the beautiful, on the true and the essential. All of negativity is a Great Teacher for you, your earthly self. It is a school. Through it you learn, you get stronger, you develop, you advance, you rise, you emerge. You are being transmuted. You are becoming the best you can be, you are becoming who You Are. You expand your love, wisdom, intelligence, and the totality of your abilities. You discover what was previously hidden, forgotten, unmanifest. You discover your strength. And with it, your essence.

Meditate on the two lists for a few moments.

Thank the angels for the entirety of your experiences, the whole of your life, the totality of your being. Thank the Divine element, the higher, the spiritual, the transcendental. Ask to receive the strength and the wisdom to love and accept everything that exists in your life, both the positive and negative, to make peace with them and understand them. To see them through a higher perspective. In a larger context. And then, to expand, strengthen, multiply the positive elements and release, transmute, reduce (or even annihilate) the negative ones.

Stay in gratitude! In awe, in great joy, in ecstatic bliss! Feel yourself becoming a source of gratitude and transcendent love. You are now vibrating at the frequency of gratitude. A Divine Frequency! Gratitude is your nature. A Divine Nature!

At every opportunity, express and act upon your gratitude in the most generous and open-hearted way!

ESOTERIC PRACTICE

Angelic Love and Blessings

Ask and invite the Angelic Love and Blessings into your heart. Ask daily, several times throughout the day. Simply call upon, ask, see, feel the love and the blessings of angels in your heart. See and feel their love to fill you completely and their blessings flow in you and through you. Engage in this practice many times daily.

Repeat silently, as often as you can, with faith and power: *"Angels of Light! I bless myself with light, peace, love, and pure angelic energies! Angels bless me with light, peace, love, and pure angelic energies! Angels of Light close to me, Angels of Light around me, Angels of Light next to me!"*

Do the same for a person who is dear to you, a person in need, or anyone you have met: *"Angels of Light! Angelic Light, Peace, Love, and Angelic Blessings! Angels bless you with light, peace, love, and pure angelic energies! Angels of Light close to you, Angels of Light around you, Angels of Light next to you!"*

You can also repeat silently: *"I send Angelic Love to myself,"* or when it is meant for another person: *"I send you Angelic Love!"*

Nourish gratitude and joy in your heart. Nourish gratitude and joy for yourself, for others, for angels, and for every single thing and for everything! Gratitude and joy and only gratitude and joy! That splendid and wondrous life, reality, and existence are! Your life, your reality, and your existence!

MEDITATION

The Love of Angels

How is the love of angels? What does it look like? Can a human being reach it? Feel it? Experience it?

Imagine endless meadows with beautiful flowers all around you. Notice the sights, sounds, and smells around you. See countless flowers and colors, smell the sweet-smelling flowers. Enjoy the exquisite and marvelous landscape, endless meadows surrounding you, a sea of colors, smells, and energies. See the celebration of nature, beauty and life in all its forms, variety, expressions and glory.

Imagine yourself in this magical and enchanting landscape, breathing deeply, taking deep breaths of beauty and life.

Breathe deeply.

Ask angels to shower you with their love.

Breathe deeply.

Ask angels for their love.

Breathe deeply.

Invite love, invite the angels.

Breathe deeply.

Inhale the love of angels.

A most wonderful, marvelous, heavenly experience of love, beauty, and life.

In your mind's eye, lie down in the meadows, between the countless flowers, colors, smells, the beauty, and life. Gently let yourself sink into the experience of Love.

ESOTERIC PRACTICE

Angels of Nature

Take a walk outdoors and open yourself to the wonders of nature: to the energy, the life, the colors, and the smells of nature. Communicate with Mother Nature, the sky, the sun, the waters, the trees, the flowers, the stones, the soil. Find a spot where you can meditate and sit there. See yourself within a brilliant white light. Feel the light surrounding you; affirm that the light cleanses you, empowers you, and illuminates you on all levels. Affirm it several times, see and feel the luminous purity and the pure luminosity on all levels of your beingness. Invite the Angels of Nature, feel them close to you. Open your eyes. Talk to them with your mind, with your heart, energetically, spiritually. Offer love to them. Allow yourself to receive energy, guidance, knowledge, and great power. Feel you are becoming one with nature and its angels. You are one with the angels of nature. Affirm it a few times more and stay with this energy.

MEDITATION

Angels of Abundance

Light a white candle and dedicate it to the Angels of Light and the Divine Source which is Infinite and Boundless.

(Caution: candles have to always be away from flammable objects and do not leave candles unattended.)

Close your eyes and visualize yourself standing under a waterfall of white light. Ask the light to permeate you, clean you, and purify you on all levels; to wash away the negative energy, to illuminate and energize you, to charge you positively. See and feel the light permeating you, cleansing you, purifying you, enlightening your beingness, your mind, and your body... The light is charging you positively and it energizes you. The light is everywhere inside you and the light is all around you. Take a few deep breaths filled with pure white light and brilliant luminosity!

Now, envision yourself within a radiant golden sun. It is a perfect sun of higher spiritual consciousness, higher spiritual light. It symbolizes the perfect wisdom, the perfect love, and the perfect power; it attunes you to these qualities of your primal, authentic, higher nature, soul, and essence. Take some deep breaths filled with pure golden light and brilliant luminosity!

"Perfect Love, Perfect Wisdom and Perfect Power." Repeat these words a few times, feel the words, their meaning, and energy within your heart and your mind.

Invoke your beloved Guardian Angel! See and feel his sweet and loving energy, his heavenly presence...

Invoke the four Archangels of light: Archangel Michael, Archangel Gabriel, Archangel Raphael, and Archangel Uriel... See and feel their powerful energy and their fiery presence...

Proceed to invoke the Angels of Abundance, of total abundance; spiritual, mental, emotional, energetic, and material abundance; abundance on all levels and all dimensions; abundance of love, wisdom, and power. And of the earthly abundance, of the material prosperity, wealth, and success.

See and feel the energy and the presence of the Angels. Abundance is here-now and now-here. Abundance is present. Ask the Angels to heal your Abundance, to cleanse and purify it, to uplift it, to harmonize it, to enlighten it, to awaken it, to energize it, and to enhance it with wisdom, love, power, and all the divine qualities. To attune your Abundance to the Divine Abundance, the Abundance of the Source, the universal, cosmic, total abundance; the ultimate, true, and real abundance.

Declare that you are open to receive and accept abundance. Declare that you are ready to recognize, become conscious of, to express, manifest, create, and co-create.

Abundance on all levels!

Stay with this energy.

Take some deep breaths.

Open your eyes.

Thank the angels wholeheartedly.

Light another white candle and dedicate it to the Divine Abundance of the angels and of yourself.

Empowerment: If you wish, you can empower your Spiritual Total Abundance by boosting this specific meditation with the high energy and focused intention of the Angelic Invocations and the Angelic Symbols. You can use either method or both of them. From the Angelic Symbols the following are suggested: *Angelic Abundance, Angelic Wealth, Angels of Abundance.* From the Angelic Invocations the following are suggested: *Invocation to the Angels of Abundance, Angelic Invocation for Abundance, Success, and Prosperity.* It doesn't matter if you will use first the symbols and then the invocations or vice versa. Follow your inspiration and intuition. Use either of them or both and then practice the meditation. You can find the Angelic Symbols and the Angelic Invocations in the respective books that are part of the same series.

ESOTERIC PRACTICE

Creating Angelic Fields

The creation of a stable, solid, and impenetrable field of angelic vibration and quality, spiritual energy and vitality, offers an ideal space for meditation, healing, rest, revitalization, introspection, and spiritual upliftment. The angelic field protects our space and generates a vital angelic dimension here on Earth (and the angels desire this)! Essentially it is all about attuning our space to the higher spiritual dimension (sixth dimension), the spiritual level of absolute clarity and illumination. By creating an angelic field, we turn our space into a small "temple" of spirit and light; a space dedicated and attuned to love, serenity, abundance, and harmony. Nothing negative can access our angelic space and we can experience our higher potential, our higher self, the highest aspect of our being which is filled with wisdom, love, and power.

We can create and open an angelic field in any space, just by using our focused intention and our creative force. It has to do with recognizing, becoming conscious, and co-creating.

To open an angelic field in your home or workplace or any other space, follow the procedure below.

Bring your hands into prayer position and focus your mind. Take a deep breath.

Visualize (see in your mind's eye and feel) a white or golden flame lighting up in the center of your space. The flame becomes gradually more intense; you see and you feel it clearly. The warm, marvelous, perfect, angelic, and radiant light of the higher and immaculate spirit becomes stronger, it spreads in your space and it fills it entirely. The powerful spiritual flame is in the center of your space and it illuminates with its dazzling angelic light the entire space!

Invoke the Angels:

"I invoke and invite all the Angels of Light, the Highest Angels of the Supreme Light to create a perfect angelic field within and around my space (e.g. 'my house'), a sublime field of pure vital energy, pure spiritual light, and pure spiritual love.

An elevated and perfect angelic field of absolute cleanness, protection, guidance, joy, vitality, luminosity, love, flow, healing, health, grace, positivity, beauty, benevolence, good fortune, unity, freedom, power, communication, creativity, inspiration, wisdom, peace, serenity, and harmony.

Supreme angelic field in my space, within and around my space!

Perfect angelic field in my space, within and around my space!

I accept it, declare it, co-create it, envision it, perceive it, and feel it.

So it shall be done and so it is! Amen and thank you! Thank you and Amen!"

Envision a luminous field of powerful and pure white or golden light to fill and surround your space. A perfect angelic field, an angelic dimension is open. The ever-loving dimension of the spirit is within your space and your space is within this dimension. It is truly wonderful and exquisite! The process is complete!

Archangelic Fields

There is the option to create additional fields with specific qualities by invoking the Archangels corresponding to these qualities. You can call upon the highest and most beloved four

Archangels of the Light, Michael, Gabriel, Raphael, and Uriel. In this way you co-create their energy fields in your space and ground more their infinite and perfect light for the common good of all!

After opening an angelic field in your space, proceed with creating the archangelic fields:

Visualize (see and feel) the flames of the Archangels arise, light up and become activated in your space; one flame after another, in the center of your space or around it. Visualize four golden flames; you can also visualize the colors corresponding to the four Archangels and their elements (fire, water, ether/air, matter): red for Michael, blue for Gabriel, purple for Raphael, and silver for Uriel. Alternatively you can envision azure, fuchsia, green, silver corresponding to the four Archangels respectively. Follow your inspiration. The energies of the Archangels are elevated, enhanced and spread all over your space.

Note: It is not necessary to visualize the colors. The intention, the assumption, and the belief – that the flames are illuminating your space with their powerful and radiant light – is enough.

Declare:

"I invoke and invite Archangels Michael, Gabriel, Raphael, Uriel to fill, surround, and illuminate my space with their supreme energies, qualities, and powers.

Archangels Michael, Gabriel, Raphael, and Uriel within my space, above my space, beneath my space, left and right of my space, front and back of my space, in all directions of my space, north and south, east, and west.

Supreme archangelic field in my space, within and around it!

Perfect archangelic field in my space, within and around it!

I accept it, declare it, co-create it, envision it, perceive it, and feel it.

So it shall be done and so it is! Amen and thank you! Thank you and Amen!"

The flames, the energies, the powers of the four great Archangels and the all-immaculate and all-illuminating field that they create, it all stays in your space.

Repeat the technique three times more (a total of four times) the same day or the following days. This technique can be repeated from time to time, once or twice a year whenever your intuition tells you.

ESOTERIC PRACTICE

Angelic and Archangelic Fields in the Body

A particularly secret (until now) and extremely powerful technique is the opening and activation of the angelic field in the space that we take up as material beings, i.e. the opening and activation of the angelic field in our body. It is an advanced concept and perception, a technique of higher energy and consciousness with various and multiple benefits on all levels!

Follow all the steps of the technique and replace the word and concept of space with that of your body.

Bring your hands into prayer position and focus your mind. Take a deep breath.

Visualize (see in your mind's eye and feel) a white or golden flame lighting up in the center of your body. The flame becomes gradually more intense, you see and you feel it clearly. The warm, marvelous, perfect, angelic, and radiant light of the higher and immaculate spirit becomes stronger, it spreads in your body, and it fills it entirely. The powerful spiritual flame is in the center of your body and it illuminates with its dazzling angelic light the entire body!

Invoke the Angels:

"I invoke and invite all the Angels of Light, the Highest Angels of the Supreme Light to create a perfect angelic field within and around my body, a sublime field of pure vital energy, pure spiritual light, and pure spiritual love.

An elevated and perfect angelic field of absolute cleanness, protection, guidance, joy, vitality, luminosity, love, flow, healing, health, grace, positivity, beauty, benevolence, good fortune, unity, freedom, power, communication, creativity, inspiration, wisdom, peace, serenity, and harmony.

Supreme angelic field in my body, within and around my body!

Perfect angelic field in my body, within and around my body!

I accept it, declare it, co-create it, envision it, perceive it and feel it.

So it shall be done and so it is! Amen and thank you! Thank you and Amen!"

Envision a luminous field of powerful and pure white or golden light to fill and surround your body. A perfect angelic field, an angelic dimension is open. The ever-loving dimension of the spirit is within your body and your body is within this dimension. It is truly wonderful and exquisite! The process is complete!

Archangelic Fields in the body:

After the opening and activation of the angelic field in your body, proceed with creating the archangelic fields.

Visualize (see and feel) the flames of the Archangels arise, light up and become activated in your body; one flame after another, in the center of your body or around it. Visualize four golden flames; you can also visualize the colors corresponding to the four Archangels and their elements (fire, water, ether/air, matter): red for Michael, blue for Gabriel, purple for Raphael, and silver for Uriel. Alternatively you can envision azure, fuchsia, green, silver corresponding to the four Archangels respectively. Follow your inspiration. The energies of the Archangels are elevated, enhanced and spread all over your body.

Note: It is not necessary to visualize the colors. The intention, the assumption, and the belief – that the flames are illuminating your body with their powerful and radiant light – is enough.

Declare:

"I invoke and invite Archangels Michael, Gabriel, Raphael, Uriel to fill, surround, and illuminate my body with their supreme energies, qualities, and powers.

Archangels Michael, Gabriel, Raphael, and Uriel within my body, above my body, beneath my body, left and right of my body, front and back of my body, in all parts of my body.

Supreme archangelic field in my body, within and around it!

Perfect archangelic field in my body, within and around it!

I accept it, declare it, co-create it, envision it, perceive it and feel it.

So it shall be done and so it is! Amen and thank you! Thank you and Amen!"

The flames, the energies, the powers of the four great Archangels and the all-immaculate and all-illuminating field that they create, it all stays in your body.

Repeat the technique three times more (a total of four times) the same day or the following days. This technique can be repeated from time to time, once or twice a year whenever your intuition tells you.

Creating the Angelic Fields for Another Person

This technique can be practiced on behalf of another person that we wish to help and support, to empower his/her energy, to improve the quality of his/her life and his/her being. The technique brings about only good because it originates from Good (the Angels) and it focuses solely on Good (the creation of angelic fields of luminous/positive energies).

Simply read the text and envision the process for the person you wish to support. Repeat a total of four times. It is advised you inform the person what you are going to do. Remember that whatever you are doing, you are doing it for one's Good, for one's Highest Good, so do it with Love, the Highest Love!

This particular technique is one of the most advanced, powerful, intense, and beneficial techniques that a person can experience. It reconstructs, restores, and manifests the spiritual health of a person (and therefore, health on all levels, since spirit is the highest, all-encompassing level) and it can be combined with all the other techniques of angelic therapy. It is indeed a true blessing!

MEDITATION

Angelic Qualities

The totality of human states, qualities and characteristics which people possess, feel and experience (e.g. joy, love, abundance, romance, or freedom) exist independently of people in a higher dimension in their angelic form. In their higher, spiritual, angelic frequency/quality. They are the states, characteristics, and qualities that the angels experience, emit and create. The energies, essences, and powers that the angels themselves are.

Can you imagine the beautiful and positive human qualities and states in their higher, spiritual, angelic form? Their pure, energetic form. Can you perceive, experience, and feel them? Or to come closer to them? Read the list with the Angelic Qualities given below:

Angelic Love
Angelic Harmony
Angelic Balance
Angelic Abundance
Angelic Flow
Angelic Freedom
Angelic Wholeness
Angelic Knowledge
Angelic Understanding

Angelic Wisdom
Angelic Power
Angelic Health
Angelic Talents
Angelic Creativity
Angelic Compassion
Angelic Intention
Angelic Will
Angelic Vision
Angelic Joy
Angelic Perception
Angelic Inspiration
Angelic Happiness
Angelic Purity
Angelic Illumination

Choose one of the above angelic qualities and close your eyes. Take a few deep breaths and relax your body and mind. Focus your intention and energy on this angelic quality. Surround and fill your body and self with the quality you have chosen. Imagine the quality to embrace and fill you, feel it within you and around you. Place it in your mind, your heart, your hands, your cells, your DNA. See it as a word written in golden letters, hear it spoken, feel it as sensation, visualize it as an image, experience it as a state. Embrace and accept this quality, share and offer it, let it out and communicate it. Connect more to it, attune more to it, become one with it. Become the quality, be the quality. Take a few deep breaths. Whenever you are ready, you can conclude the exercise and gently open your eyes.

PART V.

Angels and Esotericism

How many planes and dimensions of reality exist?

According to the great mystics and teachers of esotericism, Reality is divided into seven major planes – seven vast dimensions. Each dimension consists of seven sub-levels. Imagine that there are seven great "floors" in the immense building of Reality and each floor has seven sub-levels or departments. Each dimension, or plane of Reality, is different from one another. The difference lies in the vibration and frequency of energy that each dimension carries and emanates. The higher levels and dimensions are more light, bright and spiritual, while the lower are more heavy, dense and material. The higher we rise in the great spectrum of Reality, the more pure and illuminating states we experience, the further we move from matter and the closer we move to spirit. As we ascend into higher dimensions, there is increasingly more light, love, joy, peace, freedom, wholeness and oneness.

The difference between the various levels and dimensions of Reality is not only of a vibrational frequency (level of energy) but also of consciousness: the higher spiritual consciousness a being has, the "higher" it is in the great spectrum of Reality. Consciousness ranges from the simple consciousness of minerals, to plants' more complicated consciousness, then to the even more evolved consciousness of animals, to the self-consciousness of human beings, where consciousness is perceiving itself as being conscious. Above the ordinary states of human consciousness there is the superconsciousness of angels, Archangels and of all light beings; and consciousness perceiving itself as All-That-Is, as existential unity and oneness, as Divine and Divinity itself.

Beyond the seven major dimensions of Reality, there are more planes to be found in esoteric teachings. Some speak of nine, ten, twelve, thirteen or even more dimensions of Reality. Nevertheless, these additional planes can be included in the plan of the seven major dimensions. Mystics and esoteric seekers have taught about the causal and intuitive planes. These are sub-dimensions of the fifth dimension, the mental plane. Also in the sixth dimension, the spiritual plane, we find the dimensions or planes related to the Light, planes described as the angelic, buddhic, atmic, paradisiac, edenic realms. All concepts such as God, Godhead, Divinity, Nirvana, Theosis, Source, Creator, the Eternal, the Infinite, the Absolute, and the Supreme Reality or Beingness, belong to the seventh dimension, the highest dimension.

Do you follow? As you read and study the spiritual nature of the Great Reality, about all the higher dimensions, you may feel expanded, elated and elevated. Some students feel dizziness and a feeling of take-off, as their mind, consciousness and energy-field open up and receive higher energy and knowledge.

If you feel dizziness, fatigue, a sense of "take-off" or any other uncomfortable or peculiar feeling or state whilst you read this particular answer as well as the following one and any other spiritual information found in this book, then simply take a break. Take a few deep breaths, shake your hands and legs, move around, drink plenty of pure water and rest your mind. It takes some time to really grasp, absorb and assimilate all of this higher knowledge and energy of the higher planes, worlds and dimensions of the Greater Reality.

What are these higher dimensions and where are they?

Let's explain it as plainly and directly as possible.

Reality (All-That-Is, Existence, Beingness) exists, vibrates and manifests in seven major dimensions. These are seven planes, seven spectrums of energy, in seven different levels of frequency.

Each superior dimension is more elevated, spiritual (subtle) than the previous one and it vibrates on a higher spectrum of frequencies; it has more and higher energy, and higher and more light. Beings and consciousnesses (human beings as well) experience more happiness, freedom, and wholeness, and greater oneness, bliss and Divinity, as they find themselves in each of the higher dimensions.

The seventh dimension is the greatest, the highest, the total one (the most Divine, the Divine per se) and it includes and creates all other worlds, planes and dimensions. It is the All, the Everything, the Divine, the Godhead, God. Everything is found within this sublime and ultimate dimension or reality and everything emanates from it. Our innermost part, our core or soul, is a cell of the Divine, a ray in the sun of this Ultimate, Total and Absolute Reality. We are a ray of consciousness in the sun of the Divine Consciousness. We are all "cells" of God, Divine cells; everything is.

The sixth dimension is the dimension of Spirit and Light. It is the first and the highest expression of Divinity: the spirit, the light. Infinite, boundless and perfect spirit/light. This is where angels and our selves as higher selves reside (spirits, individualized spiritual forms of our eternal soul).

The fifth dimension is the mental or noetic world and the fourth dimension is the plane of emotions, also known as the psychic world. Each of these dimensions contains seven planes with seven sub-planes each, i.e. a total of 49 planes in the fourth dimension (psychic world, emotions and feelings) and 49 planes in the fifth dimension (mental, noetic world). All levels interconnect as the mental planes contain, permeate, surround and envelope all the emotional planes. In other words, the fourth dimension is within the greater fifth dimension, just like the fifth dimension is within the greater sixth dimension. This means that, dimensionally and energetically, spirit is higher and greater than thought and thought is higher and greater than emotion.

The higher a consciousness (a human being) is attuned within the emotional and mental planes, the better, more elevated, light, bright and luminous the stare it experiences.

The first three dimensions form the lower plane, the material physical plane. It is the world of matter where we move and the world we perceive directly. The physical plane features the time dimension, which often is called the "fourth dimension," but in esotericism, we consider and include time among the first three dimensions (material world, nature, flow of the universe) and we use the term "fourth dimension" to refer to the world of emotions, the psychic planes.

The energy and aura of matter (the physical world) is the etheric plane, which is the energy blueprint of matter. It is an energy womb that supplies and sustains everything. All material things in their pure energetic form constitute the etheric plane. Since the etheric/energy dimension or world is a part of the material world (it is its etheric form, essence and aura), we don't consider it a distinct dimension.

Now, let's go upward once more. Above and beyond the third dimension there is the fourth dimension, an immense fourth dimensional plane which is the world of feelings and emotions. This plane is dominated by the liquid element, things are more fluid here – more subjective – just as feelings are. In this dimension we experience more freedom than in the material world. For example, we travel by thought and we can fly – the most wonderful, amazing and sublime sensation to experience! We find ourselves in the fourth dimension (actually our consciousness is inside it) whenever we sleep, meditate, daydream, fantasize. Our consciousness is fully and completely transferred to the fourth dimension in between our earthly lives, right after our physical death. In reality, there is no death for consciousness, only transitions and change. There is only Life, in different levels and forms. We can never cease to exist: in the Divine Level, our core or soul level, we are Eternity, Eternal Life. The fourth dimension, a higher and greater dimension than the material physical level, is the "next world" we experience after the completion of our earthly life on the material physical plane.

There are seven planes and forty-nine sub-planes in the fourth dimension, which resonate to different vibrational frequencies. The lower planes of the fourth dimension are called "astral planes." Astral planes have lower vibrations and it is the location where we experience negative emotional and mental states. The higher planes of the fourth dimension resonate to higher frequencies; in these luminous planes we experience joy, serenity, love, freedom and peace. Between the higher and the lower planes of the fourth dimension, there is the purgatory plane: a plane of psychic purification that follows one's physical death to prepare the soul to reach the higher planes. The terms "hell" and "heaven" refer respectively to these lower (astral) and higher illuminating planes of the fourth dimension. Heaven and hell (i.e. the higher and lower planes) are in reality psychic states, the same that we also experience during our earthly life: sadness, fear, pain or joy, serenity and love. It is about misery (our hell) or happiness (our heaven). Most of all, heaven and hell are states of our own consciousness; they exist within us no matter which plane we are on. We experience heaven or hell (positive or negative psychic states) at all times, whether we are in physical form or have passed to the fourth, the psychic dimension.

Moving higher up from the fourth dimension, its seven planes and its forty-nine sub-planes, as we rise energetically and spiritually, we reach the fifth dimension of the great spectrum of Reality. Our thoughts exist in the fifth dimension, a plane even more great and free (just like our thoughts) than the previous one. It is a vast world of five dimensions, with the element of air being dominant. It should be noted that all the elements are present in all dimensions, but what differs is the ratio of the elements in each dimension. (E.g. the element of earth/

matter exists also in the fourth and fifth dimension but as an idea, a sensation. It is just like when we dream of objects but they are only ideas and sensations.)

The fifth dimension also has seven planes and forty-nine sub-planes resonating to higher and lower frequencies; these planes and sub-planes are related to the emotional/psychic planes as they actually contain them. The higher planes of the fifth dimension are called causal planes. Causal planes include the World of Ideas (Plato), the primary forms and ideas over everything and also the archetypes. In the highest planes of the fifth dimension, the higher levels of the Cosmic, Existential, Divine Mind, and the Akashic Records are located. The Akashic Records are the archives of every soul in the cosmos; they are the collective/cosmic memory.

In the highest planes of the fifth dimension (the higher mind), consciousness experiences lucidity and greater freedom, truth and luminosity; it is only a "breath" or a "thought" away from the sixth dimension – the plane of spirit and pure light.

The first five dimensions are called worlds of "good and evil" or worlds of "separation" because we experience the separation (from Unity) and the opposites. There are higher and lower feelings and thoughts, negative and positive, good and bad, just as there are higher and lower choices, actions and experiences. We experience everything as pleasant or unpleasant, light or dark, desirable or undesirable. Through the separation and the contrast between opposites, the human being receives multiple lessons and grows. Above the planes of experience, the planes of the first five dimensions, there are the planes of pure beingness, the dimensions of absolute harmony and unity, what we call the "Absolute Good," which is our true nature and essence.

The sixth dimension is the dimension of Spirit, Light, and Love. This dimension of Pure Spirit is experienced as Divine Light and Divine Love; it is an infinite plane of absolute wholeness and unity. It is here where consciousness experiences ultimate freedom. The sixth dimension of the Great Reality is the place where all angels and teachers or masters of light reside. The dominant element is fire. The sixth dimension has seven planes, with each one having seven sub-planes that extend to infinity in terms of energy, size and light. It is impossible to describe sixth dimension with images or words because language and intellect reach and are limited, up to the fifth dimension. To discover what exists beyond language and intellect, we have to use our higher power and wisdom, our intuitive and insightful perception, our energetical and spiritual sensitivity, our spiritual and psychic knowledge and awareness as well as our ability of higher attunement through projecting our consciousness outside the body, entering states of super-consciousness.

Beyond the sixth dimension extends the seventh dimension. The seventh dimension is the dimension of God/The Divine, the Transcendental, the Absolute, the Infinite, the Unknown within its Absolute Transcendence. We know only a few things (at least mentally) about this plane: we experience it in our heart, our soul and our existence as presence, consciousness, a sense of self (sense of beingness). We experience it as love, wisdom and will/power; the three primary qualities of God and all consciousnesses, angels and human beings. We comprehend that God/The Divine is Love, Wisdom and Will/Power (Creativity) in their infinite, absolute, ultimate and perfect state and form!

It is important to understand that all dimensions exist here – right here, all of them, simultaneously, now, continuously and at all times. Every cell in our body is simultaneously in all dimensions, on the fourth, fifth, sixth and seventh dimensions, as every cell has an emotional/psychic, mental/noetic, spiritual and divine counterpart, essence and beingness. Each molecule of matter has spiritual equivalence, essence and beingness as it is found within the light (and created by the light) of the sixth and seventh dimensions. The reverse is not applicable i.e. there are "things" in the higher dimensions that don't have a material correspondence, as each higher dimension is greater than the preceding ones. For example, our thoughts and mental images are beyond the material world. In the Spirit (sixth dimension) all potential and possibilities exist for everything that is or can be! We can imagine the Spirit (sixth dimension) as an infinite ocean of light with matter (the physical universe) being a lake of more visible and condensed light within the ocean. Whatever exists within the lake, it also exists within the ocean and it is of the same material as the ocean but of another vibration. However, not everything that is found in the greater ocean also exists within the lake. Angels are beings and consciousnesses of the great ocean that can visit the lake but are not limited by it.

To sum up:

A human being exists in all dimensions and all dimensions are within him.

He exists as a soul in the seventh dimension. This is his innermost sense of selfhood, his highest beingness.

As spirit/light/higher self in the sixth dimension.

As intellect/insight/imagination in the fifth dimension.

As psyche/emotions/feelings in the fourth dimension

As etheric/energy body and as a material/physical body in the etheric and the material matter level, the world of the first three dimensions.

As is now crystal-clear, it is the ultimate blessing that we exist, you and I! And the most divine aspect is that it really could not have been any other way!

ESOTERIC PRACTICE

Outline of Reality

Make a sketch, a drawing, based on the information of the previous answer. It will help you understand better the greater outline of Reality.

You can divide a piece of white paper into seven horizontal rows and color them. In each horizontal section (level), write its respective name. Begin by the first three dimensions of matter that comprise the physical/material world (use one color to depict these three dimensions). Proceed further and color the fourth, then the fifth, the sixth and at the end the seventh dimension (the Divine plane, the All). If you want, you can divide the fourth, fifth and sixth dimensions into their seven sub-levels.

Meditate upon your drawing.

Alternatively, you can draw seven concentric circles. Write inside each circle the corresponding dimension. The three inner circles represent the material world. The next circle represents the fourth dimension, the next one the fifth dimension and the next one the sixth dimension. The circle of the seventh dimension is the largest of all the circles. The drawing of concentric circles gives a better depiction of Reality, as each higher dimension includes and permeates the lower dimensions/planes/levels/worlds. Thus, all is included in the highest-of-all seventh dimension (God/the Divine). All moves and exists within it! There in nothing that is not part of the Divine, the Divine nature, the Divine essence, the Divine substance, the Divine energy, the Divine perfection, the Divine value and the Divine purpose!

What do we mean by the term "God"?

Who truly knows who and what God is? Who has seen His Face (i.e. the ultimate truth and reality)? "God" or the "Divine" doesn't have a gender or other human, earthly limiting characteristics. By using the term "God" we mean whatever it is that each one of us perceives and understands. We all are continuously seeking "what is God." We all are continuously searching and remembering a more deep, true and substantial experience of God.

We may say that God is the supreme principle of the universe and of the cosmos, the unity behind everything, the absolute reality, the All That Is, the Supreme Being, the Supreme Consciousness (energy, presence, essence) of the world (of all the worlds) and all the energies, presences, essences within it (omnipresent). God is the Supreme, the Absolute, the Total Reality behind, within and beyond all phenomena. Everything originates from the Divine Beingness, it moves within it and it returns to it.

We know that the Divine Beingness (the Supreme, Absolute and Inconceivable for the human being Reality) may also be expressed Personally (a Personal God). We know that "God is Love" and that Love is Divine. The Kingdom of God exists within each one of us, we are made in the "Image and Likeness" of God: we are all, without exception (despite our apparent differences), divine beings that re-discover their potential and their divinity through a "game" of matter and personal experience that only matter makes possible.

May we all know and experience the Divine Element, the Divine Essence, the Divine Presence, the Divine Love/Wisdom/Power, the Divine Consciousness and Reality, the Divine Unity and Wholeness; within us and around us, in everything. May we reach it soon and without pain, with the angelic wings of seeking, of awareness, of joy and of true freedom.

What if I don't agree with what I have read so far?

That is natural and totally acceptable! All the truths on Earth are relative because they are views and perspectives upon the Truths. The mind is the prism, man is the prism, human knowledge and human experience are the prism. Human beings never fully get away from the prism. However, this needn't intimidate us. All the (comparatively relative) truths need to be experienced for us to ascertain their level of validity and worth for human life and development. Man needs to study the spiritual teachings in depth, to experience them, to compare, reject, adopt, transcend them. Only then the spiritual truth will hold value in one's soul. In the journey of Life, man learns to inquire, doubt, experience and believe (and not necessarily in that order).

ESOTERIC PRACTICE

How do you perceive God?

What is your personal view of God?

How do you perceive God, the Absolute/Supreme Reality, the All That Is, the Supreme Divine Force, the Omnipotent Creator, the Source, the Beginning of All (descriptions of God by various mystics and teachers)?

Proceed with the following seemingly simple but enlightening exercises to approach this absolutely transcendental and multidimensional topic.

Exercise 1: What do you think, what do you believe about God/the Divine?

Take a piece of white paper. Write on top of the paper the word "GOD." Concentrate. Wait a little. Then write your thoughts. Read them. Fill in if you have some new thoughts. Continue the exercise for a few days more.

Exercise 2: Discovering God/the Divine within you

Take a white piece of paper. Write on top of the paper the word "GOD." Do a brief meditation: close your eyes gently, take some deep and slow breaths and relax. Focus on your heart chakra (the energy center located in the center of the chest, over the heart).Visualize a radiant golden flame. Observe it for a little while. Feel the warm golden energy it emits. Feel the wonderful energy and light of the flame. Ask your inner self about God: "What is God?" Wait a little and then open your eyes and write down whatever comes into your mind. Read what you have answered about God and fill in something more if you want. Continue this exercise over the following days.

Exercise 3: Discovering God/the Divine through nature

When you are outdoors, in the arms of Mother Nature, in a place you love, observe around you the beauty, the harmony, the life and the perfection. See and feel the countless wonderful colors, forms, sounds and smells. Ask yourself about God. Let yourself free to feel and to receive the answer. Ask Mother Nature to help you connect with the Higher/Spiritual/Divine element. Feel how nature is itself a Higher/Spiritual/Divine expression, emanation and creation. Nature is a mirror of the Divine, the All That Is, the Existence. It is truly a magnificent, magnificent, magnificent experience!

Do angels know the "Face of God," the Holy Absolute Reality?
Are angels one with the Divine Reality and how do they perceive it?

A particularly high energetic attunement that we call "at-one-ment" is needed in order to perceive what angels "think," "feel," and how they experience things. From what we know, angels are consciously, or rather super-consciously (totally conscious), one with the Divine Reality, the Divine Source and Essence, in complete unification and harmony with it. The high attunement to the angels is of great value; it is worth for someone to go deeper into it and experience it more directly through meditation, study and esoteric practice.

What do we mean by "Spirit"?

It is the beingness, the essence of the existence, of the world and of everything. It is the energy that makes up everything; the energy within, behind, above and around everything. This energy is seen clairvoyantly as Light and we feel and experience it as Love. The spirit – the spiritual dimension and beingness of the world – is experienced by us as the supreme, radiant, perfect and absolute Love. It is the highest experience of love and light one can have. Spirit IS Light and Spirit IS Love!

The dimension of the Spirit is the sixth dimension of Reality, an infinite plane of six dimensions of absolute purity, transcendence, completeness and unity. The sixth dimension of Spirit contains the five lower dimensions of separation and duality, the worlds of "good and evil" and of experience. These dimensions are the mental/noetic dimension (fifth dimension), the psychic/emotional dimension (fourth dimension) and the etheric and material world (first three dimensions).

Therefore, everything is within the Spirit and the Spirit is within everything and the Spirit (the Divine Energy, the Divine Light, the Divine Love) Is Everything.

Are God and Spirit the same thing?

Spirit, Light and Love are the closest to God (the Supreme, the Absolute) and Spirit is the Divine that we have the chance to know and experience through our self, our spirit and our soul – as our self, our spirit and our soul are in perfect harmony and unity with the Divine Spirit.

God is Spirit and Spirit is God. But God, as the highest dimension of Reality, transcends Spirit, the creative energy, substance and essence of everything. The creative energy, substance and essence – which constitutes everything – emanates from the Divine and it Is Divine, but the Divine extends to the Infinite, the Eternal, the Transcendental. God/the Divine – as the Supreme Source, Principle and Reality of All – goes beyond Spirit and includes concepts and states such as the All, Wholeness, the "Zero," the Primary, the Void, the Infinite, Nirvana and the Unknown.

What is Logos?

If Spirit is the Creative Force, Essence and Energy of the Divine, Logos ("the son") is the Divine's Consciousness, Wisdom and Love. Divine Consciousness, Divine Wisdom and Divine love are Logos. A human being holds within himself both Divine Spirit, as creative force and energy, and Divine Logos, as thought and consciousness. And by being a Soul (a Divine Monad, Divine Beingness), a person has God/the Divine within his/her inner being. This is the esoteric interpretation of being created "in the Image and Likeness of God."

I read in spiritual books that the purpose of a human being is to reach his divine nature and that our Higher Self is godlike. Could this be an illusion of the "ego"? Where do other people fit in this viewpoint? And what about God? Have we replaced God with ourselves? Doesn't this demonstrate self-centeredness, selfishness and vanity?

Man is the creation, projection, emanation of the Whole, of the All, of the One; of the existence, and of the Divine – the transcendental, supreme, absolute and infinite Divine, of God. Each human being holds within their inner being the information about their origin, beingness and essence. Each person is innately endowed with Divine essence, which is the same material that all existence is made of; not only the same material but also the same information, energy, intention and force. The Divine is everywhere and the Divine is All. Everything is a part of the Divine and everything is Divine. So is a human being. The discovery and acknowledgement of this truth is the greatest spiritual awakening that a human being may ever reach. This discovery is followed by the realization and understanding that others are also part of the Divine. The Divine exists within everyone without exception, truly and absolutely. Everyone and everything is within the Divine and the Divine is in everyone and in everything. The Divine, the Supreme Essence and Force, the Supreme Reality, has created everything and it constitutes everything (at the same time, it transcends everything).

The purpose of a human being is Theosis, the complete connection and unification with the Divine in the highest possible level and the manifestation of the Divine throughout all of life's aspects and conditions. Theosis doesn't mean that man aspires to take the role of God, to become God in the place of God, or that man believes he is in the highest/supreme state/ position, above everyone and everything else. Man's purpose is "spiritualization" and "divin- ization" i.e. to make one's life and existence complete, higher, pure, spiritual and Divine; to make oneself a part of God on all levels. Superconsciously man is already and always a part of God and a divine being. The plan is to realize it on a conscious, physical, earthly level. To become what one is: a part of God, a divine part. To discover, recognize and become con- scious of one's essence, substance and origin, one's plan and purpose: and all of these are Divine. From God, within God, through God, for God, a Divine journey, in a Divine way. And that is Divine!

The spiritually conscious and consciously spiritual person – a mystic – knows that:

It is not possible to recognize fully the Divinity within yourself, the Divine origin, substance and essence, the Divine plan and purpose of existence without recognizing fully the Divinity of others and the total Divinity of the Supreme Reality/God.

Similarly, it is not possible to recognize the Divinity of the Supreme Reality/God without recognizing the full Divinity of yourself and others.

Should a human being have spiritual confidence and strength or should he "humble himself under the mighty hand of God" as religion says (1 Peter 5:6)? Is man small or great?

One doesn't negate the other. A great teacher of light experiences awe and wonder, appreciation, humbleness and gratitude at the splendor of existence, of life, of the higher reality and of God. At the same time, being in full unity, harmony and flow with the spiritual element and the Divine, a teacher of light expresses freely, fearlessly, and abundantly the supreme power and will; he/she manifests spiritual mastery on all levels of his/her being and all levels of life, inspiring others learn and grow, supporting the highest good of all.

There are terms I come across, such as soul, spirit, Higher Self, I AM Presence, Divine Spark, Core, Monad... do these terms describe the same thing?

This is a tough question to answer, especially from a human perspective. These are the two reasons that make it difficult to answer:

Firstly, in the spiritual plane (the incorporeal/transcendental plane, behind and beyond the apparent matter), "things" are not like in the material plane. Here, in the physical plane (the material visible world), we see that a table is a table and we call it a "table" to distinguish it from other objects. In the spiritual plane – which is above and higher than the world of mind and intellect – it is difficult to define situations, to distinguish them, to describe and name them as we do in the physical plane.

In the world of spirit (sixth dimension of Reality) we have transcended the world of thought and intellect (fifth dimension) and of language (fifth dimension as well). In the spiritual world, we transcend separation and form (both separation and form are basic structural features of the first five dimensions of Reality) and enter into the light that is formless and limitless. All the terms mentioned in this question are used to describe exactly this great, inconceivable, ecstatic plane of Transcendental Reality, higher and above the separation and the forms of the first five dimensions.

The second reason that this question is difficult to answer is that various researchers, scholars, seekers, mystics and teachers may perceive the terms and concepts differently, or use various terms to describe the same situation. In esoteric traditions and bibliography, terms such as soul, spirit, Higher Self, I AM Presence, Divine Self, Godself, are used alternatively to refer to the element of our being found above the material world. The element that is imperishable, eternal, primary, sacred and divine.

However, I will try to summarize certain elements and characteristics of the terms and shed some light beyond the veil (or more precisely, shed some light from the veil toward here!):

Soul: The eternal part of our self, the core of our existence, our primary and pure part, our divine element. The first and greatest light within us. Sometimes, the term "soul" is used to describe emotional, psychological and mental states; this results in us confusing things and perceiving soul as an element of lower and limited importance: "my soul is aching," "sell my soul," "bare my soul to someone," "my soul is heavy"... etc. In esotericism and in a religious framework, the term "soul" refers to something more than a psychic/emotional state or a personality feature. It refers to our everlasting, imperishable and perfect core, above and beyond everything we experience (feelings, thoughts, choices, experiences) in the limiting earthly present. Our soul is our essence and we are our soul. Everything else is just roles, or temporary features of smaller and inferior truths (i.e. things that are less true in regard to the ultimate truth that we are eternal and imperishable soul).

Spirit: This term usually refers to the spiritual body. It is one of the bodies that our soul/ higher self creates, a body of light and spiritual essence. This spiritual body vibrates, is condensed, it manifests itself, it creates thoughts, feelings, etheric energy, and eventually it creates matter (a physical body). Our spirit is close to our soul and it includes the four lower bodies: mental (higher and lower), psychic/emotional (higher and lower), etheric (energetic) and physical/material. Above all, we are "souls" (eternal, perfect and divine beings) and subsequently we are "spirit" (unlimited light and life, with infinite creative potential on all levels).

Higher Self: The term "higher self" is used in two different ways. Firstly, "higher self" is used as a contradistinction to the lower self (our earthly self/personality). It includes anything superior: the spirit and soul. Secondly, the term "higher self" refers to a lower self (energetically) than the soul element. By this concept, higher self is our luminous spiritual side that was created with spiritual energy by the soul. Our higher self, also named "heavenly man," creates our manifested existence and the four manifested levels of our self (mental/ noetic, psychic/emotional, etheric, material) – in other words, our earthly self. Our higher self is our highest Form who keeps the records of our experiences throughout our incarnations. We can imagine our higher self as our most luminous self, our luminous spiritual self who has acquired knowledge, wisdom, love, compassion and power through all the lessons, roles and experiences of the past. It is our true spiritual wisdom and power.

Divine Monad, I AM Presence: These two terms have the same meaning. This is the innermost, supreme part of the self. Pure "I am": it is not something specific and it is potentially everything (i.e. the potential of just Being someone or something). The I Am is present: I Am I, I am present, I exist. It is the presence of existence, of beingness. It is also called a "divine monad" that we can imagine as follows: if the Divine Beingness and Divine Reality is a Sun (a super-cosmic sun), then each one of its rays is a Monad. Each Monad (soul, "I am," "I exist") is one with God, in the image and likeness of God. Reflect on it. The rays are the sun and the sun is the rays... These monads exclaim, "I am, I exist, I am present!" Each one of them manifests itself; it really becomes something! Some rays become human beings (passing through the Human Form as described in the "World of Ideas" by Plato) and other rays become Angels (passing through the Angelic Form/Idea).

The Divine Monad, I AM Presence ("I am," "I exist"), the Divine Spark, the Divine Essence, the Divine Core and Soul are all names that define the same concept: the imperishable, eternal point within us, the primary, the most pure and divine. By alternating the words and the terms, and even creating more combinations of words and new terms, we have the chance to come close to these inconceivable truths that exceed the human intellect and language. Truths of a supreme, infinite, never-ending bliss!

Note: If you read all of the above carefully and you have tried to reach a deeper understanding and experience the various concepts, stop reading. Take some deep breaths, move a bit and rest. By doing so, you will "ground" and better assimilate the information and the energies of the spiritual realities.

ESOTERIC PRACTICE

Experiencing Spiritual Concepts

Observe how you feel with each one of the following concepts:

Spirit

Soul

Higher Self

I AM Presence

Divine Monad

Divine Core

What thoughts and feelings does each of these concepts bring up? What images and colors does it bring to your mind? What do you feel with your senses? Feel and envision. Become more sensitive, focus and meditate.

Close your eyes and bring these concepts one by one into your mind. Observe. Apply this inner observation for all of the above spiritual terms.

What are spirit guides and who are the ascended masters? Are they different from angels?

Spirit guides and ascended masters are not angels; we could describe them as "angelic" (holy, enlightened) people! Just as every person has a Guardian Angel, every person has spirit guides. Spirit guides are human beings who no longer have physical form and exist in higher dimensions. They act in a guiding, supportive, empowering, counseling, and even healing way on us. The spirit guides may be relatives who have passed or people with whom we shared a deep connection. As they exist in higher dimensions and they are closer to their spiritual soul and essence, they function as our guides, mentors and protectors. For example, a spirit guide may be an ancestor, a family member, a beloved partner or friend or even a teacher. In such cases, we feel that even though the particular individual is no longer on Earth, he/she is close to us spiritually and psychically and helps us in various ways.

Ascended masters are highly advanced spirit guides. They have transcended karma (by understanding and healing it completely) and they have completed their dharma (life purpose), through a large number of incarnations on earth, receiving countless lessons in countless roles, facing countless challenges and obstacles in all levels and areas of human life. It is what we do, it our own journey as well: the understanding and healing of karma, fulfilling our life purpose, receiving lessons from all of our roles and challenges. We too are on the path to become ascended masters, masters of wisdom. To become spiritually conscious and consciously spiritual. To embody (manifest and apply) fully the Divine energy, essence and presence (supreme love, wisdom and power) and our Divine consciousness (cosmic/existential superconsciousness of absolute unity and harmony).

Ascended masters are saints and teachers who come from every tradition, culture and religion: wise teachers, mystics, healers, creators, artists, scientists... people who have abundantly served and inspired humanity with their work and presence. And even they themselves continue to evolve following an advanced plan of Divinization and Theosis (resonance and unity with the Supreme). Ascended masters are our elder siblings who have already graduated from Planet Earth's school; they have reached the Light, the destination which all human beings will eventually reach, sooner or later.

As we grow spiritually, we attune not only to our own personal spirit guides (the ones we connect with because of personal ties and relationship) but also to these higher spiritual guides, the ascended masters, who serve as teachers, guides, protectors and healers of the whole of humanity. We draw wisdom, love and power by studying their work and by following their footsteps, striving to experience and actualize their timeless and panhuman teachings.

Do God and angels know the future? How can human free will and divine predestination be compatible?

Time does not exist in the Absolute and Supreme Reality; everything has already happened in the Perfection and Wholeness of the Existence. In our plane, which is a plane of separation and conflict (it is called the world of "good and evil," where consciousness experiences contrast), we live in the present while partly remembering the past and without knowing the future. Only the limited present is our stable, constant and continuous reality. In the physical and material plane (here and now), we experience the contrasts, such as good and evil, light and darkness, pleasant and unpleasant – relative states that help us choose and reject, grow and evolve, become aware and conscious and, in the end, become complete. In this particular plane and plan, and with this particular goal and purpose, we experience the greatest gift of God, of consciousness and of spirit. We experience the Gift, the Potential of Free Choice and of Free Will. We choose continuously in the present, so the future is not pre-destined. It is as if we are standing at a single point each time (the present) and many paths lie ahead. God (and we as souls and Divine monads) knows the past, the present and the future; this fact doesn't negate the second and parallel reality of the physical plane in which we experience free will. Freedom of will and the fact that the future is unknown are both real and true in our physical plane.

There are two parallel levels of Reality and both are valid. On the one hand, Absolute Reality, God, where everything has already happened and the future is known. And on the other, relative reality, the material world, in which we experience freedom in our choices and all futures are open and possible and, for this reason, unknown. Everything is possible for the future and is dependent upon what we want to express, manifest, materialize, both on a personal and a collective level. The unknown future of the physical plane is part of the great value and beauty of Life!

Can angels help me see the future?

We do not know if angels know our future; God most probably does! Human beings experience freedom of choice and we are free to choose our individual and collective reality. The choices and circumstances we create (individually and collectively, in the past and the present, consciously and unconsciously) sow seeds for the future. The future is not predestined. It can change at any moment according to what happens and what we experience and choose in the present.

According to the tendencies we create in the present, angels can warn us about danger, negative events/situations, and poor choices but also encourage and inspire us to make better ones. By using meditation or channeling we can get images and information about the possible futures according to the tendencies we create, our current direction and what we attract in the present moment. That doesn't mean we should depend on angels or the possible future information we get. We should live in the present with as much awareness and wisdom, as much love and joy as we can and await the future as optimistically and brightly as possible, planting positive seeds, adopting positive projections, views and perceptions about the future.

Advice: Ask the angels to guide you to your most positive and bright future!

"Beloved angels, guide me to my most positive and bright future! Thank you!"

I saw in my dreams events that occur in the future, such as an accident or the death of a person. Why does this happen?

Angels often warn and instruct us about dangerous or painful events so we can either prepare for or avoid them. Our soul – our higher self who possesses great wisdom – does the same.

A few days before the soul leaves the material world behind, it knows that it will transition to a higher plane, to a more illuminating, beautiful and liberating state of bliss and completeness! The people with whom the soul is connected often receive the message in their sleep, as they are more open/receptive during that state, so as to prepare and accept this change on the level of their earthly personality. The more spiritually aware we are of life events and transitions, the less fear and sadness (grief) we experience and the more love and acceptance we experience and emit. This also assists the soul that is moving to higher planes in its journey.

If I see a negative dream, can I change its energy in order to alter my negative state of mind, the feeling that something bad will occur and the chance of the negative dream actually happening?

Yes, whenever you see a bad dream, do the following:

Close your eyes, breathe slow and deep, and relax. Once you are calm and quiet, see White Light surrounding you. Recall the dream and consciously change its course and replace the ending. It is as if you are entering the dream and rewriting the script. Do not worry, it is not some strange or negative intervention, it is purely a healing process. Simply use your imagination and focused intention to change the script of your dream.

For example, if you saw an accident or death or another painful event happening: visualize or recall the dream, when you reach the point where things begin to turn unpleasant, change the story with a new one that is pleasant and fulfilling for you. Mentally visualize, imagine vividly and feel the positive and empowering feelings that your new ending gives you. Affirm that all is well and that all works out for the best. Take a few deep breaths, continue to feel the uplifting feelings and gently open your eyes. You have transformed the dream, your negative mood and state of mind and the kind of energy you emit. You have positively and therapeutically contributed to any possible future.

If you find it difficult to visualize and feel the new ending, the intention of changing the ending works also well. Even a single minute of your time – focused on your intention to create an empowering ending – is far better than leaving the situation as it is (in your subconscious and your energy).

Wake up in a light, cheerful and positive mood of optimism, power and confidence, knowing that angels have illuminated and healed fully every single thing. It is an extraordinary technique that works every time perfectly and works for the good. Avoid getting up from bed right away when you have had a bad dream. Close your eyes and consciously re-create your dream and change its course (the change also takes place in your subconscious). You have the power and the right as well as the spiritual duty to recreate and elevate your dream. It is a part of your energetic development to consciously and spiritually choose what you want to experience and what you experience – even in your dream and subconscious state!

Can the angels assist me in learning about my previous lives?

As we human beings grow spiritually, energetically, emotionally and mentally, as we expand and illuminate on all levels, as we manifest greater love, wisdom and power, as we become conscious of our spiritual beingness (and the spiritual essence of all of existence), we start to remember past experiences of higher planes or of past earthly lives.

Our self-knowledge grows and expands multi-dimensionally! We remember ourselves in past lives and under different conditions and situations. This helps us understand the origins (roots) of our present experiences. Our self-knowledge is not merely personal but also spiritual (knowledge of the Higher and Greater Self). It is an amazing process that is accompanied by a great variety of feelings and emotions: pain, sadness, anger, regret and guilt for poor choices and negative experiences but also forgiveness, compassion, repentance and change of heart, as well as joy, awe and wonder about the splendor of existence and the imperishableness of Being.

The recollection of and having awareness of the past is a necessary process for all humanity. It has already taken place for all the enlightened souls and it will eventually be done for all. It is the soul's plan, man's plan, the Divine plan. It is guaranteed by the universal justice, the absolute one. You need to know who/what you are so you can become what you want to be and who you really Are. By remembering, becoming conscious and knowing who we are, through the perception and the understanding of both past and present, we increase not only our knowledge and wisdom, we amplify our love for our being and for the whole of existence. Love (translated as acceptance, forgiveness and unity), amplified in time and space so as to include our past lives, is our spiritual and growth index.

Angels and especially our Guardian Angel are able to support us in the process of recollecting our past lives. We can call upon our Guardian Angel as well as the well-known Archangels and ask them to guide us with truth and safety through the process; to assist us in reaching Complete Spiritual Self-knowledge, knowledge about the past and on all levels. It is safe, it is for the Good and it is worth it! It gives infinite joy and freedom! Ask for it today!

"Beloved Guardian Angel and Beloved Supreme Archangels of the Highest Light, guide me with safety and truth to reach Complete Spiritual Self-knowledge – to know myself in the past and on all levels. Thank you!"

What is the greatest secret of the existence, the highest energy of all and the greatest force of the universe?

It seems almost unbelievable, but the greatest secret, energy and force of the universe has already been revealed to humanity by the wise teachers and masters who walked the Earth. Love is the greatest secret of existence, the highest energy and the greatest force of the universe. Love is Divine and the Divine is love. It is almost impossible to grasp fully the size, quality, intensity, depth, essence, meaning, power and wisdom of love. Just like all important things, all the secrets, all the forces and energies, love needs to be experienced. The experience of love is its splendor and it is such splendor to experience love! Its experience is its value. Whoever has experienced true love has experienced God and whoever has experienced God has experienced true love. Love can go where no thought, feeling or power can go. Love can do things that no other element can do. It can penetrate and reach the deepest darkness and illuminate it, the deadliest disease and heal it, the greatest sin and forgive it, the biggest mistake and correct it. How much bliss is hidden within love; how blissful it is!

What is the White Light and what is the Golden Light?

White and Golden Light are pure spiritual energies that offer life and vitality. They create, sustain, and give health and well-being to all beings. White and Golden Light are the light of life, life energy, vital energy, and also the higher spiritual energies of love, intelligence, wisdom, will and power – the higher qualities of spirit.

White Light is the pure energy of life that regenerates and provides all good things, such as health, power and balance. It is the pure light that cleanses and purifies all lower vibrations, all darkness, and all heavy, blocked, ill, stagnant energies. The white light dissolves negative feelings and thoughts, fear, sadness and anger; all negativity. It regenerates the aura and the physical body; all the systems, all the organs and all the cells. It cleanses, rejuvenates, positively charges and energizes the aura and the chakras (energy centers) providing the optimal frequency for their function. The white light purifies, renews and protects. It includes all the colors and it can offer all the energies, all potentials, and every good. It is the creative force of the spirit, of the universe and of the self.

The Golden Light is the highest vibration: the light of consciousness, of pure spirit and soul, of the higher spiritual dimensions, the light of higher intelligence and awareness. It is the light of the great masters, angels and of all celestial beings, the Divine Light; it is of the highest frequency and it vibrates in the highest planes. Golden Light is the Light of the Divine, the Light of Perfect Love, Wisdom and Power, the Light of Infinite Love, Wisdom and Power, the Light of Divine Love, Wisdom and Power.

While the White Light is creative light and life energy, the Golden Light is the Divine Consciousness Light and the energy of Logos. While the White Light creates and restores perfect purity, cleanness, health, harmony and power on all levels of the self and in all life areas, the Golden Light connects and attunes to the Higher Self and the Soul, to the Divine Source, the Highest Dimensions, Spirit and its Divine Angels. The Golden Light expresses and manifests the spiritual beingness and essence of all, including our own.

How can we use the White and the Golden Light in our lives?

By using the power of intention, affirmations, invocations, and visualizations we can surround and fill ourselves with White Light, activating more health and vitality, harmony and vigor in our bodies. The White Light purifies us from negativity (lower vibrations) and manifests our primary and perfect purity.

Surrounding and infusing ourselves with Golden Light, we connect and attune to our Spirit and Soul, to our Higher Self and the Divine Source, to the Higher Dimensions of Freedom and Wholeness, to Angels and Spiritual Teachers. The Golden Light manifests the higher wisdom, the higher love and the higher power of our essence. It raises our vibration, our overall energetic quality and our consciousness, becoming sun-like; it offers absolute and total protection and guidance; it awakens our psychic and spiritual abilities and talents. In the Golden Light, we experience upliftment, we radiate positivity, our life improves and becomes more beautiful and wonderful – more golden! The White and Golden Light complement each other, they both are aspects and manifestations of the same Divine Power, of the Divine Spirit that we are all part of.

MEDITATION

White and Golden Light

White Light Visualization:

Sit comfortably and gently close your eyes.

Take a few deep breaths and relax.

Mentally ask your body and your mind to relax and let go of the tensions...

You feel serene...

Your mind and your heart bloom...

You experience openness and receptiveness...

Visualize a loving white light washing over you.

See and feel it clearly...

The whitest, the brightest, the most intense White Light you can imagine...

The whitest, the brightest, the most real White Light you can experience...

Your mind, your heart are opening up, they are blooming, it is wonderful...

You experience openness, you are in absolute receptivity, it is magnificent...

The White Light surrounds you...

With its whiteness, its luminosity, its purity...

The White Light permeates you...

The White Light fills you...

The White Light illuminates you...

With its whiteness, its luminosity, its purity...

The White Light cleanses you, it heals you, it empowers you...

It energizes you, it invigorates you, it charges you positively...

It offers you health, power and well-being...

It gives you balance and harmony...

White Light, the Light of Life...

Inhale and exhale, ten times, the White Light within you...

White Light, in every cell, White Light even in the most deep and distant darkness...

To all cells, White Light...

You are brimming with White Light...

The White Light has filled you completely and you radiate dazzling whiteness, pure luminosity...

White Light everywhere, only White Light and all within the White Light.

Remain in the White Light...

You feel, you see, you experience cleanness, illumination, vitality, health, well-being, harmony, positivity.

On all levels.

You feel better and you *are* better than ever; you feel and you are heavenly!

Thank the Light!

Golden Light Visualization:

After completing the previous meditation, visualize Golden Light.

Visualize Golden Light emanating from your core, your center, your soul, your spirit, from the Source, the Source within you.

See and feel it vividly.

The Golden Light expands and embraces you like a warm radiant sun.

The Golden Light, the Divine Light of supreme love, wisdom and power surrounds you.

It permeates, fills you and illuminates you.

The most gold, the most luminous, the most real Golden Light you can imagine.

The most gold, the most luminous, the highest Golden Light you can experience.

You have and you experience Perfect Protection.

You have and you experience the Highest Guidance.

You are one with the Divine Source, the Angels and the Great Masters.

You are one with your Higher Self, the Divine Monad, your Soul and your Essence.

You are fully attuned to the Supreme and Perfect Wisdom, the Supreme and Perfect Love and the Supreme and Perfect Power of the True Spirit, the Infinite, the Divine.

You experience Higher Consciousness, Superconsciousness, Infinite Light and Infinite Love.

You receive and you emanate Infinite Light and Infinite Love from a Higher Consciousness, from a state of Superconsciousness.

You manifest and you embody your Higher Potential, your Higher Aspect, your Higher Self. Golden Light, Golden Light on all levels.

You radiate Golden light, you shine like a Golden Sun.

You are Golden Light, you are Golden Sun.

You are Consciousness, you are Love.

Take ten deep breaths, inhaling and exhaling Golden Light.

You remain within the Golden Light.

You experience unity, happiness, bliss, completeness and wholeness.

You feel better and you are better than ever; you feel and are heavenly!

Thank the Light!

Optional Sequence:

The White and Golden Light meditation has been completed. If you wish, you may continue by calling upon angels, your Guardian Angel, Archangels, spirit guides and great teachers and experiencing their powerful, wise and loving energy.

Note:

Perform the meditation of White and Golden Light whenever you need overall empowerment, upliftment and balance. You may use this meditation as preparation for any other meditation/visualization. It is probably the most important energetic and spiritual meditation offering countless benefits on all levels.

21-day plan:

Follow a 21-day plan of performing daily the meditation of White and Golden Light. It is an intense program of total, energetic and spiritual rejuvenation, regeneration and restructuring on all levels. You can follow the 21-day plan once or twice a year (or more often) to keep yourself at a high vibration and a high state of clarity, health and brightness; in alignment with who you really are.

What is the Violet Flame?

The Violet Flame is a high frequency spiritual energy that protects, purifies, heals and empowers the aura, the etheric field, influencing in a positive way our body, mind, psyche and spirit. The Violet Flame is invoked through intention, invocation, prayer, visualization, meditation and affirmations. We can invoke the Violet Flame for ourselves and other people as well as to purify any space and uplift any situation. The Violet Flame brings purification, healing, higher protection and guidance. It transmutes all lower energies (thoughts, feelings) into higher light and vitality, higher wisdom, power and love.

We may perceive and visualize the Violet Flame as a fire or a light of violet, indigo, lavender or purple color. It is also known as purple or violet ray and purple or violet energy. The high healing energy of the violet flame is prominently guided, guarded and represented by Archangel Zadkiel, Archangel of spiritual healing, and the Ascended Master Saint Germain, the master of alchemy and spiritual transmutation (transformation of lower energies into higher spiritual essence).

In addition to working with Archangel Zadkiel and Ascended Master Saint Germain, we may feel, perceive, visualize and work with other Ascended Masters or spiritual entities linked to the Violet Flame. Many people studying esotericism invoke Jesus, Mother Mary, Kuan Yin, the Buddha of Compassion and Archangel Raphael. The light of the Violet Flame is one of the highest healing spiritual energies as it is associated with the sixth and the seventh energy centers (the third eye and the crown chakras) which are the seats of insight, higher perception and consciousness and, therefore, of spirituality as a whole.

MEDITATION

Violet Flame

Begin by preparing properly: take care the physical and energetic cleanliness of yourself and your space.

Light a white candle and dedicate it to the Divine Source and its Angels, and to the Violet Flame and Energy.

Attention: Always keep candles away from flammable objects and do not leave them unattended.

Sit comfortably, observe the candle flame and relax.

Gently close your eyes, relax even more, let go of the tensions, calm your body and mind.

Mentally, call forth the Violet Flame.

Visualize the violet ray descending to Earth.

Visualize the violet ray lighting a magnificent violet flame around you.

Feel the violet flame surrounding you, feel the violet flame permeating you.

Mentally, ask for the highest spiritual protection and guidance.

Ask for purification, healing and transmutation; Divine Purification, Divine Healing and Divine Transmutation.

Violet Flame, Violet Light in your mind... It grows, it burns, it purifies, it illuminates...

Ask from the Violet Flame to transmute the lower negative thoughts into pure light, love and vitality...

Violet Flame, Violet Light in your emotions... It grows, it burns, it purifies, it illuminates...

Ask from the Violet Flame to transmute the lower unpleasant emotions into pure light, love and vitality...

Violet Flame, Violet Light in your etheric field, aura, channels/meridians and energy centers/ chakras... It grows, it burns, it purifies, it illuminates...

Ask from the Violet Flame to transmute the lower energies, blockages and toxins into pure light, love and vitality...

Ask from the Violet Flame to transmute the lower negative energies, the toxins and the blockages into pure light, love and vitality...

Visualize the Violet Flame entering into your first chakra (base of the spine)... into your second chakra (genital area)... into your third chakra (solar plexus)... into the fourth chakra (heart area)... into the fifth chakra (throat area)... into the sixth chakra (third eye area)... into the seventh chakra (crown area)...

From your seventh chakra the Violet Flame descends to your first chakra once more.

The Violet Flame surrounds your whole body, it permeates it, it purifies it. A clean and powerful field of Violet Light, magnificent and sublime!

Mentally ask the Violet Flame to transmute the heavy, dark, unhealthy energies into pure light, love and vitality... All disease from all cells, organs and parts of your body.

All of your cells within the Violet Flame... Violet Flame, Divine, magnificent and sublime!

All of your organs within the Violet Flame... Violet Flame, Divine, magnificent and sublime!

Mentally, call upon the Archangel of the Violet Flame, Archangel Zadkiel... Archangel Zadkiel, Zadkiel, Zadkiel... And the Great Master of the Violet Flame, Saint Germain... Saint Germain, Saint Germain, Saint Germain...

Feel their luminous presence appearing from the infinite light in the horizon. They emerge from a ray of golden ray. See them radiating higher, Divine Light and Love!

They come closer to you...

Welcome Archangel Zadkiel and Saint Germain with awe and love, talk to them, ask them, allow them to attune you to their spiritual essence and power, to your spiritual essence and power. To the spiritual essence and power of the Supreme, the Spirit, the Divine.

Feel... receive... accept... experience... You feel, you receive, you accept, you experience purification, healing, transmutation, protection, guidance, energy, power and blessing from the Great Archangel, from the Great Master, from the Great Flame.

You feel great, boundless, true gratitude in your heart...

You entire being is pure, illuminated and beloved; your entire existence is awe, joy and gratitude!

A violet being in violet joy and violet gratitude!

Violet Flame Blessings.

What are the chakras? Is there a connection between angels and chakras?

Chakras are the energy centers of the etheric body. There are seven major chakras. The etheric body surrounds and permeates the physical body and it offers its energy, power and vitality. The etheric body is often called "etheric double" as it is an energetic copy of the human body. It features the energy centers, the chakras, as well as energy channels, called "meridians" or "nadis," and the aura, which is the outer edge of the etheric body, its protective shield.

Chakra is a Sanskrit word meaning "wheel," as the chakras resemble spinning wheels or rotating vortices distributing energy in the various parts of the body. The seven major chakras are located along the central channel/meridian of the body, known as Sushumna, which is parallel to our spine.

Following is a list with each of the seven chakras' attributes, functions and associations.

The seven major chakras:

First chakra
Color: red
Location: base of the spinal cord, coccyx, and perineum
Physical correspondence: genetic code, bones, and legs
Main themes: connection to the earth, material life, grounding, family, DNA, ancestors, physical strength, basic needs, survival, abundance, and protection

Second chakra
Color: orange
Location: pelvic area, one palm below the navel
Physical correspondence: lower abdomen, reproductive organs
Main themes: sexual energy, work, creativity, joy, relationships, vitality, energy of life

Third chakra
Color: yellow
Location: solar plexus and stomach

Physical correspondence: stomach, upper abdomen, and digestion
Main themes: will, power, self-esteem, self-confidence, acceptance, balance, ego, and personality

Fourth chakra
Color: green
Location: middle of the chest
Physical correspondence: chest, lungs, heart, the immune system, and the circulatory and respiratory systems
Main themes: emotions, harmony, peace, freedom, and love

Fifth chakra
Color: blue
Location: base of the neck
Physical correspondence: neck
Main themes: Expression, communication, truth, and peace

Sixth chakra
Color: deep blue, indigo, and purple
Location: middle of the forehead
Physical correspondence: brain, head, and face
Main themes: thought, imagination, intuition, insight, and perception

Seventh chakra
Color: white and violet
Location: top of the head
Physical correspondence: nervous system
Main themes: consciousness, awareness, and spirituality; connection to the universe, nature, and the higher power; transcendence; and oneness

When the chakras function properly, when they are open, clean and radiant, with vivid and pure colors, when they vibrate and rotate optimally, we experience well-being, health, balance, safety, completeness, joy, power on all levels of existence: spiritually, emotionally, mentally and physically. We think, we feel, we function and we are well.

When the chakras are not functioning well, when they are closed, dirty, blocked, having dull and dark colors, when they don't vibrate and rotate correctly, we experience negativity or disease, on all levels of existence.

In addition to the seven major chakras, there are countless secondary chakras found in the areas of: the palms, elbows, shoulders, cheeks, knees, soles of the feet, left and right of the forehead, the chest, abdomen and navel (i.e., there are secondary chakras left and right of the major chakras).

Another two significant energy centers are the Soul Star (chakra of the Soul) and the Earth Star (Earth chakra), often called the "Alpha" and the "Omega" respectively.

Soul chakra
Color: golden
Location: a hand's length above the head
Main themes: qualities of the soul, higher self, potential, possibilities, and divine plan

Earth chakra
Color: silver
Location: a hand's length below the feet
Main themes: physical incarnation, actualization, manifestation, fulfillment of the soul's plan and life's purpose, greater connection to Earth, and the power to adapt.

There are various methods and techniques to open, clean, charge, balance and energize the chakras: focused positive thought, positive affirmations, higher feelings such as love and joy, visualization, meditation, conscious deep breathing, movement and exercise, contact with nature and its elements, proper natural balanced nutrition, holistic healing, yoga, shiatsu, massage, aromatherapy, crystal therapy and reiki. These are simple and effective ways to achieve, experience and enjoy an optimal function of all our energy centers.

Angels – being the messengers for all the pure celestial energies and forces and of our higher potential (our infinite spirit) – can also awaken, clean, illuminate, energize and balance our chakras. Working with them is the most direct and spiritual (that is complete, profound and true) way to open the chakras.

When we have restored the optimal function and vibration of the chakras, we receive more energy and vitality (life-force energy, vital light) in our etheric body, and also in our physical body as our physical body is nourished and sustained by the etheric. As a result we experience all the good things, on all levels: spiritual, mental, emotional and physical health, harmony, freedom, wholeness, well-being, balance and cleanness. All the best on all levels!

Following is the correspondence of our energy centers to certain Archangels, according to the esoteric and spiritual teachings:

First chakra: Uriel

Second chakra: Gabriel

Third chakra: Jophiel

Fourth chakra: Raphael

Fifth chakra: Michael

Sixth chakra: Raziel

Seventh chakra: Zadkiel

Soul Chakra: Metatron

Earth Chakra: Sandalphon

In the list above, each Archangel symbolizes and represents the higher aspect of the respective chakra, its higher expression and potential. Each Archangel provides us with the necessary energy and power, help and support to manifest the optimal form and function of the respective chakra. Together with the Archangels of Light, we can co-create perfect health on all levels, through our seven pure and luminous centers, our seven sublime and beloved temples.

Note:

Apart from the list given above, we can invoke and visualize different Archangels corresponding to each chakra or more Archangels for a single chakra. For example, when we work with a severely blocked chakra: we can call upon/visualize all the Archangels and their healing energies, and we can also invoke angels or group of angels such as the Guardian Angel, the angels of healing etc...

MEDITATION

Archangelic Activation of the Energy Centers (Chakras)

This is a complete, powerful and effective technique to awaken, clean, activate and uplift your nine energy centers (the seven major chakras as well as the Soul Star and the Earth Star) with the help of the supreme and most beloved Archangels of the Infinite Spiritual Light.

Sit comfortably, gently close your eyes and relax.

Take a deep breath, full of energy, light and positivity... Bring your awareness to your first energy center located at the base of your spinal column. Visualize or feel it as a radiant red sphere, a sphere of pure red light. See or feel the sphere being cleared, empowered and brightened. See and feel the pure red light of your first chakra.

Affirm: *"I experience grounding, empowerment and a healthy and strong body! I adapt and I function perfectly in all circumstances! My family is healed, uplifted and illuminated! My genetic code is crystal-clean and bright, perfect and Divine! I love the Earth and I am totally and perfectly grounded!"*

Mentally, call upon Archangel Uriel – supreme angel of the supreme light – and ask him to further clear and activate your first chakra and your feet to a higher vibrational frequency. Archangel Uriel, with his supreme flame and power, heals, energizes and illuminates your first energy center and your feet totally! You see it, you feel it, you experience it, it is a fact! It is a most luminous and positive change! You feel boundless joy! Take another deep breath and your first chakra is perfect as never before! Archangel Uriel, Uriel, Uriel!

Gently bring your awareness to your second energy center situated a palm below the navel. Visualize or feel it as a radiant orange sphere, a sphere of pure orange light. See or feel the sphere being cleared, empowered and brightened. See and feel the pure orange light of your second chakra.

Affirm: *"I experience pure, balanced, healthy, bright, loving and Divine relationships with other people! I overflow with love, joy, romance and passion! I love people and I connect and relate to people in the best way possible!"*

Mentally, call upon Archangel Gabriel – supreme angel of the supreme light – and ask him to further clear and activate your second chakra and your pelvis to a higher vibrational frequency. Archangel Gabriel, with his supreme flame and power, heals, energizes and illuminates your second energy center and your pelvis totally! You see it, you feel it, you experience it, it is a fact! It is a most luminous and positive change! You feel unconditional joy! Take another deep breath and your second chakra is perfect as never before! Archangel Gabriel, Gabriel, Gabriel!

Now bring your awareness to your third energy center, at your solar plexus in your upper abdomen. Visualize or feel it as a radiant yellow sphere, a sphere of pure yellow light. See or feel the sphere being cleared, empowered and brightened. See and feel the pure yellow light of your third chakra.

Affirm: *"I experience self-confidence, power, protection, safety and balance! I accept and love myself and everything is going perfectly and divinely! I feel good and I am good!"*

Mentally, call upon Archangel Jophiel – supreme angel of the supreme light – and ask him to further clear and activate your third chakra and your abdomen to a higher vibrational frequency. Archangel Jophiel, with his supreme flame and power, heals, energizes and illuminates your third energy center and your entire abdomen totally! You see it, you feel it, you experience it, it is a fact! It is a most luminous and positive change! You feel brilliant joy! Take another deep breath and your third chakra is perfect as never before! Archangel Jophiel, Jophiel, Jophiel!

Now bring your awareness to your fourth energy center, in the middle of your chest. Visualize or feel it as a radiant green sphere, a sphere of pure green light. See or feel the sphere being cleared, empowered and brightened. See and feel the pure green light of your fourth chakra.

Affirm: *"I experience love and serenity in my heart! My heart opens and turns to the light, to good, to the Divine! I love peace, I love love! All is Good!"*

Mentally, call upon Archangel Raphael – supreme angel of the supreme light – and ask him to further clear and activate your fourth chakra and your chest to a higher vibrational frequency. Archangel Raphael, with his supreme flame and power, heals, energizes and illuminates your fourth energy center and your chest totally! You see it, you feel it, you experience it, it is a fact! It is a most luminous and positive change! You feel the most loving joy! Take another deep breath and your fourth chakra is perfect as never before! Archangel Raphael, Raphael, Raphael!

Now bring your awareness to your fifth energy center, located at the base of your throat. Visualize or feel it as a radiant blue sphere, a sphere of pure blue light. See or feel the sphere being cleared, empowered and brightened. See and feel the pure blue light of your fifth chakra.

Affirm: *"I experience higher communication and expression of love and truth! I am able to express myself, my beingness and my soul easily, freely and unconditionally! I love freedom!"*

Mentally, call upon Archangel Michael – supreme angel of the supreme light – and ask him to further clear and activate your fifth chakra and your throat to a higher vibrational frequency. Archangel Michael, with his supreme flame and power, heals, energizes and illuminates your fifth energy center and your throat totally! You see it, you feel it, you experience it, it is a fact! It is a most luminous and positive change! You feel true joy! Take another deep breath and your fifth chakra is perfect as never before! Archangel Michael, Michael, Michael!

Now bring your awareness to your sixth energy center, located at the center of your forehead. Visualize or feel it as a radiant purple sphere, a sphere of pure purple light. See or feel the sphere being cleared, empowered and brightened. See and feel the pure purple light of your sixth chakra.

Affirm: *"I experience a clear and bright mind, filled with love and truth! I have a perfect intuition, awareness and perception! I love truth!"*

Mentally, call upon Archangel Raziel – supreme angel of the supreme light – and ask him to further clear and activate your sixth chakra and your head to a higher vibrational frequency. Archangel Raziel, with his supreme flame and power, heals, energizes and illuminates your sixth energy center and your head totally! You see it, you feel it, you experience it, it is a fact! It is a most luminous and positive change! You feel blissful joy! Take another deep breath and your sixth chakra is perfect as never before! Archangel Raziel, Raziel, Raziel!

Now bring your awareness to your seventh energy center, located at the top of your head. Visualize or feel it as a radiant white sphere, a sphere of pure white light. See or feel the sphere being cleared, empowered and brightened. See and feel the pure white light of your seventh chakra.

Affirm: *"I experience perfect unity and harmony with the universe, existence and the Divine! My spirituality is blossoming! I love the universe, existence, the Divine!"*

Mentally, call upon Archangel Zadkiel – supreme angel of the supreme light – and ask him to further clear and activate your seventh chakra and your entire body to a higher vibrational frequency. Archangel Zadkiel, with his supreme flame and power, heals, energizes and illuminates your seventh energy center and your entire body totally! You see it, you feel it, you experience it, it is a fact! It is a most luminous and positive change! You feel absolute joy! Take another deep breath and your seventh chakra is perfect as never before! Archangel Zadkiel, Zadkiel, Zadkiel!

Now bring your awareness to your Soul Star, located a palm above your head. Visualize or feel it as a radiant golden sphere, a sphere of pure golden light. See or feel the sphere being cleared, empowered and brightened. See and feel the pure golden light of your Soul Star.

Affirm: "*I experience the purity, the power, the wisdom and the love of my soul! I experience all my spiritual potential! I am my Higher Self! I love my soul!*"

Mentally, call upon Archangel Metatron – supreme angel of the supreme light – and ask him to further clear and activate your Soul Star and your potential to a higher vibrational frequency. Archangel Metatron, with his supreme flame and power, heals, energizes and illuminates your Soul Star and your potential totally! You see it, you feel it, you experience it, it is a fact! It is a most luminous and positive change! You feel absolute joy! Take another deep breath and your Soul Star is perfect as never before! Archangel Metatron, Metatron, Metatron!

Lastly, bring your awareness to your Earth Star, located a palm below your feet. Visualize or feel it as a radiant silver sphere, a sphere of pure silver light. See or feel the sphere being cleared, empowered and brightened. See and feel the pure silver light of your Earth Star.

Affirm: "*I experience the manifestation of my life's purpose! As spirit and soul I am able to create and actualize whatever I desire! The good, the bright, the true, the perfect, the Divine! I love my incarnation!*"

Mentally, call upon Archangel Sandalphon – supreme angel of the supreme light – and ask him to further clear and activate your Earth Star and your powers to a higher vibrational frequency. Archangel Sandalphon, with his supreme flame and power, heals, energizes and illuminates your Earth Star and your powers totally! You see it, you feel it, you experience it, it is a fact! It is a most luminous and positive change! You feel absolute joy! Take another deep breath and your Earth Star is perfect as never before! Archangel Sandalphon, Sandalphon, Sandalphon!

The Archangelic Activation of your Chakras has been completed. Slowly open your eyes and move your body gently. Drink lots of water, rest or continue your everyday activities.

Instructions:

To experience constant positive change and improvement in your energy system, carry out the meditation described above for nine or more days. You can read or visualize it three times a day (consecutive or morning/noon/evening). Follow the schedule that fits you best, every day for nine days. Later, once per month will be sufficient to reap the benefits of the Archangelic Activation of the Energy Chakras.

Alternative method:

If you are not able to apply the complete meditation due to its length and intensity (it is an advanced and powerful meditation), do one chakra/one activation daily. On the first day, apply the meditation to activate the first energy center, on the second day, activate the second energy center... and so on, until you reach the ninth day and the activation of the earth star energy center. Read three times daily the meditation text corresponding to the chakra you wish to activate, give yourself time to visualize, experience and assimilate the process (approximately ten minutes per day are enough). Repeat the nine-day plan two more times, reaching 27 days overall.

What are our higher bodies? What is the relation between angels and our higher bodies?

Man is true miracle of the existence. He is a multidimensional beings and there are many levels of expression and manifestation within his beingness. Beyond his visible, physical, material body, man has more invisible, higher, immaterial bodies. These are the etheric body, the emotional body, the mental body and the spiritual bodies. Our Higher Self and our Soul are both within and beyond these bodies and they create them so as to exist and have experiences on the different planes of Reality. The Soul (our supreme divine essence and our core), the Higher Self (our supreme spiritual manifestation) and their bodies comprise a single and perfect unity. It may seem unbelievable that we are all these different forms and levels of manifestation and expression. There is so much more than what meets the eye or what the mind can see.

The etheric body or etheric double is an energetic copy of the physical body. The etheric body surrounds like a cocoon the physical body and permeates it providing it with vital energy. It is our life-force, our vitality and power.

The emotional or psychical body is the emotional world (fourth dimension) where we experience feelings and desires. The emotional body includes the astral body which is the lower psychical plane.

The mental body is the world of intellect and mind (fifth dimension). It includes the higher mental body also called the causal body. The causal body is where the causes of our thoughts and actions lie.

The spiritual body is our spiritual essence, our spiritual energy and light (sixth dimension). We are able to create many spiritual bodies in increasingly higher and greater levels of light-love-wisdom-power.

All these bodies – the physical, the etheric, the emotional, the mental, and the spiritual – are created by the Higher Self (i.e. our selves in the sixth dimension, in spirit and light) and they comprise our manifested form, our personality, temporarily here on Earth.

These bodies live, breathe, grow and evolve through the experiences and the roles we have in life. The more pure, luminous, advanced and evolved the subtle bodies are, the more energy/light/love/wisdom and power they contain and emit, and the higher intelligence the subtle bodies possess, the closer we are – consciously – to our higher existence, to what we truly and essentially are, to our Divine Beingness (infinite spirit and perfect eternal soul).

The purpose of a human being is to personally and directly experience the Divine (the supreme, the absolute, the whole, the true) on all levels of one's existence.

All our subtle bodies and all the levels of our beingness are created by our Higher Self through spiritual energy and with the help of Archangels: Michael (spirit, light, fire) constructs and maintains our spiritual and mental bodies; Gabriel (psyche, water) constructs and maintains the emotional bodies; Raphael (air and ether) constructs and maintains the etheric double. Together with Uriel (balance, manifestation, matter/earth), all four Archangels create and maintain the material/physical body.

MEDITATION

Archangelic Activation of our Bodies

Sit comfortably and gently close your eyes. Take some deep breaths and mentally ask your body and mind to relax, to loosen and let go of the tensions, to calm completely...

Bring your attention to your mind, the space of your thoughts...

Wait a little...

Call upon Archangel Michael.

"Archangel Michael, Michael, Michael..."

Visualize (see, feel) his golden flame.

"Infinite Love, Infinite Wisdom, Infinite Power...

Divine Love, Divine, Wisdom, Divine Power..."

See the flame becoming red (the energy of fire)...

Ask Archangel Michael to fully purify, heal, illuminate and activate your mind. On all levels.

Archangel Michael fully purifies, heals, illuminates, activates and attunes your mind and even its causal level (the causes of thought and behavior) to a higher, more pure and luminous vibration.

Archangel Michael, the Divine Fire, gives you a clear, healthy, illuminated mind full of love and truth!

Bring gently your attention to your psychic body, the space where you experience feelings and emotions...

Wait a little...

Call upon Archangel Gabriel.

"Archangel Gabriel, Gabriel, Gabriel..."

Visualize (see, feel) his golden flame.

"Infinite Love, Infinite Wisdom, Infinite Power...

Divine Love, Divine, Wisdom, Divine Power..."

See the flame becoming azure or blue (the energy of water...)

Ask Archangel Gabriel to fully purify, heal, illuminate and activate your psychic body, your emotional body. On all levels.

Archangel Gabriel fully purifies, heals, illuminates, activates and attunes your psychic body and even its astral level (emotional states of lower vibration that you have experienced in the past) to a higher, more pure and luminous vibration.

Archangel Gabriel, the Divine Water, gives you a clear, healthy, illuminated psychic/emotional full of love and peace!

Now bring your attention to your aura, your energy/etheric body.

Wait a little...

Call upon Archangel Raphael.

"Archangel Raphael, Raphael, Raphael..."

Visualize (see, feel) his golden flame.

"Infinite Love, Infinite Wisdom, Infinite Power...

Divine Love, Divine, Wisdom, Divine Power..."

See the flame becoming violet/purple (ether, the energy of life)...

Ask Archangel Raphael to fully purify, heal, illuminate and activate your etheric body. On all levels.

Archangel Raphael fully purifies, heals, illuminates, activates and attunes your aura, your energy centers and meridians to a higher, more pure and luminous vibration.

Archangel Raphael, the Divine Energy of Life, gives you a clear, healthy, illuminated etheric body full of love and vitality!

Bring your attention to your material/physical body...

Wait a little...

Call upon Archangel Uriel.

"Archangel Uriel, Uriel, Uriel..."

Visualize (see, feel) his golden flame.

"Infinite Love, Infinite Wisdom, Infinite Power...

Divine Love, Divine, Wisdom, Divine Power..."

See the flame becoming white/silver (the energy of earth/matter)...

Ask Archangel Uriel to fully purify, heal, illuminate and activate your physical body. On all levels.

Archangel Uriel fully purifies, heals, illuminates, activates and attunes your bodily systems and organs, even your cells to a higher, more pure and luminous vibration.

Archangel Uriel, the Divine Light and the Divine Earth, gives you a clear, healthy, illuminated physical body full of love and power!

Bring your attention to your spiritual body.

Wait a little...

Call upon the Archangels of Light and Pure Spirit, the Highest Archangels...

Call upon Archangel Michael, Metatron, Zadkiel, Chamuel, Jophiel, Tzaphkiel, Jeremiel, Raziel and all the Highest Archangels of the Supreme Light and Pure Spirit.

"Archangel Michael, Metatron, Zadkiel, Chamuel, Jophiel, Tzaphkiel, Jeremiel, Raziel and all the Highest Archangels of the Supreme Light and Pure Spirit ..."

Visualize (see, feel) their golden flames.

"Infinite Love, Infinite Wisdom, Infinite Power...

Divine Love, Divine, Wisdom, Divine Power..."

Ask the Archangels to fully activate the Spiritual Wisdom, Love and Power within you. To awaken, energize, advance and attune your spiritual body to the highest vibration.

The Highest Archangels of the Supreme Light and Pure Spirit awaken and activate your spiritual body, the higher love, wisdom and power within you, the infinite love, wisdom and power within you... the supreme, total, absolute, Divine love, wisdom and power within you...

Wait a little...

You feel and you are your Higher Self and soul!

Now all the Archangels align, attune and balance all your bodies and all levels of your existence... You are a perfect union of purity, harmony and luminosity... You are a unity of light, a unity of love!

The Archangelic Activation of your Bodies has been completed. Slowly open your eyes and gently move your body. Drink lots of water, rest or continue your everyday activities.

To experience more intense and immediate benefits, practice this meditation for seven consecutive days.

Check also the meditations: "The Archangels in the Human Body" and "Infusing the Body with Archangelic Energies for Optimal Health" in the chapter about Archangels.

What are thought-forms?

Human personality (essentially, man's mental and emotional body) is comprised of thought-forms, clusters of thoughts and feelings that intertwine, creating a psychonoetic mass: the personality itself. These thoughts and feelings have shape and form that can be seen clairvoyantly. We experience some thoughts as light, luminous and pleasant, while others are heavy, dark and unpleasant.

Positive thought-forms include our virtues, thoughts of kindness and benevolence, creativity and offering, but also feelings such as joy, peace, delight and love. Clairvoyantly, positive thoughts and feelings appear luminous because they have higher energy and vibration. Negative thought-forms include our flaws, our addictions, thoughts of control, selfishness and fear, but also heavy and dense feelings such as rage, guilt and sorrow. Clairvoyantly, negative thoughts and feelings can be seen as dark as they have lower energy and vibration.

Thought-forms possess their own kind of intelligence and consciousness (just like our body organs do). This is the reason we often feel we don't entirely control them and that instead they are the ones controlling us – like when "we don't feel ourselves" because we are dominated by our addictions, vices, obsessions, and negative elements and have a sense of not being in control of our lives.

We are able to discard the negative thought-forms and empower the positive ones (to give them more space and energy within our personality) by using esoteric, energetic and spiritual methods: meditation, visualization, invocation, prayer, symbols, initiations, holistic and energy healing (reiki and others), and positive thought and affirmations. We can also empower this positive change by engaging in the following: physical exercise, deep and proper breathing, healthy diet, frequent contact with Mother Nature, loving and giving, creativity and joy, esoteric study and observation, self-knowledge and self-development, and counseling and psychotherapy.

Parallel to these suggestions, you can apply the energy clearing of negative thought-forms with the Forces of Light – the Archangels and especially Archangel Michael.

MEDITATION

Clearing Thought-Forms with Archangel Michael

First method: Clearing a particular thought-form

Light a white candle and dedicate it to the Highest Angels of the Supreme Light.

Attention: the candles always have to be away from flammable objects, and do not leave the candles unattended.

Observe the warm candle flame for a few moments and relax. Take a few deep breaths and gently close your eyes.

Mentally, ask yourself:

"If there was some negative energy within you, what would that be...?"

Wait a little, until you hear, see or sense the answer to your question.

"What size does this negative energy have? What shape, what form? What color, what texture? When did it appear there? What is its influence on you?"

Ask the negative thought form what it can teach you. Wait a little, until you hear, see or sense the answer.

Then, declare to this thought-form that it has to go. Declare that your body, your personality and your energy belong to you, to the Higher, to the Light!

Call upon Archangel Michael – the Fire, the Power, and the Will of God – and ask him to remove the negative thought-form, to uproot it and send it to the Light.

See and feel the Power of Fire and Light, Archangel Michael removing, uprooting the negative thought-form and sending it to the Light.

Wait a little.

Then, call upon Archangel Raphael (air, ether/energy), Gabriel (water, emotions), Uriel (light and matter, physical body) and the Angels of Healing to heal, empower and fill the spot (where the thought-form used to be) with light, love, etheric power and energy.

Visualize (see, feel) the golden-white light filling the spot, healing it and empowering it.

Wait a little.

Thank the Powers of Light for their help and support.

Gently open your eyes and look at the candle flame. The warm and wonderful light of the candle surrounds you.

Repeat the exercise two times more so that the results will be actualized, manifested and realized on all levels.

Second Method: General Personality Clearing

Light a white candle and dedicate it to the Highest Angels of the Supreme Light.

Attention: the candles always have to be away from flammable objects, and do not leave the candles unattended.

Observe the warm candle flame for a few moments and relax. Take a few deep breaths and gently close your eyes.

Call upon the four Archangels of Light – Michael, Gabriel, Raphael, Uriel – and ask them to clear and purify your personality.

Imagine your personality as a mass of mental and emotional energy. It is comprised of many thought-forms; some are light, luminous and positive, while others are heavy, dark and unhealthy.

Visualize the golden flame of spirit lighting up within you, within your personality. It is the quality and the power of your Higher Self, the quality and the energy of the Supreme, of the Purely Divine. The golden flame emits energy, light, love, and power...

Infinite energy, infinite light, infinite love, infinite power, infinite wisdom...

Supreme energy, supreme light, supreme love, supreme power, supreme wisdom...

Perfect energy, perfect light, perfect love, perfect power, perfect wisdom...

Divine energy, Divine light, Divine love, Divine power, Divine wisdom...

The golden flame of spirit illuminates your personality. Your thought-forms receive light. The heavy, dark, unhealthy thought-forms are burned, purified and eliminated; they lose their power, they are released and transmuted, they are sent into the Spirit, into the Light.

The positive thought-forms (thoughts and feelings), positive prototypes and patterns are empowered, enhanced and rekindled.

Call once more upon the four Archangels of Light, Michael, Gabriel, Raphael and Uriel. Ask them to clear and purify your personality, your body and your life, to clear and purify you completely and on all levels.

Take ten slow and deep breaths.

The golden flame continues to burn within you.

You feel and you are your clearest, healthiest, most luminous self!

Thank the Forces of Light for helping you.

Gently open your eyes and look at the candle flame. The brilliant light of the candle surrounds you.

Repeat the exercise two times more so that the results will be actualized, manifested and realized on all levels.

A note of advice about both methods:

After these particularly advanced, intense and deep cleansings, help yourself by taking an unrefined sea salt bath (use 3-4 fistfuls of salt). Natural sea salt enhances and facilitates the purification process. Alternatively, take a shower and gently rub the sea salt on your body with circular movements. Afterward rinse your body off with water and feel the water cleansing you on all levels. Also make sure to drink lots of water, eat healthily and rest as much as you can.

What is karma? Can angels help me release negative karma?

Most people perceive *karma* as something negative. But it is the Greatest Law of Life and the Greatest Cosmic Law. It is a True Gift from Spirit to Matter. It is actually the Spirit itself Manifested in Matter, the Perfection, Justice and Balance manifested. It is the absolute Justice and the Absolute Balance. The Absolute Love expressed as Law.

Karma is the pan-universal law of cause and effect: everything has a cause, a source and a purpose to exist. What happens each moment is the result of a huge chain of cause and effect; effects that become the causes for new effects and so on. Karma is perfectly expressed in the saying, "You reap what you sow."

We perceive karma – the effects and the conditions in our lives as well as their causes in the past – either as good, positive and pleasant or bad, negative and unpleasant. Pleasant events and situations are called "positive or good karma," and unpleasant events and situations are called "negative or bad karma." (We say that negative/bad karma caused them.)

A spiritually conscious/consciously spiritual person understands the Law of Karma and recognizes it within all human conditions. He/she observes and notices karma in personal as well as social, global and universal life. Every thought, feeling, choice, word and action has a cause and also an effect. There is no action without a reaction. The conscious choice and expression of thoughts (since thoughts antecede everything else), feelings, words and actions are the greatest tools of happiness and illumination for each human being – on a personal as well as on a collective, social and universal level.

If you feel that you experience negative "things" in your life as a result of bad karma (poor choices and negative events in the past), then you can transmute it in the following two ways:

Change your direction by being more conscious/aware and through the great power of repentance (the changing of opinion and perception) by choosing thoughts, feelings, words and actions that are more positive and luminous, more healing and empowering, and that create and support a new, better, desirable reality.

Invoke the angels of karma and all the angels of light to clear the negative influences and release limiting negative patterns (recurring patterns of energy, feeling, thought and behavior). The meditation described below can help you with the process of transmuting negative karma.

MEDITATION

Angelic Cleansing of the Negative Karma and Activation of the Positive Karma

Light a white candle and dedicate it to the Divine Source, the Highest Good.

Gaze at the candle flame for a while. Feel the warmth of the flame surrounding you.

Close your eyes and visualize white light surrounding you, pure and radiant white light.

Take a few deep breaths.

Let the light permeate you, fill you and illuminate you on all levels.

You experience purity, cleanness, vitality, joy, power and clarity on all levels.

Feel your Guardian Angel close to you, by your side.

Open your heart.

Call upon the angels of light, the highest angels of the highest light.

Call upon Archangels Michael, Gabriel, Raphael and Uriel; the Angels of Purification; and the Angels of Karma.

Feel their higher light, higher vibration and higher quality, their Divine Love and Wisdom.

You are also emitting golden light from your spirit, your soul and your heart... You are your spirit, your soul and your higher self!

Ask the Angels to purify, clear and release your karma. To heal and transmute it. To purify in their Divine Fire all the bad and negative choices of the past. Your choices and the choices of others. Conscious and unconscious choices. From this lifetime and from all past lifetimes. From earth and from all other planes of existence.

Stay in this powerful spiritual energy. Feel the purification of karma taking place – on all levels.

Inhale deeply.

Wait for a while.

Now, ask the Angels and the Archangels to activate your higher, bright and positive karma. To empower your positive and good choices with Divine Light. To empower with Divine Light all the thoughts, feelings and actions that advance you and that offer good to others.

Feel the boosting of your positive karma is truly taking place, and stay in this hyperclear, hypervivid and hyperluminous energy.

Take a few deep breaths.

Thank wholeheartedly the Angels and the Archangels for their help.

Open your eyes and look at the candle flame for a few minutes more while the loving angelic energies continue to work around you, on you and within you...

Feel infinite joy, the joy of absolute and perfect release.

Your soul is smiling, your body is smiling... It is the joy of freedom!

The change has been made.

Nothing is impossible for the Spirit.

All is possible and attainable for you.

MEDITATION

Removing Karmic Ties with the help of Archangel Michael

This is one of the most popular techniques in esotericism and spirituality but also in energy healing methods: removing karmic ties with the help and power of Archangel Michael (Fire, Power of God).

Preparation:

Light a white candle and dedicate it to the highest angels of the highest light. Gaze at the candle flame for a while and relax. Feel the flame surrounding you. Take a few deep breaths. Close your eyes. Feel that your Guardian Angel is close to you, right by your side.

Mentally, call upon Archangel Michael – the Fire, the Will and the Power of God.

Visualize a perfect Golden Flame.

See and feel the golden flame of spirit burning within and around you.

Feel Archangel Michael close to you, his Light, Love and Power.

Ask Archangel Michael to cut all the dark and negative ties connecting you to situations that no longer serve the highest good, your good and the good of others.

Archangel Michael cuts the negative ties with people...

Archangel Michael cuts the negative ties connecting you to objects...

Archangel Michael cuts the negative ties connecting you to places...

Archangel Michael cuts the negative ties connecting you to situations...

Archangel Michael cuts all karmic bindings...

Archangel Michael cuts all karmic ties from all your energy centers...

Archangel Michael removes all karmic ties from all your higher bodies...

Archangel Michael removes all karmic ties from all parts of your physical body, in front, behind, on the left, on the right, below and above your body...

Archangel Michael removes all karmic ties from all the organs of your physical body, from your cells and your genetic code...

Archangel Michael removes all karmic ties from the higher levels of your existence, the unseen and unknown levels...

Archangel Michael cuts, removes, dissolves, burns, purifies, transmutes.

He illuminates and hyper-illuminates with his light and hyperlight...

He purifies, he purifies fully, truly and completely...

He heals, he heals fully, truly and completely...

See and feel again the golden flame of spirit burning within and around you.

The golden flame of spirit emits energy, light, wisdom and power.

Infinite energy, infinite light, infinite love, infinite wisdom, infinite power.

Supreme energy, supreme light, supreme love, supreme wisdom, supreme power.

Perfect energy, perfect light, perfect love, perfect wisdom, perfect power.

Divine energy, Divine light, Divine love, Divine wisdom, Divine power.

Wholeheartedly thank Archangel Michael and all the Angels of Light, Spirit and Love.

Take a few deep breaths.

Open your eyes and look at the candle flame for a few minutes more.

A note of advice:

After this particularly advanced, intense and deep clearing, help yourself by taking an unrefined sea salt bath (use 3-4 fistfuls of salt). Natural sea salt enhances and facilitates the purification process. Alternatively, take a shower and gently rub the sea salt on your body with circular movements. Afterward, rinse your body off with water and feel the water cleansing you on all levels. Also make sure to drink lots of water, eat healthily and rest as much as you can.

What is the purpose of life?

The purpose of life is life itself: joy, creation, manifestation, happiness. The purpose is experience. Living and experiencing things is the purpose, and it encompasses all other purposes. More specifically, on a human level, the purpose of life is self-knowledge, knowing one's self in all aspects and on all levels, as well as self-development, spiritual evolution and actualization. It is the unfolding and the expression of our potential, the discovery and manifestation of our abilities and talents. It is the journey toward freedom, fulfillment and awareness. And Love! Love is the ultimate purpose! Love, as it is experienced spiritually, as a higher perspective and consciousness of cosmic harmony and unity, and as it is experienced in everyday life, as compassion and sympathy, care and giving, selflessness and benevolence, help and service.

What is the purpose of my life?

The purpose of your life is to express the potential, desires and abilities of your soul and your – full of love, wisdom and power – spirit! To be the best version of yourself each moment, to be in contact with the divine (the higher, the spiritual) element within and around you, recognizing, inspiring and encouraging its expression in everything and everyone. The illumination, spiritualization, divinization, unification of all parts of your being and all aspects of your life.

We may say that the purpose of your life is exactly that: to discover the purpose of your life! To find, to create (co-create) your own identity, your own value, your own plan and purpose. Who are you? What are you? How far can you go? What do you want to experience? How do you perceive, process and assimilate life experiences? What goals and plans have you set? How much knowledge can you take in? How much power can you handle? How much wisdom and love can you receive and give? Can you put the pieces of the puzzle together? Can you see the puzzle of your life? How far can you go when it comes to boldness, sincerity, acceptance, humbleness, gratitude, respect, honesty, truth, detachment, freedom, forgiveness, compassion, creativity, kindness, helping others and service to the greater good?

Can the angels assist me in finding my life purpose?

Angels can assist you not only in finding your life purpose but also in fulfilling it! Simply ask them from deep within your heart and soul to help and guide you.

What are the Rays? How are the Angels related to the Rays?

The Divine Rays are twelve streams of divine energy, twelve expressions of the great spectrum of Light. You can find information about the Rays in relevant esoteric texts. Nevertheless, man can understand and experience few things in relation to the Rays. The Angels of the Rays represent, oversee and manifest these Divine Streams and Qualities of Light.

Below you will find a short presentation of the twelve Rays, their colors and qualities as well as the Angels corresponding to each one. You are invited to meditate on this list and go deeper into each Ray.

1st **Ray (Red): Will & Power.** Archangel Michael and Lady Faith.

2nd **Ray (Blue): Love-Wisdom.** Archangel Jophiel and Lady Constance.

3rd **Ray (Yellow): Active Intelligence.** Archangel Chamuel and Lady Charity.

4th **Ray (Green): Harmony, Beauty, Art, Will.** Archangel Gabriel and Lady Hope.

5th **Ray (Orange): Concrete Knowledge & Science.** Archangel Raphael and Mother Mary.

6th **Ray (Indigo): Devotion, Idealism, Inner Wisdom.** Archangel Uriel and Lady Grace.

7th **Ray (Violet): Transmutation, Alchemy, Ceremonial Order.** Archangel Zadkiel and Lady Amethyst.

8th Ray (Aquamarine, Sea-Foam Green): Catharsis and Purification. Archangels of Psychic Clearing, Haniel.

9th Ray (Turquoise): Lightbody Attraction. Archangels of Emotional Intelligence and Creativity, Tzaphkiel.

10th Ray (Pearl White, Golden): Lightbody Grounding, Connection to the Soul and Monad. Archangels of the Holy Spirit, Sandalphon.

11th Ray (bright Pink-Orange with golden touches): Bridge to the New Age. Archangel Metatron.

12th Ray (Golden): Grounding of the New Age and of the Christ Consciousness. Archangels of Christ, Jeremiel.

MEDITATION

Attunement to the 12 Divine Rays

Sit comfortably with your back straight. Gently close your eyes. Take ten breaths, slowly and deeply, and fill your entire body with energy and positivity. Discard anything that you no longer need... Ask your body and your mind to relax and let go of the tension... Feel that you are within a bright white light... Imagine being in serenity and harmony... You are surrounded by serenity and harmony... Serenity and harmony all around you... Bring yourself into a state of openness and receptiveness, open your heart to light and love... Your Guardian Angel is with you, by your side! It is a splendid, sacred moment... Light and Love, All is Light and All is Love!

Call upon the First Divine Ray. Envision the Red Ray of Power and Will. See and feel it – the First Ray surrounds you, permeates you and fills you with its energy... Archangel Michael and Lady Faith offer you the red light, the energy and power of the First Divine Ray... You are fully attuned and connected to these highest angels of the supreme light and the First Divine Ray, the Red Ray of Divine Power and Will. Take a deep breath and wait a little.

Call upon the Second Divine Ray. Envision the Blue Ray of Love and Wisdom. See and feel it – the Second Ray surrounds you, permeates you and fills you with its energy... Archangel Jophiel and Lady Constance offer you the blue light, energy and power of the Second Divine Ray... You are fully attuned and connected to these highest angels of the supreme light and the Second Divine Ray, the Blue Ray of Divine Love and Wisdom. Take a deep breath and wait a little.

Call upon the Third Divine Ray. Envision the Yellow Ray of Active Intelligence. See and feel it – the Third Ray surrounds you, permeates you and fills you with its energy... Archangel Chamuel and Lady Charity offer you the yellow light, energy and power of the Third Divine Ray... You are fully attuned and connected to these highest angels of the supreme light and the Third Divine Ray, the Yellow Ray of Divine Active Intelligence. Take a deep breath and wait a little.

Call upon the Fourth Divine Ray. Envision the Green Ray of Harmony, Beauty, Art and Will. See and feel it – the Fourth Ray surrounds you, permeates you and fills you with its energy... Archangel Gabriel and Lady Hope offer you the green light, energy and power of the Fourth Divine Ray... You are fully attuned and connected to these highest angels of the supreme light and the Fourth Divine Ray, the Green Ray of Divine Harmony, Beauty, Art and Will. Take a deep breath and wait a little.

Call upon the Fifth Divine Ray. Envision the Orange Ray of Concrete Knowledge and Science. See and feel it – the Fifth Ray surrounds you, permeates you and fills you with its energy... Archangel Raphael and Mother Mary offer you the orange light, energy and power of the Fifth Divine Ray... You are fully attuned and connected to these higher angels of the supreme light and the Fifth Divine Ray, the orange Ray of Divine Concrete Knowledge and Science. Take a deep breath and wait a little.

Call upon the Sixth Divine Ray. Envision the Indigo Ray of Devotion, Idealism and Inner Wisdom. See and feel it – the Sixth Ray surrounds you, permeates you and fills you with its energy... Archangel Uriel and Lady Grace offer you the indigo light, energy and power of the Sixth Divine Ray... You are fully attuned and connected to these higher angels of the supreme light and the Sixth Divine Ray, the Indigo Ray of Devotion, Idealism and Inner Wisdom. Take a deep breath and wait a little.

Call upon the Seventh Divine Ray. Envision the Violet Ray of Transmutation, Alchemy and Ceremonial Order. See and feel it – the Seventh Ray surrounds you, permeates you and fills you with its energy... Archangel Zadkiel and Lady Amethyst offer you the violet light, energy and power of the Seventh Divine Ray... You are fully attuned and connected to these higher angels of the supreme light and the Seventh Divine Ray, the Violet Ray of Transmutation, Alchemy and Ceremonial Order. Take a deep breath and wait a little.

Call upon the Eighth Divine Ray. Envision the Aquamarine (Sea Foam Green) Ray of Catharsis and Purification. See and feel it – the Eighth Ray surrounds you, permeates you and fills you with its energy... The Archangels of Psychic Clearing/Purification and Archangel Haniel offer you the aquamarine light, energy and power of the Eighth Divine Ray... You are fully attuned and connected to these higher angels of the supreme light and the Eighth Divine Ray, the Aquamarine Ray of Catharsis and Purification. Take a deep breath and wait a little.

Call upon the Ninth Divine Ray. Envision the Turquoise Ray of Lightbody Attraction. See and feel it – the Ninth Ray surrounds you, permeates you and fills you with its energy... The Archangels of Emotional Intelligence and Creativity and Archangel Tzaphkiel offer you the turquoise light, energy and power of the Ninth Divine Ray... You are fully attuned and connected to these higher angels of the supreme light and the Ninth Divine Ray, the Turquoise Ray of the Divine Lightbody Attraction. Take a deep breath and wait a little.

Call upon the Tenth Divine Ray. Envision the Ray of Lightbody Grounding and the Connection to the Soul and Monad in White and Golden color. See and feel it – the Tenth Ray surrounds you, permeates you and fills you with its energy... The Archangels of the Holy Spirit and Archangel Sandalphon offer you the golden-white light, energy and power of the Tenth Divine Ray... You are fully attuned and connected to these higher angels of the supreme light and the Tenth Divine Ray, the Ray of the Divine Lightbody Grounding and the Connection to the Soul and Monad in the Pearl White and Golden color. Take a deep breath and wait a little.

Call upon the Eleventh Divine Ray. Envision the Pink-Orange-Golden Ray of the Bridge to the New Age. See and feel it – the Eleventh Ray surrounds you, permeates you and fills you with its energy... Archangel Metatron offers you the pink-orange-golden light, energy and power of the Eleventh Divine Ray... You are fully attuned and connected to these higher angels of the supreme light and the Eleventh Divine Ray, the Pink-Orange-Golden Ray of the Divine Bridge to the New Era. Take a deep breath and wait a little.

Call upon the Twelfth Divine Ray. Envision the Golden Ray of Grounding of the New Age and the Christ Consciousness. See and feel it – the Twelfth Ray surrounds you, permeates you and fills you with its energy... The Archangels of the Christ and Archangel Jeremiel offer you the golden light, energy and power of the Twelfth Divine Ray... You are fully attuned and connected to these higher angels of the supreme light and the Twelfth Divine Ray, the Golden Ray of the Divine Grounding of the New Age and the Christ Consciousness. Take a deep breath and wait a little.

Inhale and exhale deeply. The attunement to the twelve Divine Rays has been completed. Gently open your eyes. Drink plenty of water, rest or continue your everyday activities.

Instructions:

To experience constant positive change and upgrade in your energy system, carry out the meditation described above for 12 or more days. You can read or visualize it three times a day (consecutive or morning/noon/evening). Follow the schedule that fits you best, every day for 12 days. Later, once per month will be sufficient to reap the benefits of the Alignment with the 12 Rays.

Alternative method:

If you are not able to apply the complete meditation due to its length and intensity (it is a very powerful and advanced meditation), use it for one ray/one attunement daily. The first day, apply the meditation to achieve alignment with the first ray, and the second day align with the second ray...until you reach the twelfth day and the alignment with the twelfth divine ray. Read the meditation text corresponding to the ray you wish to align with three times daily, giving yourself time to visualize it, to experience and assimilate the process (approximately ten minutes per day are enough). Repeat the 12-day cycle another two times, reaching a total of 36 days.

Is there a connection between angels and planets?

According to esoteric (spiritual) teachings, each planet of our solar system – and each celestial body in the universe – is ruled by one or more angels. Conversely, each angel is responsible for a celestial body. The following list shows the correspondence between angels and planets.

Sun: Michael, Raphael

Moon: Gabriel

Mars: Chamuel, Uriel

Mercury: Raphael, Michael

Jupiter: Zadkiel, Zoviahel

Venus: Anael, Haniel

Saturn: Oriphiel, Cassiel, Anahiel

Uranus: Uriel

Pluto: Azrael, Samael

Neptune: Azariel, Sachiel

The angels mentioned above are the rulers and protectors of the respective planets. They represent the planets and manifest their higher spiritual energy, essence and value. They bring the spiritual meaning, lesson and knowledge of those planets to humanity. As we advance spiritually and psychically, we connect more and more to Mother Earth (our home) and also to the rest of the planets and the celestial bodies of our solar system. The solar system, the galaxy and the whole universe are ever-larger aspects of the greater self, parts of the supreme Divine Selfhood. We attune and connect more and more to the energies, the lessons, the challenges and the gifts (potential, power, abilities, knowledge) that they (the planets, celestial bodies, solar system, galaxies...) symbolize, represent and express. The angels and Archangels corresponding to each planet help us make this connection, to resonate and receive all the gifts that the celestial bodies hide in the higher levels of the solar-galactic-universal-cosmic-divine evolution, of our own evolution, our journey from matter to the ultimate spirit, from the limited to the unlimited, from the apparent to the true, from ego to Beingness, to the One, to the Whole, to All-That-Is.

MEDITATION

The Journey of Consciousness through the Universe

Imagine a person who awakes energetically and spiritually, who attunes to higher frequencies and potential. As the person acquires more and more awareness, knowledge, wisdom, power, light, and vital energy, his aura, essence and radiance expand, increase and strengthen. Gradually, the person embraces energetically and spiritually the place where he lives, his entire country, continent and planet. As the person's aura, energy and essence continue to grow and expand, he embraces (energetically, spiritually) the neighboring celestial bodies/satellites/planets and the star of our solar system (the sun). He embraces the entire solar system and then the neighboring stars and the entire galaxy! While continuing the journey of spiritual illumination, the person will "embrace" the neighboring galaxies and ultimately the entire universe, the entire space and time continuum! We can say that Theosis, the ultimate connection to the Divine, the Divine superconsciousness, is this supreme and ultimate expansion and unification of energy, spirit and consciousness, where the human spirit embraces (attunes and connects to, becomes) the entire universe and beyond – the entire Cosmos, the Existence, the One, the Whole, the All. And the One, the Whole, the All, the Divine, God are infinite – infinite bliss, infinite love and infinite light. Words are too poor and short to express What They Are!

A Question for Thought, Meditation, and Further Study

How did you feel when you read the above text? Meditate upon the journey into the universe, growing, embracing and becoming conscious of greater parts of existence, of Beingness, of the All and the Divine.

MEDITATION

Connecting with Planets and Their Angels

Sit comfortably with your back straight. Gently close your eyes. Take ten slow and deep breaths, filling your entire body with energy and positivity while discarding anything you no longer need... Ask your body and your mind to relax and let go of the tension... Feel that you are surrounded by a bright white light... Imagine being in serenity and harmony... You are surrounded by serenity and harmony... Bring yourself into a state of openness and receptiveness, open your heart to light and love... Feel that your Guardian Angel is with you! It is a splendid, sacred moment... Light and Love, All is Light and All is Love!

Solar Attunement... Ask to attune to the Sun and Archangels Michael and Raphael... You receive the pure, higher, spiritual energy of the Sun and its most high and luminous Angels, and you receive all their divine gifts... You receive, receive, receive... The Sun and its Angels offer you healing... It is a true and profound experience... You experience empowerment, upliftment and expansion... You enjoy and absorb the energy... Solar Illumination... Take a deep breath and wait a little.

Planetary Attunement... Ask to attune to the Moon and Archangel Gabriel... You receive the pure, higher spiritual energy of the Moon and its most high and luminous Angels, and you receive all their divine gifts... You receive, receive, receive... The Moon and its Angels offer you healing... It is a true and profound experience... You experience empowerment, upliftment and expansion... You enjoy and absorb the energy... Planetary Illumination... Take a deep breath and wait a little.

Planetary Attunement... Ask to attune to Mars and Archangels Chamuel and Uriel... You receive the pure, higher, spiritual energy of Mars and of most its high and luminous Angels, you receive all their divine gifts... You receive, receive, receive... Mars and its Angels offer you healing ... It is a true and profound experience... You experience empowerment, upliftment and expansion... You enjoy and absorb the energy... Planetary Illumination... Take a deep breath and wait a little.

Planetary Attunement... Ask to attune to Mercury and Archangels Raphael and Michael... You receive the pure, higher spiritual energy of Mercury and of its most high and luminous Angels, and you receive all their divine gifts... You receive, receive, receive... Mercury and its Angels offer you healing... It is a true and profound experience... You experience empowerment, upliftment and expansion... You enjoy and absorb the energy... Planetary Illumination... Take a deep breath and wait a little.

Planetary Attunement... Ask to attune to Jupiter and Archangels Zadkiel and Zovahiel... You receive the pure, higher spiritual energy of Jupiter and of its most high and luminous Angels, and you receive all their divine gifts... You receive, receive, receive... Jupiter and its Angels offer you healing... It is a true and profound experience... You experience empowerment, upliftment and expansion... You enjoy and absorb the energy... Planetary Illumination... Take a deep breath and wait a little.

Planetary Attunement... Ask to attune to Venus and Archangels Anael and Haniel... You receive the pure, higher spiritual energy of Venus and of its most high and luminous Angels, and you receive all their divine gifts... You receive, receive, receive... Venus and its Angels offer you healing... It is a true and profound experience... You experience empowerment, upliftment and expansion... You enjoy and absorb the energy... Planetary Illumination... Take a deep breath and wait a little.

Planetary Attunement... Ask to attune to Saturn and Archangels Oriphiel, Cassiel, and Anahiel... You receive the pure, higher spiritual energy of Saturn and its most high and luminous Angels, and you receive all their divine gifts... You receive, receive, receive... Saturn and its Angels offer you healing... It is a true and profound experience... You experience empowerment, upliftment, and expansion... You enjoy and absorb the energy... Planetary Illumination... Take a deep breath and wait a little.

Planetary Attunement... Ask to attune to Uranus and Archangel Uriel... You receive the pure, higher spiritual energy of Uranus and its most high and luminous Angels, and you receive all their divine gifts... You receive, receive, receive... Uranus and its Angels offer you healing... It is a true and profound experience... You experience empowerment, upliftment and expansion... You enjoy and absorb the energy... Planetary Illumination... Take a deep breath and wait a little.

Planetary Attunement... Ask to attune to Pluto and Archangels Azrael and Samael... You receive the pure, higher spiritual energy of Pluto and its most high and luminous Angels, and you receive all their divine gifts... You receive, receive, receive... Pluto and its Angels offer you healing... It is a true and profound experience... You experience empowerment, upliftment and expansion... You enjoy and absorb the energy... Planetary Illumination... Take a deep breath and wait a little.

Planetary Attunement... Ask to attune to Neptune and Archangels Azariel and Sachiel... You receive the pure, higher spiritual energy of Neptune and its most high and luminous Angels, and you receive all their divine gifts... You receive, receive, receive... Neptune and its Angels offer you healing... It is a true and profound experience... You experience empowerment, upliftment and expansion... You enjoy and absorb the energy... Planetary Illumination... Take a deep breath and wait a little.

Solar Attunement... Ask to attune to the entire Solar System and its Archangels... You receive the pure, higher, spiritual energy of the Solar System and its most high and luminous Angels, and you receive all their divine gifts... You receive, receive, receive... The Solar System and its Angels offer you healing... It is a true and profound experience... You experience empowerment, upliftment and expansion... You enjoy and absorb the energy... Solar Illumination... Take a deep breath and wait a little.

Galactic Attunement... Ask to attune to the entire Galaxy and its Archangels... You receive the pure, higher spiritual energy of the Galaxy and its most high and luminous Angels, and you receive all their divine gifts... You receive, receive, receive... The Galaxy and its Angels offer you healing... It is a true and profound experience... You experience empowerment, upliftment and expansion... You enjoy and absorb the energy... Galactic Illumination... Take a deep breath and wait a little.

Universal Attunement... Ask to attune to the entire Universe and its Archangels... You receive the pure, higher spiritual energy of the Universe and its most high and luminous Angels, and you receive all their divine gifts... You receive, receive, receive... The Universe and its Angels offer you healing... It is a true and profound experience... You experience empowerment, upliftment and expansion... You enjoy and absorb the energy... Universal Illumination... Take a deep breath and wait a little.

The planets, the solar system, the galaxy, the universe and all their Archangels assist you in your healing, empowerment and upliftment and the completion of your beingness on all levels. They support your freedom, fulfilment and illumination. There is infinite energy, infinite light, and infinite love in the solar system, the galaxy and the universe! You are one with the solar system, the sun and its planets, you are one with the galaxy, and you are one with the universe! Planetary, solar, galactic and universal alignment and unity!

The attunement has been completed. You are and you feel amazing, exquisite and divine! Give thanks, take some deep breaths and open your eyes. Drink plenty of water, rest or continue your everyday activities.

Secret tip:

Try to practice this particular meditation at night under the starlit sky. It is truly a universal experience!

How are angels related to the zodiac signs?

According to esoteric teachings, each zodiac sign is overseen and ruled by an Angel. There are several correspondences, and the lists of protector Angels of each zodiac sign vary. Below, I give two lists connecting the twelve sun signs with their ruling angels.

The 12 zodiac signs and their ruling Angels:

ARIES: Camael

TAURUS: Hagiel

GEMINI: Raphael

CANCER: Gabriel

LEO: Michael

VIRGO: Raphael

LIBRA: Hagiel

SCORPIO: Asrael and Camael

SAGITTARIUS: Zadkiel

CAPRICORN: Asariel

AQUARIUS: Uriel and Cassiel

PISCES: Asariel and Zadkiel

(Source: *The Angel Bible* by Hazel Raven, Godsfield Press)

ARIES: Machidiel

TAURUS: Asmodel

GEMINI: Ambriel

CANCER: Muriel

LEO: Verchiel

VIRGO: Hamaliel

LIBRA: Uriel

SCORPIO: Barbiel

SAGITTARIUS: Adnachiel

CAPRICORN: Hanael

AQUARIUS: Gabriel

PISCES: Barchiel

(Source: *A Dictionary of Angels* by Gustav Davidson, Free Press)

MEDITATION

Connecting with the Angels of our Zodiac Sign

To practice this meditation, you may utilize the angels ruling your zodiac sign. (See the two lists above.)

Prepare yourself appropriately: Sit comfortably with your back straight. Gently close your eyes. Take a few deep breaths and relax. Visualize pure white light all around you. Feel serenity and harmony. Feel your soul rejoicing and smiling. Visualize even more light surrounding you, and stay in this uplifted state.

Now, ask to connect to all the angels governing the zodiac cycle. Receive their potential and their gifts, energies and qualities. You relate to the entire zodiac cycle; all sun signs reflect you and have an influence on you and your life. Take a deep breath and wait a bit.

Then, bring to your mind the ruling angel(s) of your zodiac sign. Ask to be able to manifest the higher energy/quality of your sun sign and of the Archangel governing it.

Ask to be fully connected to the angels overseeing your zodiac sign.

Continue to inhale and exhale deeply. Stay in this energy and quality that has been created.

Thank the angels and open your eyes.

Empowering the Attunement:

Below, you will find two simple techniques to empower the alignment with the zodiac signs and their ruling angels.

Light up 12 white candles. As you light the candles, dedicate each candle to one of the 12 zodiac signs and its ruling angel. Do it with great awe, wonder and love. Proceed with the meditation above. Complete the meditation by blowing the candles out.

Attention: the candles always have to be away from flammable objects, and do not leave the candles unattended.

Alternatively, you may dedicate 12 crystals to the 12 zodiac signs and their respective governing angels. You can use white quartz, rose quartz, amethyst or other crystals and gemstones. Before you use any crystals, it is necessary to clean and charge them. Form a circle with the 12 crystals and sit inside the circle. Proceed with the meditation given above.

If you wish, you can apply both techniques.

Do I have to do all these meditations to connect with angels? Isn't the intention, the love and the faith in angels enough? Can I just call upon them whenever I am in need?

The love we have for angels is the primary force which connects us to them. Intention, desire, hope and faith activate the sacred process of angelic attunement and connection. Various meditations, advanced techniques and exercises, regular and systematic study are also essential elements of our spiritual journey to the Divine. They are important tools of spiritual upliftment, holistic empowerment and personal (and collective) advancement. We cannot advance much further without daily spiritual study and practice (through meditations, invocations and exercises). We long to move past the apparent and superficial elements... to reach the supreme one, the Divine. In this process, we will use every available means, and each tool is important and precious.

Do I have to do all the meditations found in this book? Meditations about the Archangels, the chakras, the rays, the zodiac signs, the planets, the Guardian Angel, etc.? Which meditations are right for me?

In spirituality – and in the Spirit as well – there is no such thing as "have to." You may freely and intuitively choose the meditations you like or the ones that leave a strong impression on you. You may apply the exercises, techniques and meditations of this book however you see fit, as many times as you want. (Though there are suggestions in certain meditations about their practice frequency.) Read the whole book one or more times and then follow your intuition and inner guidance. As with all things in life: the more time, energy, effort, love and passion you invest into your spiritual study and practice, the greater results, experiences, essence and power you will gain.

You don't need to practice all the meditations and all the exercises. They are different roads to reach spiritual perception of angels, spirit and the Divine. They are tools of illumination and happiness, self-knowledge and self-improvement, expansion and advancement (of energy, spirit and consciousness), tools of joy, knowledge and love. The goal of all spiritual exercises and practices is to inspire and mobilize us to discover who we truly are, what exists behind and beyond the material phenomena, what exists on a deeper, higher, more essential and total level.

What are the angelic centers or angelic chakras?

The *angelic chakras* or *angelic centers* are our superiorly cosmic, purely spiritual energy centers. They have higher vibrational frequencies and potential. The angelic chakras open and become activated when we are ready to enlighten ourselves, our lives and our beingness; to become conscious, to heal, to unite wholly and cosmically, 100%, from the alpha to the omega; to attune and connect to the supreme, the divine; to manifest and express the perfect and infinite wisdom, love and power of the divine. It is the highest transformation and the highest transmutation that our essence, our core, our soul, our true and deepest being longs for.

The angelic chakras/angelic centers are also called *angelic stars*. We can imagine and visualize them as extensions of the seven major chakras, as the roots or the cores of the seven chakras. We can also envision the angelic chakras as the seven *higher chakras*, the *higher self*, the higher aspect of the seven major chakras or the seven spiritual/cosmic chakras located above and beyond the crown chakra (seventh chakra).

As we become awakened and we expand energetically, spiritually and consciously, our energy centers become open, activated and illuminated and we experience higher states of insight, freedom, bliss and fulfilment. And vice versa, these states awaken and activate the angelic chakras of our spirit.

MEDITATION

Opening the Angelic Centers

Sit comfortably with your back straight and gently close your eyes. Take some deep breaths. Feel your breath filling your entire body with energy, vitality, light and positivity... high, pure vibrations. Your body is filled and radiates energy, vitality, light and positivity... high, pure vibrations. Dive into the absolute serenity and harmony of your essence, of your primary and authentic essence, absolute serenity and harmony... You are one with the divine source, the brightest and highest infinite source. You are one with your soul, your pure, clean, free and divine soul.

Mentally ask your higher self, the higher intelligence of your spirit and soul, and your Guardian Angel to open and activate the angelic centers in your body and spirit. Envision, see and feel the dazzling stars being awakened and activated to shine brightly. Ask the angels – the pure, free and supreme spiritual intelligences – to help you, the highest angels of the highest light. Ask them to open the angelic chakras in your body and spirit... Visualize, see and feel the luminous stars being awakened and activated, to radiate and shine within you, to emit the Divine Light... the Light of Life, the Light of Spirit, the Light of Consciousness – the primary, the perfect, the Divine Light.

Feel the emotional and spiritual upliftment, the expansion and the elevation that the angel chakras bring. You feel and you experience emotional and spiritual upliftment, expansion and elevation, hyper-luminous light and illumination, hyper-luminous clarity and power, and hyper-luminous joy and bliss on all levels. Stay in this state... After a few minutes, take a few deep breaths, energetic and spiritual breaths – full of energy, vitality, light, life. Open your eyes.

Your angelic centers, the dazzling angelic stars of your spirit are open and activated. They emit their higher, pure, luminous vibrations, potential and powers.

Do human beings have "angel wings"? What is that?

Angel wings are a natural and vital part of our higher spiritual anatomy. The opening of our angel wings is a milestone in our energetic and spiritual advancement and evolution. It is a true celestial blessing, a blessing directly from the spirit (the divine essence of existence), a precious gift from Angels and the Divine Source.

Angelic wings symbolize freedom and express our spiritual maturity and inner completeness. It is a symbol and an expression of the higher spiritual wisdom, love and power that we have realized, reached, gained, created, emitted and offered. All people can recognize and become aware of their angel wings, of their freedom and power to open their wings and co-create the real, the good, the beautiful, and pure happiness, for themselves, for others and for all.

Our wings, our higher spiritual aura, our constantly evolving spiritual body, can be awakened, opened and activated either automatically (due to spiritual awakening and maturity) or through intense esoteric work (spiritual study, meditation, spiritual practices and initiations) focused on our self-knowledge and self-development as well as the advancement, healing and illumination of all.

The experience of opening our angel wings brings great euphoria, bliss and ecstasy. It is a spiritual explosion, a spiritual orgasm of energy and love, of light and fire, of wonder and awe – a true illumination! When our angel wings are open, all our psychic and spiritual potential and powers expand, and we are able to ascend to a higher level of multidimensional work, such as travelling to other dimensions, experiencing superconsciousness, performing advanced meditations and visualizations, gaining access to powerful and immediate healing on all levels... and many other things, all of which are beyond amazing and splendid!

MEDITATION

Opening Our Angel Wings

Can you imagine yourself with angelic wings? Can you see yourself with wings of infinite freedom and spirit? With wings of transcendence and divinity? With wings of great power and wisdom, of true bliss, of supreme light and illumination? Can you imagine the most magical, the most beautiful, the most splendid, the most bright and radiant, the most beloved angel wings? Angel wings, the wings of angels...

Feel your wings around your shoulders and your back. Visualize, imagine, see and feel your wings. There is no need to hurry; take your time...

Visualize an angel of supreme light standing behind you. See and feel the angel, a supreme angel of light. He is approaching you; he is standing behind you... More and more clearly, you see and feel the angel behind you...

Ask the angel to help you open your wings... With serenity, with joy, with love...

Invoke your spirit, your soul, your higher self, your divine monad, your divine essence and origin.

"My beloved higher self, my beloved soul and spirit, I open the angel wings of my higher divine beingness. I open my true wings, my angel wings!"

Imagine, visualize, see and feel your angel wings open up... slowly...

With the help of the highest angel behind you, with the help and energy of your higher self, your spirit and soul... you open your wings!

You are awakened, uplifted, expanded, liberated...

Feel the psychical and spiritual awakening, upliftment, expansion and liberation...

You now have wings; your angel wings are open! You may use them psychically and spiritually for your own good and the good of others, the highest good of all!

Your being is now filled with light and love, with joy and bliss! You are light and love, you are joy and bliss! Your wings are the great gift of angels to you, your divine gift.

Stay in this blessed state of bliss and illumination, a sacred blessing of love, freedom and joy.

Can the angels change or improve our DNA?

As we awaken our consciousness to love, light, the all and the divine and as we evolve and advance on all levels (mentally, emotionally, energetically, spiritually), our growth is also reflected on our material part: our physical, biological body. The changes (bright, positive and vital as the sun!) manifest in our matter. Our mater becomes conscious, uplifted, enlightened, "spiritualized." We ground and express the wisdom, love and power of our spirit. We ground and express our spirit itself – our essence – in the material world, right here, right now on earth. It is an amazing, transformative, divine experience!

During this process, our genetic code – the primary/creative code of matter – is changing. Our DNA gets purified, cleared, healed, enhanced, reconstructed and expanded so it can hold our greater beingness, our higher essence – our truthfulness, our reality, truth and reality themselves.

The inadequate, poor, sore, unhappy, wounded (by ancestors and karma) and partly dark DNA with its two-strand double helix transforms into... complete, overabundant, infinitely joyful and blissful, supremely luminous and radiant, absolutely beloved DNA with 12 (true, spiritual) strands. We regain our primary and ultimate, true and highest genetic code: the genetic code of the Divine beingness, essence, consciousness; the genetic code that expresses the Divine on all levels. It is the Divine expressed in matter and matter in its most Divine (energetically and consciously, the highest) expression.

As a bridge between heaven and earth, the material and the spiritual world, and the visible and the invisible, and also as our faithful and luminous companions on our spiritual journey, angels guide, support and provide the energy, wisdom and power for this important evolution, the transformation/spiritualization/activation of our genetic code. It is true bliss to express in your genetic code the higher spiritual wisdom, love and power of your spirit and soul and of the divine source, your essence, the light and the good. It is true bliss that your genetic code becomes the symbol and the base of this new, higher and greater Reality that you are and that you experience at last!

MEDITATION

Angelic & Divine DNA Activation

Bring your attention deep within yourself... Imagine you are going deep into the core of your being... deep, very deep within you... into yourself, into the center of your beingness. You are going very deep into the core of your existence; you are going to your Divine core... divine center, divine core... You are travelling deep inside... You are getting closer and closer to the core...

Divine center, divine core...

Now, you are deep, very deep within yourself... It is a place of absolute love, absolute serenity and absolute harmony. It is a place where divine wisdom, love and power flow abundantly – all the divine energies! It is a most bright place... All Light... All in the Light... All from the Light... All Light... All the Light...

You can see your genetic code... the code of spirit and of your body, of your material form, of your earthly life. It is your spiritual and physical code. You see it clearly.

Mentally ask the forces of light, spirit and the Divine to surround you...

See and feel the angels surrounding you... Heavenly beings of heavenly light... Supreme beings of supreme light!

Now, focus on your DNA once more... Observe if there are any dark spots. If there are, ask for their clearing and purification... Are there any cut or wounded spots? If there are, ask for their healing and restoration... Take a deep breath.

Full awakening and complete activation of the highest, spiritual, angelic and Divine genetic code in your body and spirit!

Visualize, see and feel a shower of light cleaning your DNA, a powerful shower of pure, cleansing light. The changes occur on all levels of your existence.

You feel it and it is happening – a new and clean DNA, improved, healthier, brighter than ever. Take a deep breath.

Full awakening and complete activation of the highest, spiritual, angelic and Divine genetic code in your body and spirit!

And now visualize, see and feel your genetic code under a shower of angelic and divine love. Your DNA receives love... it is filled with abundant love, quintessence and energy of love... It is illuminated on all levels. You feel it. It is a fact. Take a deep breath.

Full awakening and complete activation of the highest, spiritual, angelic and Divine genetic code in your body and spirit!

Ask the forces of light and the angels to attune your DNA to higher frequencies... to inscribe angelic codes and symbols on your DNA, angelic qualities and energies. Ask your DNA to connect and align fully with the Divine Source. Take another deep breath.

Full awakening and complete activation of the highest, spiritual, angelic and Divine genetic code in your body and spirit!

Ask Archangel Michael, Archangel Gabriel, Archangel Raphael and Archangel Uriel to touch your DNA...to hold it, to illuminate it with their infinite energy, infinite power and infinite wisdom... You see it, you feel it and it is happening. It is a fact – a most positive and Divine change of your genetic code!

Full awakening and complete activation of the highest, spiritual, angelic and Divine genetic code in your body and spirit!

Ask from the Highest Archangels to enable the highest programs of your spirit and soul, of the divine source and of the highest good. See and feel the Highest Archangels infusing your DNA with their Archangelic Divine Flames... You see it, you feel it. It is happening on all levels. It is a fact! Take a deep breath.

Full awakening and complete activation of the highest, spiritual, angelic and Divine genetic code in your body and spirit!

And now visualize, see and feel a perfect celestial sphere of supreme golden light surrounding your DNA. It is perfect and absolute protection, guidance, love and illumination. It is the power of good, bringing all good things, all the good in the world. Take a deep breath.

Full awakening and complete activation of the highest, spiritual, angelic and Divine genetic code in your body and spirit!

So it be done...! Amen...! So it is...! Amen!

Whenever you are ready, take some deep breaths and gently move your body. Mentally, see your body surrounded by an intense, powerful and dense golden light. See the golden light permeating you. Feel it. It is a fact. All your cells are filled with golden light. Absorb this magnificent energy and open your eyes.

You are and you feel better than ever, you are and you feel amazing, sublime, divine!

Drink plenty of water, rest or continue with your daily activities.

For more direct and steady energetic results and spiritual benefits, apply the above meditation twelve days in a row.

There are situations and behaviors that bother me in spiritual traditions, such as dogmatism, fanaticism, commercialization, rivalry, control and exploitation. What do you think about that?

My answer to this question is quite simple: spirit is perfect, but spirituality is imperfect. Spirit is infinite, but spirituality limited. Spirit is Divine, and spirituality is human. Keep this in mind to start differentiating. Research and study. Avoid what you don't like (ways of thinking or behaving) and embrace what you admire and love. Keep your mind and your heart open, observe, wait, be the last to judge.

Together with your open mind and your open heart, your sensitivity and intuition, and your logical, observing and inquiring view, unfold your compassion and understanding for human spirituality. Remember that all spiritualities are perspectives upon the Spirit, different paths. See human spirituality as a great master, your higher self or an angel would!

A Question for Thought, Meditation, and Further Study

If you could choose (and you can!) your spirituality, how would it be? Write its main elements and characteristics...! (This is a wonderful exercise, and I urge you to try it out!)

What is esotericism and mysticism? Are they the same thing?

Esotericism and *mysticism* are closely related concepts that often intertwine with one another. They are characterized by an interest and study of eternal spiritual truths as they exist in religions and beyond them – since many truths were hidden or compromised to serve certain interests or intimidate people, etc.

An esoteric is a person with an intense inner thirst for seeking and studying the esoteric truths. A mystic is a person who is initiated to the esoteric mysteries and has personal experiences of the esoteric truths. Every spiritually conscious – awakened from the lethargy of materialism – human being follows and practices a combination of both: the systematic study of spirituality and inner truths (esotericism) and the personal experience of inner mysteries and truths (mysticism).

A Question for Thought, Meditation, and Further Study

You are on the quest of seeking the truth, the truth beyond what you see with your eyes. You seek your own happiness and the happiness of other people. You seek answers to your questions. You seek knowledge, joy, freedom and completeness. You seek illumination, self – actualization, enlightenment. You seek what is righteous, fair and good. From the moment you begin to seek, you are already an esoteric and a mystic! How much of an esoteric and how much of a mystic are you? When it comes to spirituality, are you more drawn to theory or experience? Develop both sides equally if you want to Know and to Experience.

What Is Kabbalah?

Beyond the four most known Archangels – Michael, Gabriel, Raphael, Uriel – the tradition of Kabbalah offers a great body of information about other angels, their names and their respective qualities. Kabbalah is an esoteric discipline of spiritual quest and growth with intense mystical elements and apocryphal concepts. It is the esoteric part of Judaism, the mystical aspect of Judaic philosophy and religion.

Even though Kabbalah is closely intertwined with Jewish religious beliefs and philosophy, it can offer useful and enlightening esoteric teachings and practices to the modern seeker. The modern seeker can find valuable material concerning spiritual teachings and practices even if one is not of Jewish faith. Kabbalah, just like all esoteric and mystical parts of all religions, is about the direct and personal experience of the Divine (through spiritual practices such as meditation, prayer and the use of mantras) and not about the rigid dogma. Dogma is used by the outer part of religion, the part of religion intended for the masses, often used to intimidate and control the masses on various levels.

Kabbalah teaches about angels, and a central concept of its teachings is the Tree of Life (a spiritual symbol and archetype). According to Kabbalists (the researchers and mystics of Kabbalah) the Tree of Life is the Spiritual Map that God gave to man after his exit from Eden, which is the fall of his consciousness from heavenly unity and wholeness into the material world, so he would be able to return one day. The Tree of Life is a guide of personal and collective spiritual fulfillment and a map for the elevation of consciousness. The Tree of Life consists of ten worlds (levels) called Sephirot to assist man to arise from the material world and earthly life to the Spiritual and Divine level, i.e., to reach Theosis (the unification of consciousness with the All-That-Is and absolute bliss). Symbolically, Theosis is expressed as "the return to Eden" or "the return of the prodigal son."

The study of Kabbalah is hard and demanding, as it includes several apocryphal concepts, but it offers great wealth to the ones truly interested in the esoteric truths beyond the dogma of the "socially acceptable religion" and its superficial approach.

Would I benefit from following Kabbalah or another philosophical or esoteric discipline so as to experience spiritual truths and the angels?

Follow the truth. Follow the light, love, every single thing "good, beautiful and true." Truths exist in all religious and philosophical systems and disciplines. However, a truth that is not experienced personally and not understood profoundly is a useless truth, a dead truth. Study and research spiritual texts, doubt and wonder, think and feel, believe in what you experience and keep your mind and heart open to the unknown, the unfamiliar, the new.

Personally, I always liked studying various religions and see their possible similarities and differences. I liked studying their historical evolution, the influence they have on people (psychologically, socially...), their moral and philosophical principles, their dogmas, their views on human nature, good and evil, the purpose of life and life after death. Even though I was open (mentally and energetically) to the potential existence of angels, I became a believer when I experienced their presence and power firsthand so directly and intensively that I could not ignore or doubt it. The same goes for all the spiritual truths: I have studied, questioned and doubted them, I have meditated upon them and I have experienced them.

God (and angels) doesn't see religions or other labels. God sees only the purity of the heart, the giving, the actions, the energy and the vibration we emit with everything we think, feel or do; how willing we are to experience these truths, help ourselves and others. God is only Love. The road I have followed with complete freedom and fiery joy, going beyond fear, guilt and blind attachment to dogma, is the road I would lovingly and respectfully suggest to every person who wants to proceed to the discovery (how much joy a discovery holds!) and the experience of one's own essence and true beingness.

What Is the Tree of Life?

The Tree of Life is a symbol found in many ancient cultures and traditions (Greece, Egypt, Middle East, China, the Aztecs and the Mayans, Norse mythology...). It is usually depicted as an Eternal Life Tree located in a Heavenly Garden, a higher plane of reality. The Tree of Life is usually guarded by an angel holding a flaming sword, a Cherub, often believed to be Archangel Gabriel or Uriel.

The Tree of Life represents and symbolizes various levels of creation, spirit (divine energy) expressed in various planes (worlds, emanations), the connections between these planes (the "branches" of the tree) and, in this way, the oneness of all existence.

The Tree of Life is a central concept in the Jewish esoteric tradition of Kabbalah. It serves as a map of creation, with ten worlds emanating from the Supreme, the Divine. The Tree of Life is a map of consciousness for spiritual self – knowledge and fulfilment, a cosmic map that leads to Eden, Divine Enlightenment and Consciousness, and unification with the Supreme Source of All.

According to Kabbalah, the Tree of Life consists of ten worlds (planes, levels), namely the Sefirot (Sefira in singular). Every Sefira has an essential energy/quality that a person needs to develop on his journey to Theosis. Every Sefira is related to an Archangel who represents the respective level and its essential energy/quality. The ten Sefirot interrelate one to another through 22 paths.

The list given below shows the names of the ten Sefirot of the Tree of Life, their respective energies/qualities and the Archangels linked to them.

The Sefirot, the Divine Energies/Qualities and the Archangels of the Kabbalistic Tree of Life:

Sephirot	Quality	Archangel
Kether	**Crown**	**Metatron**
Chokmah	**Wisdom**	**Raziel**
Binah	**Understanding**	**Tzaphkiel**
Chesed	**Mercy, Kindness**	**Zadkiel**
Geburah	**Strength**	**Chamuel**
Tiphareth	**Beauty**	**Raphael**
Hod	**Glory**	**Michael, Jophiel**
Netzach	**Victory**	**Haniel**
Yesod	**Foundation**	**Gabriel**
Malkuth	**Kingdom**	**Sandalphon, Uriel**

There is an additional hidden Sefira named Daath (knowledge and a place of miracles). Daath is a combination of the energies of Chokmah and Binah, and it represents Shekinah or the Holy Spirit.

Looking beyond the Kabbalistic frame, we can perceive the Tree of Life as an ancient, universal, panhuman and multidimensional Archetype, a Symbol providing knowledge and energy. We can meditate upon the importance, meaning, symbolism, essence and potential (spiritual and energetic) it offers.

The study and meditation upon the Tree of Life (Kabbalistic or not) not only offers higher spiritual energy and power but also knowledge and insight on the world of angels, the nature of creation and reality and the potential within each human being. All human beings are full of gifts and potential in their consciousness and spirit and even in their bodies, as the human body is also a map... A Tree of Life!

A Question for Thought, Meditation, and Further Study

Can you imagine your body as a "Tree of Life"? As a spiritual map to Eden, to the Divine? Can you imagine your body as a perfect and complete miniature of the All, of the World and of the Existence? The body is such a sacred, amazing and great miracle! See and love it as such!

MEDITATION

The Sacred Tree of Life

With the help of the archangels, this specific meditation takes us (spiritually and energetically) on a journey through Creation, through the Divine spheres, to the highest dimension and the highest consciousness, the Absolute Superconsciousness – that of Absolute Oneness, Completeness and Bliss. The meditation is inspired by the Kabbalistic Tree of Life, but it is not narrowed only to the people studying Kabbalah. The meditation doesn't use Kabbalistic concepts or terms (e.g., Sefirot) and can be practiced by anyone as a journey to the Divine. However, if you wish, you can add to the meditation the names of the Sefirot or other Kabbalistic concepts or practices (mantras and others). It is a complete meditation of upliftment, illumination and attunement to various levels of Creation.

Sit comfortably and gently close your eyes. Take ten deep breaths. Feel your breath filling your entire body with energy, vitality, light and positivity. Exhale, discarding anything you no longer need. Release every thought and worry... Ask your body and mind to relax and let go of the tension... You feel freer, lighter, more ethereal. You experience more clarity, more harmony, more peace...

Bring into your mind the Tree of Life. Visualize it as a sacred map of creation with ten golden worlds shining like ten bright stars, ten suns, ten universes, ten Divine dimensions, ten Divine worlds of immense beauty, wisdom, power... of infinite luminosity. How magnificent, sublime and Divine the Sacred Tree of Life is! You approach the Tree of Life with awe and wonder, with humbleness and gratitude...

Your intention is to arise to the Divine Worlds, the Divine Dimensions, the Sacred Tree of Eternal Life; to receive energy, power, knowledge and wisdom, all good things; to attune to and unite with the highest consciousness, the source, the all, the perfection, the absolute, the divine. This is your intention, and you are fully mobilized!

Take a deep breath, and visualize yourself surrounded by a bright white light... See and feel the bright light... All around you... You have absolute, complete and perfect protection. You receive the highest guidance. Your Guardian Angels is always close to you, next to you. You are together; you are one.

Envision yourself going up a celestial stairway together with your Guardian Angel. You are going up, ascending... The celestial stairway guides you to luminous worlds and dimensions, through the Divine Tree of Life...

You are ascending to the first world... In the first world you meet Archangel Sandalphon and Archangel Uriel, who provide you with the gifts of Mother Nature, of matter, of earth. They offer you steadiness, power, grounding, manifestation, adaptability, ease, the power of creation and re-creation, the potential of actualization. The Archangels offer you the secrets, the keys to matter, the keys to Mother Earth. You receive their energy and blessings... You feel splendid, perfect and divine!

You take a deep spiritual breath, and you are filled with energy and light... You resume your journey, continuing to ascend the stairway through the Heavenly Tree of Life... You reach the next hyper-luminous world, where you meet Archangel Gabriel... Archangel Gabriel offers you a solid foundation, the best that there is: the gift of Emotional Power and Wisdom, a vigorous, strong, clean and luminous emotional body. You receive the blessing and the energy of Archangel Gabriel... You receive with great love and gratitude... You feel splendid, perfect and divine!

You take a deep spiritual breath, and you are filled with energy and light... You resume your journey, continuing to ascend the stairway through the Heavenly Tree of Life... You reach the next hyper-luminous world, where you meet Archangel Haniel... Archangel Haniel offers you the gift of Victory, his energy and blessing. You feel you have fulfilled your dreams, reached your goals and purpose. You receive with great love and gratitude... You feel splendid, perfect and divine!

You take a deep spiritual breath, and you are filled with energy and light... You resume your journey, continuing to ascend the stairway through the Heavenly Tree of Life... You reach the next hyper-luminous world, where you meet Archangel Michael... Archangel Michael offers you the gift of Glory, of Splendour and Pure Power. You receive Michael's energy and blessing. You receive with great love and gratitude... You feel splendid, perfect and divine!

You take a deep spiritual breath, and you are filled with energy and light... You resume your journey, continuing to ascend the stairway through the Heavenly Tree of Life... You reach the next hyper-luminous world, where you meet Archangel Raphael... Archangel Raphael offers you the gift of Beauty and Healing. You receive Raphael's energy and blessing. You receive with great love and gratitude... You feel splendid, perfect and divine!

You take a deep spiritual breath and you are filled with energy and light... You resume your journey, continuing to ascend the stairway through the Heavenly Tree of Life... You reach the next hyper-luminous world, where you meet Archangel Chamuel... Chamuel offers you the gift of Dominion and Strength. You receive Chamuel's energy and blessing. You receive with great love and gratitude... You feel splendid, perfect and divine!

You take a deep spiritual breath, and you are filled with energy and light... You resume your journey, continuing to ascend the stairway through the Heavenly Tree of Life... You reach higher, the next hyper-luminous world, where you meet Archangel Zadkiel... He offers you the gift, the blessing, the energy of Love and Compassion. You receive Zadkiel's energy and blessing. You receive, you experience and you feel splendid, perfect and divine!

You take a deep spiritual breath, and you are filled with energy and light... You resume your journey, continuing to ascend the stairway through the Heavenly Tree of Life... You reach even higher, and you ascend to the next hyper-luminous world, where you meet Archangel Tzaphkiel... Tzaphkiel offers you the gift of Understanding. You receive Tzaphkiel's gift, his energy and blessing. You receive with great love and gratitude... All is splendid, perfect and divine!

You take a deep spiritual breath, and you are filled with energy and light... You resume your journey, continuing to ascend the stairway through the Heavenly Tree of Life... You keep on reaching higher, and you ascend to the next hyper-luminous world, where you meet Archangel Raziel... Raziel offers you the gift of Wisdom. You receive Raziel's gift, his energy and blessing. You receive with great love and gratitude... All is splendid, perfect and divine!

You take a deep spiritual breath, and you are filled with energy and light... You resume your journey, continuing to ascend the stairway through the Heavenly Tree of Life... You now reach to the highest, the supreme hyper-luminous world... There, on top of The Tree of Life, you meet Archangel Metatron... Metatron offers you the gift of the Crown, of the Principle, of the Source. Metatron offers you his energy and blessing: superconsciousness, enlightenment, completion, oneness, wholeness, divinity, the infinite, the absolute, the eternal, the transcended. You receive and experience with love and gratitude... With Divine love and Divine gratitude... Splendid, perfect and divine!

You experience Divinity, Wholeness, Unity, Joy, Completion, Bliss, Ecstasy, Illumination, Splendour, Power, Awareness, Freedom, Love and Gratitude on all levels of your beingness, on the entire Celestial Tree, the Sacred and Divine Tree.

Stay in this state as much as you wish.

After a while, see and feel yourself descending the celestial stairway through the Celestial Tree of Life. You return, coming back fully. You are grounding. Feel yourself being fully grounded. You have received all the gifts, the energy and the power of the Tree of Life and its Archangels. You have unlocked all its Divine Potential and Qualities, all your Divine Potential and Abilities! The map is now in your hands, the path is open, the tree is alive and sacred, the fruits of the tree are supreme and golden. Have a good journey, and have a good return! With Love, from Love, to Love.

What do we mean when we say, "God is Love"?

The existence and the entire reality is made up of energy, light and vibrations. It is an essence (spirit) of various frequencies manifested in different forms. All Reality (all and everything) is comprised of this essence, and therefore it is One. All is one, and the one is in all, and it is all. The Divinity, the Divine created everything and permeates everything and is everything. More than that, the Divine, God, transcends everything that exists. It transcends all worlds and the whole of creation: God is the Absolute Ultimate Reality behind, above and beyond everything. So all is within God, and everything has a divine essence and source. All is divine.

If we could perceive this Divine Aspect of Reality of all and of everything, we would see and experience Light, Infinite Light. It would be as if we were on the sun with our physical body, and we would see the dazzling radiant Light emerging, emanating, exploding, expanding, radiating in all directions with tremendous intensity, force and brilliance.

If we could feel this Divine Aspect of Reality, of all and of everything, we would feel and experience Love, Infinite Love. Imagine and remember the strongest moments of Love in your life, the ultimate absolute love you have experienced. Multiply this feeling by 1,000,000 or by infinity! This is the essence, the Divinity of the World! This is the Divine Love! And this is what "God is Love" means!

Love is the top feeling of upliftment, safety, completeness, wholeness, joy, bliss, happiness and freedom that people experience in their minds, hearts, souls and bodies. (Even our cells experience love and rejoice in it.) As the top feeling and experience of happiness, Love is the closest concept, the closest state, the closest experience to the Supreme, the Absolute, the Perfect, the Whole, the Infinite, the Real, the Divine.

The sum of all man's actions, endeavors, and deeds aims at receiving and experiencing happiness, completeness, acceptance, fulfilment, wholeness; feeling protection, safety, harmony; experiencing creativity, joy, self-actualization; feeling love, experiencing love. The Love of God (of Life, of Existence, of the Supreme, of All-That-Is), the Love of the Self, the Love of Others. And Love contains and is manifested as acceptance, grace, care, support, appreciation, acknowledgment, communication, sharing and mutuality. Those are things that all people wish and need to experience.

Through the highest love we experience Oneness, Fulfilment, Completeness, Happiness, Bliss – different names for the Spirit, what we call the "Divine." Love (in its highest form) is the mirror and the experience of the Divine. The experience of the Divine – through meditations, higher energy techniques, initiations, attunements, prayer and invocations – is an experience of absolute transcendence and supercosnciousness, of absolute fulfilment and completeness, as well as of absolute love. It is a blissful unity and a unified bliss! The experience of the Divine is Love in its purest, highest, most profound and intense form.

It may seem a paradox, but even all negative actions, endeavours and expressions of humanity still aim at experiencing love. Even war, violence, hate, conflict, control, greed, possessiveness and rivalry are vicious circles of people's efforts to gain and experience Love (and all that love is – safety, joy, fulfillment, completion, bliss). Those efforts are unintelligent, unconscious and doomed to fail. The truth is that Love and its infinite attraction is always behind everything.

Love, this highest feeling of happiness, fulfilment and oneness that each person needs, desires and tries in so many ways to experience, is Divine and the Divine. God is Love.

A Question for Thought, Meditation, and Further Study

Do you love? Do you love to love? Do you love Love? How much do you love it? Loving is the energy, the motion and the action; love is the result, the state, the final experience. If you love boundlessly, infinitely, and absolutely, then the love you experience is boundless, infinite, and absolute. This happens because the energy, the motion and the action defines what you experience, the "final result." The one emanates from the other and the one defines the other, as they are both aspects (action and state, energy and essence) of Love. How much and how you Love shows the Love you experience.

How is it possible that "God" – the highest absolute reality – is also Love, Happiness, Wholeness and Bliss as it is mentioned in several writings and meditations? Is it possible that God corresponds to a human feeling or state?

When we speak of Love, Joy, Happiness, Bliss and Completeness using spiritual terms, we refer to states of the soul and existential states rather than emotions. We refer to states existing in higher dimensions in the form of their pure divine vibrations, more superior, complete, profound, intense, true and substantial than feelings. Feelings are influenced and depend upon various factors and circumstances, and they usually alternate with great frequency.

God, All-That-Is and Reality (the highest, the absolute Reality) are not even those higher states of the soul – the Divine is so much more than that. But through these states of higher consciousness, euphoria and oneness, human beings experience the Supreme, the Spirit, the Divine. We as human consciousnesses have the chance to experience the higher, the ultimate and the absolute Reality. When we attune to the essence of existence, to the Divine, we experience Love, Joy, Wisdom, Bliss, Power, Serenity, Harmony, Freedom, Happiness and Completeness. And vice versa, when we experience these superior states of consciousness, we experience the Divine, the spiritual and the essence of the existence! This is the experience of the Divine, and the experience of the Divine is this.

MEDITATION

Divine Love

Bring into your mind the concept of "Divine Love." Open your heart...

Divine Love... What is it...? Is it real...? Where is it...? Can a person feel and experience Divine Love...? How...?

In another dimension of the infinite reality, in a higher and greater reality than the one you experience on earth, all is energy, light and love. You are energy, light and love: Divine Energy, Divine Light, Divine Love – Divine, meaning supreme and sublime, ultimate and whole, absolute and perfect, transuniversal and panuniversal, transdimensional and pandimensional.

Begin to resonate and vibrate with this higher level of reality. Feel yourself elevating...

You elevate, resonate, vibrate, exist in this higher and greater plane of reality... You perceive, feel, see, breathe, experience...

You elevate, resonate, vibrate, exist within Light and Love. Divine Light and Divine Love... You perceive, feel, see, breathe, experience... Divine Light, Divine Love...

Mentally, ask this energy, this light and love to flow through every part of your physical body.

Let light and love permeate you, fill you and overflow you. Let every cell of your body become fully illuminated and loved. Ask this energy, light and love to flow through every part of your life. Let light and love permeate, fill and overflow your life. Let your life become fully illuminated and loved.

Take ten deep, conscious and slow breaths.

Inhale love, exhale love...

Repeat...

Breathe in love, breathe out love...

With your intention and will...

Breathe in love, breathe out love...

With your imagination and visualization...

Breathe in love, breathe out love...

With your aura and your luminous body...

Breathe in love, breathe out love...

With your mind and your spirit...

Breathe in love, breathe out love...

With your heart and your soul...

Breathe in love, breathe out love...

With your Higher Self and your Guardian Angel...

Breathe in love, breathe out love...

With the divine flame, the divine within you...

Breathe in love, breathe out love...

In all dimensions and levels of existence...

Breathe in love, breathe out love...

Envision, see and feel an exquisite celestial pink/fuchsia flame of pure light burning in your chest, in the most sacred spot... Divine Love... of supreme divine vibration, of supreme divine quality, of supreme divine essence, of supreme divine origin and purpose... You see and you feel it.

And now, visualize, see and feel an exquisite celestial pink/fuchsia sphere of light surrounding you... Divine Love... of supreme divine vibration, of supreme divine quality, of supreme divine essence, of supreme divine origin and purpose... You see and you feel it.

You emit, radiate and transmit love... love to all your loved ones and to all human beings...

You become Love... love to all beings, love to the whole earth, love to the whole universe...

Love to all aspects of yourself, love to your entire life...

You become Love, and you are Love...

Call upon the Highest Angel of Love, of Divine Love...

Feel the Divine Presence...

A ray of radiant golden light coming from the Divine Presence reaches your chest, the sacred center of your beingness...

The golden light energy of the Divine Presence enfolds you, swirling around you...

You are being initiated... You are being attuned to... Divine Love, Love of the Divine Dimension... You accept, and you receive... Divine Love, Love of Divine Essence...

All is Love and Love is All.

You experience freedom, happiness, wholeness and bliss that expand to infinity...

Take a few more deep, substantial and spiritual breaths.

Stay in this blissful state, take your time and assimilate your experience. Keep this consciousness. Open your eyes. You experience and manifest your better, higher, purer, cleaner, more luminous and loving, more conscious and spiritual self!

Ground yourself, drink water and rest. Do the things you like. Keep your heart light and your mind clear. Radiate, express and spread love and blessings all around you. Spiritually and consciously, choose thoughts, feelings, words and actions of love, of Divine Love.

Who are the Solar Archangels?

The sun is the spiritual center of our solar system, the core and the source of life and of all energy, the center and source of fire and light. The heat, the light and the positive vital energy of the sun are essential for any life. The element of fire is the highest good given to all living beings on earth. It provides life, vitality, and liveliness on all levels. It is the highest element of life; it is life itself! More than this, fire is Spirit's greatest gift to earth, as its increasing use fueled the evolution of intelligence, consciousness and the creation of human civilization. The control of fire and heat by humankind gave human beings protection, helped them survive and develop beyond any expectation, and helped them advance on all levels. It is not coincidental that the sun was glorified and worshiped as a god in many civilizations and traditions all over the world and throughout the ages.

Solar Archangels are the highest angels of light that "reside" in the sun. They represent the sun in terms of energy, spirit and consciousness and express the sun's qualities and power. The Solar Archangels reside in a higher and broader spectrum of Reality (the sixth dimension known as the dimension of spirit). The sun symbolizes the Divine Source, the Divine Wisdom, the Divine Love and the Divine Power on a physical, material and universal level. The sun consciousness is also called Christ Consciousness: the consciousness of the highest wisdom, infinite love and Divinity. It is the ultimate absolute consciousness, the Divine Superconsciousness that all human beings journey toward.

Solar Archangels are angelic beings of a very high energy and vibration (solar vibration). They are emanations of the Christ/Solar Consciousness. The Solar Archangels guide and energize us toward the "solarization" of our earth, in other words, the spiritualization of our matter and the "divinization" of our "humanness."

Human beings cannot grasp or imagine how wonderful it is for a spiritual consciousness to be, to reside in the Sun! Yet the following meditation will give a first solar taste!

MEDITATION

Attunement to the Solar Archangel

This is a powerful meditation of resonance and connection to the Solar Consciousness and the Solar Archangel. It is a meditation of higher consciousness and energy, offering total upliftment, ecstasy and spiritual expansion. Because it is a long, complete, powerful and special meditation, the day that you practice it, don't practice other meditations, techniques or exercises. Make sure to rest after the completion of this meditation.

Light up a white candle and dedicate it to the Light, the Fire, the Energy and Power of the Sun; to the Archangelic Superconsciousnesses of the Sun and its Supreme Angels.

Attention: the candles always have to be away from flammable objects, and do not leave the candles unattended.

Sit comfortably, and gently close your eyes. Notice the twinkling light behind your closed eyelids.

Take some slow, deep and steady breaths. Breathe in through the nose and breathe out through the mouth, slow and gradually, without haste. Take ten deep breaths.

Ask your body to relax, to become tranquil... Ask your mind to relax, to become tranquil... Your body and mind let go of the tension... Your body and mind become peaceful... You experience a wonderful state of harmony and serenity... You let yourself into serenity... All becomes peaceful, all becomes serene...

Visualize and see your aura, your energy, the light and the power you emit and you are. Visualize your aura awakening, coming to life, becoming stronger and stronger... A bright, sweet white-azure-colored light pours out of the sky like divine nectar. The light illuminates you more than ever... Light, more light... Your aura is shining... Soak in this bright celestial light... Enjoy the flow of this sweet white-azure light...

Divine nectar! It is an exquisite state, and you experience sublime moments...!

You receive perfect protection and guidance, high spiritual protection and high spiritual guidance. You feel and you experience greater liberation and freedom, more and more lightness, illumination, lucidity, insight and clarity. You are arising and elevating...

You are elevating and you are being transferred to a higher dimension... With your consciousness, you are traveling in a higher level, in a higher plane of existence, a higher plane of consciousness and awareness, freedom and completeness... Illumination... You are liberated, elevated, uplifted... You arise higher and higher... And you reach...

...There... In that very high dimension, in that very high plane there is a Sun, a Spiritual, Cosmic, Supreme Sun... You are there... You are Here... All Light...

...All Light... See and feel yourself entering the Sun... You enter the Sun energetically and spiritually, with your entire beingness... All Light... A superluminous, hyperluminous, fiery Sun. A thousand times bigger than what you see, feel or perceive... A thousand times bigger, a thousand times brighter, a thousand times fierier... All Light...

You are entering Sun, this amazing, transcendent, fiery sphere of divine fire and creative golden light...

And then... You truly feel it! You see it! Clearly, without a doubt. It is all around you and you are truly there, in the Divine Fiery Golden Light! All Light... Ecstasy, ecstasy of Light...

All Light... You breathe with your entire beingness, and gradually you feel more at ease... You perceive... You perceive, see, hear. You move, you can walk, you can fly using your thought and intention. You float. Your senses become acute and heightened. You are able to experience what is happening, what exists in a broader spectrum...

All Light... You are inside the Divine Fiery Golden Sun! Enjoy this ecstatic transcendence, meditate and let go: experience, receive and enjoy the Light. The Divine Fire, the Power of Spirit burns any negative element. The Divine Light, the Energy of Life is healing you profoundly; it revitalizes and awakens your soul and spirit. You are also light, you are also a flame, a sacred golden flame, within the Supreme Spiritual Sun, within the Divine...

All Light... You let go, you meditate... You perceive, you experience... Infinite Light, Infinite Love, Infinite Wisdom, Infinite Power, Infinite Life, Infinite Energy, Infinite Potential, Infinite Infiniteness... a state of absolute bliss, moments of absolute bliss...!

See... Inside the Light, inside the Sun... An angel of light... The angel of light is approaching you; he is surrounding you with his golden aura and his dazzling warm love... Your mind and your heart open, bloom, rejoice and sing.... The angel is a Solar Archangel of the greatest wisdom and love, of golden wisdom and love, of fiery wisdom and love, of solar wisdom and love, of cosmic wisdom and love. He is coming closer to you... Welcome, feel and experience the energy and vibration of the Solar Archangel. The Solar Archangel emits incredible vibrations, waves of ecstasy and nirvanic energies... It is the most profound experience you have ever had...

Waves, golden waves... A golden wave of light coming from the Solar Archangel permeates you and cleanses you deeply... Waves, golden waves... Another golden wave of light... and another one... The waves permeate you, one by one, cleansing you deeply... Cleansing you more intensely, more profoundly, more substantially and truly than ever before... It is a profound change, restoration, and catharsis...

You surrender to the infinite beauty and ecstasy of the golden waves... It is the most beautiful and ecstatic experience you have ever had... Your energy, your body, your chemistry transform... They become spiritualized, angelized, divinized... Total dominion of bliss and light...

Within your heart and soul, you feel, recognize and experience the absolute purity, wholeness and perfection of the Divine, of the Transcendental and Infinite...

Within your mind and spirit, you feel, recognize and experience the absolute purity, wholeness and perfection of the Divine, of the Transcendental and Infinite...

Within your body and cells, you feel, recognize and experience the absolute purity, wholeness and perfection of the Divine, of the Transcendental and Infinite...

The Solar Archangel of the highest fiery wisdom and love embraces, permeates and infuses you. He illuminates your entire existence.

Flow of Divine, fiery, golden wisdom, love and power...

Flow of divinity, transcendence and "infiniteness"...

Feel the outpouring of completeness and joy. You emit completeness, wholeness and joy as the infinite flows within you, as the transcendental flows within you, as the divine flows within you. The infinite, the transcendent, the Divine is you, and you are it. You were, you are and you will be it...! A cosmic recognition, primal and existential... A cosmic unification, primal and existential... Simply, truly, totally: A Divine recognition, a Divine unification!

Stay in the Cosmic-Spiritual Sun, in the infinite fiery golden light, and take ten deep breaths. Breathe in and out with your entire beingness. You are grateful and thankful... You receive and emit love, wisdom, power, gratitude... From all existence, to all existence. What great compassion, respect, humbleness, sacredness, awe and wonder emanate from this state.... And how effortlessly, freely, abundantly and naturally. What a Divine alignment, what a Divine communication, what a Divine sharing that was and is...! What a Divine Experience!

You received and keep receiving all the good things of the world. The world is full of good! You experienced and emitted all the good. You are full of good!

You are a golden cell of happiness on the Cosmic, Transcendental Body, the Divine Body... A golden cell of happiness!

Gently move your body. Take your time and slowly ground yourself. Assimilate the energy, the change, the good. It is a splendid state, a magnificent and amazing moment of true blessing!

Spread your consciousness throughout your body. Spread the energy, the light, the awareness, the power, the intelligence. Spread your beingness. Spread yourself within your body.... You are inside your body again. You are your body! Your body is a part of you! How easily you arise and travel. How effortlessly you expand and experience. How naturally you change forms! How easily you return and ground yourself and all energies!

Thank the Spiritual Sun and the Solar Archangel for this existential, transcendental and Divine experience! The experience of the Existence, of the Transcendental and of the Divine.

Solar Love to all. Solar Love to everything!

ESOTERIC PRACTICE

Connecting with the Consciousness
and Wholeness of the Sun

Whenever you look at the sun and soak in its warm vital light, connect with and attune to its essence on a spiritual level, connect and attune to the Solar Consciousness, and through it connect to the existential, cosmic and highest consciousness, the Divine Consciousness. Bring into your mind, mentally recognize and greet the Angels of the Sun, the supreme Archangels of fire and light (physical and spiritual) that reside in the Sun! Talk to them, communicate, connect, call upon and love them with all your heart and being, with the fire and the light that you have within. You also have a flame within you; you are also a solar part! Consciously connecting on a spiritual and energetic level to the Sun is connecting to the Source of Life, the Divine Source (in its material correspondence), as well as connecting to yourself!

A Question for Thought, Meditation, and Further Study

Do you know that your higher self is for your earthly self what the sun is for the earth? It is a sun over your earth, over your matter, over your body. Meditate upon this, visualize and feel it! It is the conscious, energetic alignment with your higher spiritual side! Bring it into your mind whenever you can and meditate upon it.

How can I be sure if a "spiritual truth" is indeed true?

Ask your heart; it knows. How do you feel when you read or hear something? Excitement, joy, awe, upliftment, release, expansion? Or fear, insecurity, tension, misery, contraction? Most probably when you read something "true" you form a positive impression. Notice how you experience this particular truth. Do you experience it...? In any case, keep as truth what speaks directly to your heart, mind and entire being and what you personally experience.

At the same time, keep your mind and your heart open, as all truths are relative; there is always a superior truth than the current familiar and acceptable truth! The only exception to this principle is the highest/absolute/ultimate truth, what we call God, the Divine, the Divine Beingness, the Absolute Reality. Whether human beings can experience this absolute truth, the Divine, while being in a material form here on earth, and in what way, it is again something relevant! In any case, the effort to reach it is worth more than anything else and more than all other things combined!

A Question for Thought, Meditation, and Further Study

How will you know if a spiritual truth is indeed true? If others validate/confirm it? If society, education, religion, tradition, history tell you so? If your family, a friend or a person of trust tells you? If you read it in a scientific magazine or hear it in the news? Would you believe a truth that you have experienced personally? What proof would be enough for you?

ESOTERIC PRACTICE

Superconsciousness

There are multiple levels of higher consciousness and many stages of superconsciousness. Consciousness ranges from the higher insight and awareness, the angelic and archangelic consciousness, to the universal, cosmic, existential and total, supreme, absolute, Divine Consciousness. This is consciousness, in other words perception, awareness and experience, expanding into higher dimensions and a greater spectrum of Reality, with more light (the spiritual essence of everything) clarity, wisdom, and truth.

Ask the angels to raise your consciousness beyond the familiar perception and flow. To raise it higher than everyday reality, higher than matter and what is apparent, ask to enter the state of Superconsciousness, which is a greater, higher, more expanded, total and multidimensional state of perception and awareness. Can you reach this state of perception? Can you reach this state of awareness? What is it like?

MEDITATION

Divine Meditations, Meditations of Transcendental Reality

The meditations given below are of very high energy, vibration and consciousness. They are Superconsciousness meditations. They offer insight of the Divine essence and the Divine nature of Reality, the "infiniteness," the transcendence, the absolute perfection and its absolute oneness. These Divine meditations give insight to the superior potential and possibilities we can experience as the infinite spirits and eternal souls that we actually are, so we can experience true illumination.

Instructions: Dedicate a day to each one of the meditations given below. Read the text slowly and with awareness at least three times. Experience and feel all the states and energies the meditation describes. Enjoy it fully and give yourself time to experience.

The All

Close your eyes and take some deep breaths.

Feel you are one with the infinite and pure love, wisdom and power within you. Feel you are one with the Divine Source and the angels of light. Feel you are your higher self, your essence and your soul, your true spiritual self. You Are Becoming and You Are: pure and crystal – clear existence, bright and luminous existence, intelligent and wise existence, conscious and superconscious existence...

Imagine you are expanding, growing... extending to the infinite, growing infinitely... Expanding... Gradually you become the Universe, the World, the Existence, the Pure Beingness. Gradually... The Divine All, the Divine One... You become one with the All, one with the One, one with the Source, one with the First Principle. You think about it, you see and you feel it... Slowly and gradually. You grow, you expand, you resonate and unite. You become and you are... Supreme, eternal, infinite, perfect existence. All and everything. The great, the total, the highest reality. The All and the One.

Stay in this state of being, this thought, this perception and experience.

Take some more deep breaths, and when you are ready, open your eyes.

The Highest Dimension

Close your eyes and take some deep breaths.

Feel you are one with the infinite and pure love, wisdom and power within you. Feel you are one with the Divine Source and the angels of light. Feel you are your higher self, your essence and your soul, your true spiritual self. You Are Becoming and You Are: pure and crystal – clear existence, bright and luminous existence, intelligent and wise existence, conscious and superconscious existence...

Imagine, see and feel that you are travelling in higher dimensions... You are travelling, arising... Ascending, passing through various levels, you are rising higher and higher... Gradually you reach a very high dimension of light, a dimension of Spirit... And from there, you continue to rise to an even higher dimension. To the highest of all dimensions. Supreme light, supreme energy, supreme consciousness. You reach the top... The Divine Reality, the Divine Dimension embracing, permeating and creating everything. The Dimension that Is everything. The Highest and Supreme Dimension.

Once more: slowly and gradually you rise higher and you ascend the levels of energy, light, and spirit, the levels of consciousness... You are aligned and united... You become and you are... The Apex, the Highest Dimension, the Divine One...

Stay in this state of being, this thought, this perception and experience.

Take some more deep breaths, and when you are ready, open your eyes.

In The Beginning

In the Beginning... The Beginning...

Can you remember the Beginning...?

How was it in the Beginning? Who/What were you? Where were you?

Bring your attention to that memory... Try to remember the beginning of your existence... Were you energy, essence, soul? Were you an entity, a monad, a beingness? Were you a divine being, a divine state, a divine child? A divine parent? A divine creation? Were you close to the Divine Creator, the Creative Force? Were you one with it? Were you the beginning or what followed after? Try to remember the very first, the primal beginning of your existence, of your being... Before everything....

It is possible! You are able to remember! Remember, remember the beginning... Where were you?... What were you?...

In the Beginning. The Divinely Primal Beginning, the Divinely Divine Beginning.

"Where was I, who was I, what was I in the Beginning...?"

In the Absolute Center

Bring your awareness to your chest. Focus your attention there. Slowly imagine, see and feel you are traveling toward your core... You are traveling toward your center, the absolute center of your existence and of yourself. Your absolute and perfect core... You are traveling... You're getting closer and closer... And you are there...! In your Center! It is the most perfect spot in the whole wide world! A place of ultimate serenity and harmony! From there, you can activate all the Wisdom, Love and Power of your Self... And you are activating it!

Stay in the center of your Self.

Take some more deep breaths, and when you are ready, open your eyes.

The Zero, the One and the Infinite

The One, the Infinite and the Zero are all concepts linked to the Divine, the Supreme and Ultimate Reality.

Zero, as a circle, contains all the possibilities and potential; it is the womb of creation. It is the void and the fullness, the absence and the presence. Everything that exists, wholeness, and everything before it.

One is the unity of existence. Everything emanates from one. One is everything, and it is contained in everything. Everything is contained in one, and everything is one! There is no place where one is not present. One is all that exists.

The infinite is the true nature of the great reality, as the spirit, the energy, the light, the love and the Divine are infinite. Just like numbers. Just like thoughts. Just like phenomena. Just like possibilities and probabilities. As below, so above: The immaterial, the spiritual, the Divine are all infinite.

Meditate upon the zero, the one and the infinite. These high mental concepts (great achievements of human consciousness!) connect to the spiritual essence and nature of existence, to the Transcendental and the Divine.

Bring these concepts to your mind and feel their energy. Stay in each one of them and experience it.
Zero.

Infinite.

One.

ESOTERIC PRACTICE

Highest & Divine Attunements

The powerful practices/techniques given below are initiations of a very high energy, consciousness and superconsciousness. They are divine attunements with the highest celestial orders, such as the Seraphim (Divine Love) and the Cherubim (Divine Wisdom), and also higher spiritual entities such as the Elohim (Highest Angels Creators) and the Shekhinah (the Divine Source, the Source of Life, the Female Aspect of the Divine All). These four divine attunements have a similar form and expression. They attune us to various aspects of the Divine, the All, the One, to the infinite, ultimate and absolute dimension and reality.

Each initiation offers boundless light and the most pure and powerful spiritual empowerment that illuminates and permeates all levels of our being. It is a huge step in our personal evolution, as it raises our energy to a much higher frequency of vibration and infuses us with supreme light. It is a great blessing that brings only good, a great gift that empowers the good and leads us to it. Similarly to the previous advanced meditations of superconsciousness, each divine attunement gives an experience of true illumination!

Instructions: Practice one attunement each day. Read the text slowly and with awareness at least three times. Experience and feel all the states and energies it describes. Enjoy it fully and give yourself time to experience each attunement.

Begin the first day by doing the attunement to the Seraphim, the second day attune to the Cherubim, the third day to the Elohim and the fourth day to the Shekhinah. Repeat the attunements whenever you wish, intuitively, or repeat them every few months or once a year. It is possibly the greatest angelic and spiritual attunement a human being can experience!

Seraphim: Attunement to Divine Love

The Seraphim are Supreme Divine Consciousnesses and Flames expressing, manifesting and emitting the Highest Love, the Divine Love – Eternal, Absolute and Unlimited Love.

To align with the Seraphim and to increase (become conscious of) the spiritual love within you, begin by taking some deep breaths, and relax.

Envision, see and feel a Golden Divine Flame coming to life within you. Observe it. It is the energy of your spirit, of your higher beingness and of your soul. It is your higher consciousness. It emits its sweet, warm, wonderful and magnificent light...

Open your heart and your beingness. Become fully receptive. Ask to be attuned to the Seraphim at the highest level possible. Ask to connect with the Highest, Divine Love at the highest level attainable. Ask the Seraphim to surround you, permeate, infuse and fill you with their loving energy. Ask the Divine Love itself to permeate, infuse and fill you, to illuminate you fully and completely, to illuminate you from Alpha to Omega.

Envision, see and feel your beingness, your existence within the Transcendental Red Flame – Ray of the Seraphim and of the Divine Love. You are One. All One. One. Experience the oneness, experience the power, experience the energy of Seraphim and of Divine Love.

Take some more slow, full, deep breaths.

Stay for a while in this supreme Divine energy, in this supreme Divine experience.

When you are ready, return to the here and now.

Cherubim: Attunement to Divine Wisdom

Cherubim follow Seraphim in the celestial hierarchy and are also supreme angels of spirit. Cherubim express, manifest and emit the Divine Wisdom, the Highest, Infinite, Eternal, Absolute Wisdom.

To attune to the Cherubim and increase (become conscious of) the spiritual wisdom within you, begin by taking some deep breaths and relaxing.

Envision, see and feel the Golden Divine Flame coming to life within you. Observe it. It is the energy of your spirit, of your higher beingness and of your soul. It is your higher consciousness. It emits its sweet, warm, wonderful and magnificent light...

Open your heart and your beingness; become fully receptive. Ask to be attuned to the Cherubim at the highest level possible. Ask to connect with the Highest, Divine Wisdom at the highest level attainable. Ask the Cherubim to surround, permeate, infuse and fill you with their loving energy. Ask the Divine Wisdom itself to permeate, infuse and fill you, to illuminate you fully and completely, to illuminate you from Alpha to Omega.

Envision, see and feel your beingness, your existence within the Transcendental Blue Flame – the Ray of the Seraphim and Divine Wisdom. You are One. All One. One. Experience the oneness, experience the power, experience the energy of Cherubim and Divine Wisdom.

Take some more slow, full, deep breaths.

Stay for a while in this supreme Divine energy, in this supreme Divine experience.

When you are ready, return to the here and now.

Elohim: Attunement to the Divine Creative Force

Together with the Seraphim and the Cherubim, Elohim are viewed by esoteric traditions as supreme angel creators helping God to build worlds, the Majestic Creation. Elohim are considered to have Absolute Divine Consciousness.

To attune to the Elohim and increase (become conscious of) the creative wisdom, will and power within you, begin by taking some deep breaths and relaxing.

Envision, see and feel the Golden Divine Flame coming to life within you. Observe it. It is the energy of your spirit, your higher beingness and your soul. It is your higher consciousness. It emits its sweet, warm, wonderful and magnificent light...

Open your heart and your beingness; become fully receptive. Ask to be attuned to the Elohim at the highest level possible. Ask to connect with the Highest, Divine Wisdom at the highest level attainable. Ask the Elohim to surround you, permeate, infuse and fill you with their loving energy. Ask the Divine Creativity itself to permeate, infuse and fill you, to illuminate you fully and completely, to illuminate you from Alpha to Omega.

Envision, see and feel your beingness, your existence within the Transcendental Flame – the Ray of the Elohim and of Divine Creativity and Will, the Ray of all colors of Creation. You are One. All One. One. Experience the oneness, experience the power, experience the energy of Elohim and of Divine Creativity and Will.

Take some more slow, full, deep breaths.

Stay for a while in this supreme Divine energy, in this supreme Divine experience.

When you are ready, return to the here and now.

Shekhinah: Attunement to the Source of Life

According to esoteric and mystical traditions and sources, Shekhinah is the Mother of Angels who provides energy and light to the entire angelic kingdom, to the entire spiritual plane and all other planes. It is the Source of Life itself, the Source of Life for all beings. It is considered the female aspect of Existence and of the Divine, the aspect that is full of love, compassion, care and affection.

To attune to the Shekhinah, begin by taking some deep breaths and relaxing.

Envision, see and feel within you a Golden Divine Flame lighting up and coming to life. Observe it. It is the energy of your spirit, of your higher beingness and your soul. It is your higher consciousness. It emits its sweet, warm, wonderful, and magnificent light...

Open your heart and your beingness; become fully receptive. Ask to be attuned to the Shekhinah at the highest level possible. Ask to connect with the Highest, Divine Source at the highest level attainable. Ask Shekhinah to surround, permeate, infuse and fill you with her loving energy. Ask the Divine Source itself to permeate, infuse and fill you, to illuminate you fully and completely, to illuminate you from Alpha to Omega.

Envision, see and feel your beingness, your existence within the transcendental Flame – the Ray of Shekhinah, of the Divine Source, of the Source of Life, the Ray in all colors of Life. You are One. All One. One. Experience the oneness, experience the power, experience the energy of Shekhinah, of the Divine Source, of the Source of Life.

Take some more slow, full, deep breaths.

Stay for a while in this supreme Divine energy, in this supreme Divine experience.

When you are ready, return to the here and now.

Epilogue: Eden

The journey has reached its end. You are now in Eden, the celestial Eden of angels, the heavenly Eden of your spirit, your celestial and heavenly Eden. In this level of perception, in this plane of existence, you have the absolute freedom to be anything, whatever you choose to be. In this paradisiac plane, you have absolute freedom to experience love and happiness, wisdom and peace, joy and bliss. Unconditionally... Purely... Boundlessly... Absolutely!

Love Eden, love your Eden. It is your own paradise, your own perfection. It is you in perfect harmony, unity and oneness with perfection. And you do love your Eden, you do love Eden. Eden is in your heart, and your heart is within Eden. It always was and always will be.

Live your life on Earth having the knowledge, power, and love of Eden in your heart. And keep your heart in the love, power, and knowledge of Eden.

When you are back in Eden, I will be there also and all your loved ones as well. We will reminisce, envision, recall and relive: yes, life on earth was a magnificent moment in our eternity, a golden-white ray of our Eden's most luminous sun.

...Perhaps... Perhaps, we already are in Eden having this recollection...?

How immense and unknown, how Divine Reality truly is!

From Eden,

with Love!

Recognition, Remembrance, Revelation

All this time... I was you and you were me!

Now and Always... I Am You and You Are Me!

How infinitesimally small everything is... And how infinitely great!

Appendix

Angelic Hierarchy: The Angelic Order

Heaven is truly infinite. Reality surpasses and transcends any mind and imagination, its nature being infinite. Reality expands into infinity...It is Infinity...Infinitely Infinite, Infinite Infiniteness!

Similarly, there are countless Angels and celestial beings of great energy and light; beings of great Wisdom, great Power, and great Love; of great and of the Greatest, of high and of the Highest; of superior and of the Supreme Love, Power, Wisdom, Consciousness, Light, and Energy.

There are Angels for everything, for every single thing in Existence: Angels for anything immaterial and spiritual, and Angels for all things physical and material. Angels represent, express, manifest, guide, protect, compose, decompose, form, and reform everything that exists—anything spiritual or physical. Angels are one with God, and they are projections, emanations, energetic embodiments, vibratory expressions, and luminous creations of Divinity—that is, of the Whole and Absolute, of the Transcendent and Supreme, and of the Infinite and Eternal Reality, Source, Principle, and Power that is beyond all space, time, and matter, and beyond what is apparent and visible to the human eye or familiar and known to the human mind.

There is a substantial body of esoteric writings describing Angels and Archangels and their special names and qualities. Each Angel or Archangel performs a multiplicity of duties on Earth and throughout the universe. There are different Orders of Angels depending on the various duties, attributes, qualities, energies, or colors they radiate. It is natural that there are different experiences and point of views about Angels among various scholars, writers, mystics, and esoteric traditions, but there are also many similarities. Depending on the source in which Angels are mentioned, an Angel's name may be spelled in different ways, an Angel may have different qualities, or various Angels may be reported as having the same or similar attributes, qualities, and duties.

For example, Archangel Michael may be described as blue or azure flame/energy when Divine Power and Divine Will are perceived, but viewed as red flame/energy when protection, catharsis, and struggle against darkness and evil are at the forefront. Similarly, when Archangel Michael represents the Divine Consciousness, the Logos, and the Highest Wisdom, he is felt and perceived as a golden flame/energy. It must be understood that all the Angels and the Archangels are so much more than what we think, feel, see, or perceive them to be. It would not be wise to consider or anticipate that angelic beings will manifest merely as blue, green, or some other single color. These characteristics capture only aspects of their vast essences. Angels are not smaller, simpler, or less than humans, being truly amazing and magnificently complex multidimensional wonders of supreme divine art!

Angels encompass and contain all aspects, all colors, and all energies. However, we envision them as blue, red, golden, or green to attune ourselves mentally and spiritually to their luminous, divine energies. It is a process helpful for us human beings—a first, small, easy-to-follow, safe, steady, and stable step toward the Infinite!

What follows is a presentation of the Angelic Orders, the Angelic Hierarchy, and the celestial kingdom according to the relevant literature, esoteric teachings, and mystical experiences of great teachers. This presentation is a mere introduction to these wonderful celestial beings. Regular study of this material, and regular practice of relevant meditative and spiritual exercises, will enable you to tap into the Infinite Wisdom and Power of the heavens, discovering your own unique and special path to the Light.

The Angelic Hierarchy

The most universally accepted classification of the ranks of Angels is that of Pseudo-Dionysius the Areopagite, a philosopher of the fifth to sixth centuries AD; it was later adopted by Thomas Aquinas, whose life spanned between 1225–1274 AD. According to this angelic classification, celestial incorporeal spiritual beings are divided into definite Orders, each with different duties and separate frequencies and vibrations of energy. The Angelic Realm is divided into nine distinct Choirs or Orders of Angels within three major groups, known as Heavenly Spheres.

The nine Angelic Choirs or Orders are as follows:
• *Seraphim*
• *Cherubim*
• *Thrones or Ophanim*
• *Dominions*
• *Virtues*
• *Powers or Authorities*
• *Principalities or Rulers*
• *Archangels*
• *Angels*

Each Sphere contains three Orders or Choirs:

• *First Sphere (closest to the Divine): Seraphim, Cherubim, and Thrones or Ophanim*
• *Second Sphere: Dominions, Virtues, and Powers or Authorities*
• *Third Sphere (closest to Earth and humanity): Principalities or Rulers, Archangels, and Angels*

First Sphere:
Seraphim, Cherubim, Thrones

Seraphim

Seraphim comprise the highest Angelic Order and the closest Angels to God, in direct communication with Him. The name Seraphim means "the burning ones" or "the fiery ones." Their essence is of supreme divine fire, light, and love. The Seraphim, or Seraphs, are transcendent spiritual flames of Divine Love, and they are often referred to as "fiery serpents." They are represented by the serpent, symbol of healing. Their name possibly comes from ser (higher being) and rapha (healer).

They surround and protect God's Throne while continuously chanting the Trisagion—"Holy, Holy, Holy" and "Holy, Holy, Holy is the Lord of Hosts, the whole Earth is full of His Glory"—unceasingly praising the Divine. They protect the Divine Planes from evil and lower, negative vibrations. They were created with full knowledge and understanding of the Creator, and they move the heavens, as they emanate from the Divine.

The Seraphim encircle the throne of God and burn eternally with Love for the Creator. They establish and transmit the energy, the vibration, of Love. They are the supreme beings or Powers of Divine Love, as they emit and radiate the fiery light of God's Love to all worlds, all dimensions, all beings, and all the rest of the Angels. They are the Supreme Angels of Love, purifying humanity and inspiring us to perfect the internal flame of love and to move closer to the love of God.

Their transcendental light is so radiant that not even the members of the other Orders can look upon them, not even the Ophanim or the Cherubim; if human beings were to face them, we would be incinerated. However, Seraphim are also of such subtlety that they rarely are perceived by human consciousness; no being (human or angelic) can completely perceive or align with the Seraphim. They are the first and supreme emanation and creation of Divine Love, Power, and Wisdom, and they represent the full Glory, Grandeur, Miracles, and Splendor of the Divine Creative Source of All-That-Is.

According to the Third Book of Enoch (26:9–12), there are only four Seraphim, each one corresponding to the "four winds of the world." The Second Book of Enoch describes Seraphim as having four faces and six wings that correspond to the six days of creation. A Seraph covers its four faces with two of its wings, its feet with two others; with the remaining two wings, it flies. Each wing is the size of Heaven. Usually the Seraphim are depicted with the red color.

According to different texts and sources, the Seraphim Angels include Seraphiel ("Lord of Peace"), Michael, Metatron, Jehoel, Nathanael, and the fallen Angel Lucifer (known as Satan after his fall), who was the only Seraph with twelve wings. It is said that Satan, along with Sammael and Dubbiel, writes down on tablets the sins of humanity and then tells the Seraphim to transfer the tablets to God for humanity to be punished; however, the Seraphim know that God does not will this punishment, so they burn the tablets—symbolically, they purify, heal, and burn all of humanity's sins.

Cherubim

Cherubim comprise the second-highest Angelic Order after the Seraphim. They are the first Angels to be mentioned in the Old Testament (Genesis 3:22) and the ones mentioned most frequently in the Bible—as guardians of Eden and the Tree of Life, bearers of God's throne, or winged creatures of fire. According to Assyrian and Akkadian sources, their name means "fullness of God's knowledge," "one who prays," or "one who intercedes." Dionysius the Areopagite thought the word Cherubim denoted their power to know and behold God.

Cherubim are the Manifestations of Divine Wisdom and Knowledge. They are the keepers of the Knowledge of Heaven and of the Worlds, the voices of Divine Wisdom. They keep the Book of Life, the Akashic Records, which contain the details of all souls in the cosmos. Cherubim Angels manifest and guard Harmony; they are the Angels of stars, sun, and moon; and they act as guardians of stars and light.

Cherubim are depicted as four-winged beings having four faces—usually those of a man, ox, lion, and eagle. Their wings are joined one to another, so they can travel to any direction without having to turn. Their whole bodies and wings are covered with eyes, and they are associated with the color blue. Cherubim are also often depicted as huge, winged creatures with the faces of humans and the bodies of eagles or sphinxes, resembling Egyptian sphinxes. The Bible describes the upper lid (Mercy Seat) on the Ark of the Covenant as being adorned with golden Cherubim whose wings stretched over the Mercy Seat. When Adam and Eve were expelled from the Garden of Eden, God assigned Cherubim and a flaming sword to guard the Garden of Eden and the way to the Tree of Life.

Cherubim are often confused with putti, the baby Angels depicted especially in Renaissance art holding golden trumpets.

Cherubim are considered to be beings of ultimate protection. They guide humanity through the Tree of Life back to the Garden of Eden and the Throne of God (the Divine Source).

Chief Cherubim Angels include Cherubiel, Ophaniel, Zophiel, Raphael, and Gabriel.

Thrones (or Ophanim)

Thrones are also known as Ophanim or Erelim. They stand under God's Throne, hence their name. The Hebrew word Ophanim means "wheels" or "spheres." They have the most unusual appearances of any celestial beings: big fiery wheels with hundreds of eyes. They are Higher and Holy Spirits of Divine Wisdom and Divine Will. They make known the Will of God and manifest His Decisions. They are also Angels of Divine Justice. Their mission is to inspire faith in the power of God and bestow Divine Justice. They manifest Peace, Objectivity, and Humbleness.

Thrones are assigned to guard the planets. Thrones are also closely connected to the Cherubim because they travel together; they are the actual wheels beneath the Merkabah (the chariot-throne of God) driven by the Cherubim. Thrones, along with the Seraphim and Cherubim, never sleep but always guard the throne of God.

Chief Angels of this Order include Oriphiel, Zaphkiel, Zadkiel, and Raziel.

Second Sphere:
Dominions, Virtues, Powers

Dominions

The Dominions get their name from dominatus, the Latin word for "domination," and from a translation of the Greek word kyriotites, meaning "lordships." In Hebrew they are also known as Hashmallim, and it is through them that God's majesty is revealed. They are ministers of God's justice to the cosmos. They manifest spirit in physical form; their purpose is to integrate the spiritual and material worlds. Each Dominion is perceived to be carrying a scepter and a golden rod or the seal of God. They are Divinely Beautiful. They are assigned to teach and oversee the duties and activities of all other Angels and to maintain cosmic order. Dominions preside over Nations, and they rarely appear to human beings. They also govern the natural world and the elements. It is said that Hashmal and Zadkiel are among the Dominions.

Virtues

Virtues are called "the shining ones" because they radiate the most luminous light. They govern the sun, stars, planets, moon, and galaxies to maintain harmony and order in the cosmos. On Earth they oversee the seasons and every facet of natural life. Their purpose is to transfer spiritual energy to the earthly plane and the collective human consciousness. They are the Angels that work great miracles since they are able to surpass the laws of nature. They are Angels of Divine Grace and Divine Mercy; they bestow grace and valor within the human heart. They are closely connected to saints, and they offer them the ability to work healing miracles. The two Angels present at Jesus Christ's Ascension and the ones comforting him before his crucifixion were from the Order of Virtues. Members of the Order of Virtues include Michael, Raphael, Barbiel, Usiel, Peliel, and Haniel.

Powers (Authorities)

Powers have been credited as being the very first Angels created by God. They are guardians of cosmic order and peace, and they constantly fight evil. They have been assigned to record human history and to be present during the births and deaths of all humans. The Powers include the mighty Lords of Karma (Karmic Angels) and the Angels of birth and death. The Karmic Angels keep the collective history of humanity and planet Earth; they also guard and maintain the Akashic Records (database of all souls and their journeys). They constantly protect the world from being taken over by demons and evil. They guard the path to the celestial realms and maintain the border between Heaven and Earth. Powers protect souls from evil; it is believed that when we die, these Angels guide our safe transitions to the celestial realms. They assist each soul to overcome temptations, and they give strength to people. It is said that Samael and Camael belong to the Order of Powers.

Third Sphere:
Principalities, Archangels, Angels

Principalities (Rulers)

Principalities collaborate with Powers in issues of authority and power. Their symbols include the scepter, the cross, and the sword. Principalities are the guardians and protectors of such large groups as nations, countries, cities, towns, and organizations. They have a direct impact on the affairs of humanity, and they inspire ideas. They protect science and art and also have religion and politics under their care. They teach and empower groups and people, they are rulers of time, and they manifest higher divine blessings in the physical world. Members of this Order include Aniel and Camael.

Archangels

Archangels, sometimes referred to as Archangeloi, are Angels of High Order, the most important mediators between humanity and the Divine. The word Archangel means "chief or leading Angel." They are the better-known celestial beings that act on various levels, realms, and dimensions. They carry messages of the Divine to people and carry out the Divine Will. They emit the Infinite Love, Wisdom, and Power of the Divine Creator. They represent, express, and manifest Divine Energies, Aspects, and Qualities, and also the Elements of Nature. Archangels oversee and guide the Angelic Orders, which include countless benevolent and pure celestial beings of Divine Light and Divine Love. They also oversee the Guardian Angels. Archangel Michael, Archangel Gabriel, and Archangel Raphael are the most-known Archangels. They have been the closest to humanity, guiding our multidimensional, spiritual, and earthly paths of advancement to higher states of consciousness, light, love, wisdom, wholeness, and oneness.

Michael and Gabriel are the only Archangels mentioned in the Bible. Raphael is mentioned in the Book of Tobit and Uriel in the apocryphal Book of Enoch. Archangels Michael, Gabriel, and Raphael are venerated in the Roman Catholic Church on September 29 and in the Orthodox Church on November 8.

Islam recognizes the existence of four Archangels: Mikhail (Michael, Angel of Mercy), Jibril, (Gabriel, responsible for revealing the Quran to Muhammad and communicating with the prophets), Israfil (Raphael, responsible for signaling the coming of Judgment Day) and Azrael (Angel of Death, responsible for parting the soul from the human body).

Zoroastrianism (founded in the sixth century BC) was formerly among the most primal and important monotheistic religions (most probably the first monotheistic religion), and possibly the first to mention Angels. It had a profound influence on the three largest monotheistic religions of today: Judaism, Christianity, and Islam. Zoroastrianism passed on several parables, philosophical and moral principles, and other elements to these three large religions, among them the distinction between good and evil and the battle between good and evil. In Zoroastrianism, the Sublime Force is Ahura Mazda, who created six Archangels called the Amesha Spentas (meaning "Bounteous Immortal") that represent aspects of the Divine (the noncreated Creator). Amesha Spentas are Emanations and Divine Sparks of the Creator, Ahura Mazda. Those are perhaps the earliest references to Archangels. In addition, Zoroastrianism mentions Fravashi, the guardian spirits or Guardian Angels that all people have.

There are respective references to Archangels in Eastern religions and philosophies: Buddhist tradition has Devas (celestial beings) and Dharmapalas (Karma protectors), while Hinduism has Devas and Mahadevas.

It is highly intriguing, from a philosophical and metaphysical point of view, that Lucifer—whose name means "light bearer," but who is also known as Satan, which means "the opposer, the adversary" in Hebrew—was initially an Archangel! Lucifer was the most beautiful and luminous Archangel. Then he exalted himself against God and fell from grace. Archangel Michael was the one that led the battle against Lucifer and succeeded in casting him out of Heaven, along with the Angels who had chosen to follow him. This parable has many layers; one can reflect upon the correspondence of this parable to the course of man on Earth and his life in the material world.

The Archangels are countless. The most-known Archangels to be assigned and devoted to humanity include Michael, Gabriel, Raphael, Uriel, Haniel, Jophiel, Zadkiel, Tzaphkiel, Chamuel, Raguel, Raziel, Ariel, Jeremiel, Samael, Azrael, Sandalphon, and Metatron.

Archangel Michael

The most-known Angel of Heaven is Archangel Michael, who is as close as it gets to the Divine and also to humanity. He is the most prominent Angel in Christian, Jewish, and Islamic lore. His name means "who is as God," and he protects and guides all humanity. Archangel Michael is the Power of God (Divine Source and Reality) manifested in form and action. According to Stylianos Atteshlis (known as Daskalos), Michael comes from maha (meaning "great" in Sanskrit) and el (meaning "God" in Sanskrit, Ancient Egyptian, and Hebrew).

Archangel Michael fights and defeats the evil; he is the Light that negates darkness. He is the Archangel of Protection and Purification, of the Divine Guidance and Will. His element is Fire, and usually he is depicted holding a sword. He is considered to be the leader of the Archangels and the Order of Virtues; he is called the prince or lord or commander of the heavenly host, the master of all Angels. Michael is one of the Seven Archangels of the Throne (the highest ranks in the Order of the Archangels) and also the Angel of Presence, Justice, and Mercy. He is the keeper of the Keys of Heaven, ruler of the Fourth Heaven, and, according to various sources, a ruler of the Seventh Heaven as well. Michael's mystical name is Sabbathiel, his ancient Persian name is Beshter, and he is also called the Prince of Light.

Michael is the Chief Warrior fighting Evil and Satan, the Archangel of battle and defender of Heaven. In the War in Heaven, he cast Lucifer (Satan) out of Heaven after defeating him. Michael is referred to as the Angel of Death, for he takes the souls of the dead to the afterlife, leading them to Heaven. Michael taught Adam how to farm and care for his family after being expelled from the Garden of Eden and persuaded God to allow Adam's soul to return to Heaven after he died.

Orthodox Christians refer to him as Taxiarch Archangel Michael, and Roman Catholics as Saint Michael the Archangel. Perhaps Archangel Michael is the highest, most direct, and best-known manifestation of the Divine on Earth.

In the Tree of Life, Archangel Michael presides over Hod, the eighth Sephirah.

Archangel Gabriel

Archangel Gabriel, the second-most-known Angel of Heaven, is second in rank only to Archangel Michael. Gabriel's name means "God is my strength." According to Stylianos Atteshlis, Gabriel (Ka-Vir-El) means "Divine Soul Element" because ka is "soul" in Ancient Egyptian, vir is "element" in Ancient Egyptian, and el is "God" in Sanskrit, Ancient Egyptian, and Hebrew.

Gabriel is the Archangel of the Water Element, of the Soul, of Emotions, of Serenity, of Love, of Joy, and of Divine Grace. He is considered to be the Angel of Sleep and of the Fourth Dimension. He is the Divine Messenger. He is the one who announced to Mary that she would be the mother of Jesus Christ and to Elizabeth that she would be the mother of John the Baptist. He is also the Angel of Annunciation, of Resurrection, of Mercy, and of the Revelation (he will blow the trumpet to signal the Judgment Day). In Judaic lore, Gabriel is believed to be a female Archangel. Gabriel has been accredited as the Angel who instructs the newly incarnating souls to be birthed into the material world. The entirety of his collective roles is quite complex. He is regarded as the Angel of First Heaven and the one who sits on the left hand of God. He is the Angel of Justice and Truth.

Archangel Gabriel presides over Yesod, the ninth Sephirah in the Tree of Life.

Archangel Raphael

Archangel Raphael is one of the highest-ranking Archangels, and he is known as the Angel of Healing. He has in his care the healing of Earth and of humanity. His name means "God heals." According to Stylianos Atteshlis, Raphael (Ra-Fa-El) means "God of the Vital Power and Energy of the Sun" because ra is "sun" in Ancient Egyptian, fa is "vibration and energy" in Ancient Egyptian, and el is "God" in Sanskrit, Ancient Egyptian, and Hebrew.

Raphael is the Archangel of Etheric Vitality, of Life-Force Energy, of Healing, of Medicine, and of all Sciences, and the Angel of the Sun. He is known to be the ruling prince of the Second Heaven and guardian of the Tree of Life in Eden. He is one of the Seven Archangels of the Throne (the highest rank in the Order of the Archangels) and also the Angel of Presence. He is the Archangel connected to the elements of Ether and Air.

Archangel Raphael presides over Tiphareth, the sixth Sephirah in the Tree of Life.

Archangel Uriel

Uriel links humanity to the spiritual realms and to the understanding of the Divine. His name means "Light of God" or "Fire of God," and he is the most radiant of all Angels. According to Stylianos Atteshlis, Uriel (U-Ra-El) means "God of Light and of Earth, of the Material Plane" as the letter U means "space and matter" in Ancient Egyptian, ra means "sun" in Ancient Egyptian, and el means "God" in Sanskrit, Ancient Egyptian, and Hebrew.

Uriel is the Archangel of Balance and Harmony; he keeps in balance all Elements and all Bodies of Man. As the Angel of Repentance, he helps us to understand the universal laws of Karma. He is the Archangel of Manifestation and Grounding, the Great Harmonizer of All. Uriel is the Angel of Mental Clarity and also the Angel of Music, the Heavenly Melodies, and the Music of the Spheres. He is also called Angel of the Sun, Angel of Presence, Angel of Salvation, interpreter of prophecies, Seraph, or Cherub. He is also equated with Phanuel, and he is the guardian of planet Mars.

He is considered to stand at the gate of the Garden of Eden with his flaming sword.

Uriel is connected to the weather elements of thunder and lightning and to the Element of Earth.

Archangel Sandalphon

Archangel Sandalphon is responsible for carrying the prayers of people to the Divine Source. He is said to have been incarnated on Earth as the prophet Elijah and to have become an Archangel after his Ascension to Heaven.

Sandalphon's name may be derived from Greek, meaning "co-brother," a possible reference to his twin brother Archangel Metatron, who was also once incarnated, as the wise scribe Enoch. They are the only two Archangels whose name doesn't end in -el, which means "God" in Sanskrit, Ancient Egyptian, and Hebrew.

Sandalphon is the Archangel of Nature and of Earth, bringing harmony to the nature elements. He is the Archangel of Balance and Harmony; we invoke Sandalphon to help us with grounding and healing of the Earth. He is also associated with music and all forms of music therapy, while being also a patron Angel of Music and Heavenly Song.

Sandalphon is considered to be a Sarim Angel (i.e., an Angelic Prince), Angel of Prayer, Angel of Tears, and Fighter of Evil, similar to Archangel Michael. He is the one responsible for deciding the gender of a baby. He is said to be the tallest of all Angels and ruler of the Seventh Heaven.

Archangel Sandalphon presides over Malkuth, the tenth Sephirah in the Tree of Life.

Archangel Metatron

Archangel Metatron is responsible for recording everything that happens upon Earth, keeping the Akashic Records or Book of Life. His name has various possible etymologies. Metatron is made up of two Greek words, meta and thronos, which combined together mean "the one who stands next to or before the throne of God." He is called Prince of the Divine Face, Angel of Presence, and Chancellor of Heaven. Metatron is the only Archangel (except his brother, Archangel Sandalphon) within the angelic realm who was once human before becoming Archangel. His name doesn't end in -el, which means "God" in Sanskrit, Ancient Egyptian, and Hebrew. On Earth, Metatron was known as Enoch, a prophet and a wise scribe, the seventh patriarch after Adam. Enoch ascended to Heaven and transformed into Archangel Metatron.

Metatron might be the greatest Archangel of all; he is called the King of Angels. He is the Archangel of Enlightenment and Ascension. He has in his care the sustenance of human life and acts as a direct link between the Divine Source and humanity. Metatron receives daily orders from God regarding the souls to be taken that day, and he transmits them to Gabriel and Samael; he is the Supreme Angel of Death. He is the Archangel of Platinum Energy and Ray and Keeper of the Inner and Outer Light of God. Metatron has been credited with such majesty and Power that he is even referred to as Lesser YHWH, that is, the lesser God. He possesses seventy-two other names as well.

Metatron is said to be the tallest Angel in the Angelic Hierarchy and also the youngest one. He resides in the Seventh Heaven, where he records all heavenly and earthly events.

Archangel Metatron presides over Kether, the first Sephirah in the Tree of Life.

Archangel Haniel (Anael, Aniel)

Haniel is the Archangel of Joy. His name means "Grace of God" or "Joy of God." He is one of the chief Angels in charge of the Angelic Order of Principalities, and he takes care of all nations on Earth. Haniel is the Archangel of Grace, of Healing, and of Natural Intuitive and Psychic Abilities. His presence facilitates Emotional Communication and Divine Communication.

Haniel is also said to have escorted the scribe Enoch to the spiritual realm before he became Archangel Metatron. Haniel rules the planet Venus. He is listed as one of the seven Archangels of the Divine Throne. He collaborates on various tasks with Archangel Metatron.

Archangel Haniel presides over Netzach, the seventh Sephirah in the Tree of Life.

Archangel Chamuel (Camael, Khamael, Camiel)

Archangel Chamuel embodies the principle of unconditional pure love. His name means "He who seeks God" or "He who sees God." He is the Archangel of Divine Love and Human Relationships; he works on bringing love to all people. He is considered to be the patron Angel of people going through rough times in relationships and people working for world peace. Chamuel is the chief of the Angelic Order of Powers and one of the Seven Archangels of the Divine Throne. He is said to have comforted Jesus in the garden of Gethsemane on the night before his arrest. He is associated with the planet Mars. Chamuel represents the qualities of Love, Tolerance, and Gratitude. He offers Courage, Patience, and Strength.

Archangel Chamael presides over Geburah, the fifth Sephirah in the Tree of Life.

Archangel Raziel

Archangel Raziel is the Keeper of Universal Secrets and the Angel of Mysteries. His name means "Secrets of God." He is the possessor of all celestial and earthly knowledge. He reveals holy secrets only when the Divine Source allows him to do so.

Raziel stands so close to God that he hears and writes down everything God says, and then he writes God's secret insights about the entire universe. Raziel is credited with writing the Book of Raziel the Angel, a book where in all divine secrets about celestial and earthly knowledge are set down. Raziel gave the book to Adam and Eve after they were expelled from Eden, so they could better understand God and find their way back home to Eden.

According to various teachings, Raziel is the chief Angel of Erelim and an Archangel of metaphysical teachings.

Archangel Raziel presides over Chokmah, the second Sephirah in the Tree of Life.

Archangel Ariel

Archangel Ariel is aligned with the Natural World, Air, Water, Nature Spirits (Elementals), and Animals. His name means "Lion of God." Ariel is associated with cleansing and purifying the Earth; he is often called the Guardian and Lord of the Earth. He oversees the protection and healing of wild and domestic animals and of Earth's elements. He is the Archangel of Environment and Wild Animals, ruler of Earth and its elements.

Ariel, as a Healer Archangel, works with Archangel Raphael in the healing arts, and, as a Protector Archangel, he works with Archangel Michael. Sometimes he is associated with Archangel Uriel.

Archangel Tzaphkiel

Archangel Tzaphkiel is known as the Angel of understanding and compassion. His name has various meanings, such as "Contemplation of God" and "Knowledge of God." Tzaphkiel embodies the feminine aspect of Creation, and he is considered the Archangel of Higher Love and Maternal Love. According to Jewish tradition, he belongs to the Angelic Order of Erelim. Tzaphkiel is called the Watchtower of God because he observes God's Love and passes it along to humanity. He is the Archangel of Divine Contemplation, of Universal Insight and Lucidity, and of Connection to Angelic and Spiritual Realms.

Archangel Tzaphkiel presides over Binah, the third Sephirah in the Tree of Life.

Archangel Zadkiel

Archangel Zadkiel is the Archangel of Mercy, Freedom, Justice, and Forgiveness. His name means "Righteousness of God" and "Justice of God." He embodies the spirit of the Divine Violet Ray (the Seventh Ray), and he is the Archangel of Transmutation, of Benevolence, of Healing, and of Purification.

According to Kabbalah, Zadkiel is one of the two Archangels (the other is Jophiel) who assist and follow directly behind Archangel Michael when he fights evil. Zadkiel is considered to be the unnamed Angel who stopped Abraham from killing his son, Isaac, as a sacrifice to God. He is also an Angel who presides over matters such as prosperity and forgiveness; he is often associated with helping women during pregnancy and birth. He is one of the Seven Archangels of the Divine Throne, and he is chief of the Angelic Order of Dominions (in Jewish tradition equated with the Order of Hashmallim). Zadkiel rules the planet Jupiter.

Zadkiel is known as the Divine Alchemist and Angelic Lord of the Violet Flame of Alchemical Transformation. He works with Ascended Master St. Germain as guardian of the Violet Flame. The workings of the Seventh Ray (violet ray) focus on purifying and transmuting the lower energies of human beings into more evolved energies and spiritual states at all levels of being. Zadkiel teaches us the use of violet flame and helps us to heal the human mind, body, soul, and aura. The violet flame and energy of Archangel Zadkiel offers protection, strength, and spiritual guidance.

Archangel Zadkiel presides over Chesed, the fourth Sephirah in the Tree of Life.

Archangel Jophiel

Archangel Jophiel is the Archangel of Beauty and Art, the patron Angel of artists and intellectuals. His name means "Beauty of God." It is Jophiel's duty to transmit Divine Inspiration into the minds of people and help them co-create beauty and art on Earth. He is the chief of the Angelic Order of Seraphim, and he assists Archangel Michael in battle. He is said to work closely with Archangel Metatron. Jewish tradition considers Jophiel as the Angel who guarded the Tree of Knowledge and drove Adam and Eve away from the Garden of Eden.

Jophiel serves on the Second Ray of Love and Wisdom. He is the Archangel of Wisdom, Knowledge, and Illumination.

Archangel Jeremiel

Archangel Jeremiel is the Archangel of Clairvoyance, Prophecy, Intuition, and Dreams. In Judaic tradition, Jeremiel is listed as one of the seven core Archangels. His name means "Mercy of God." Jeremiel helps the souls newly crossed over into Heaven to review their earthly lives and learn from their experiences. He also guards the knowledge of the exact day of the final judgment.

Archangel Samael

According to Christian mystic Stylianos Atteshlis (known as "Daskalos"), the name of Samael comes from sam, which means "venom," and el, which means "God" in Sanskrit, Ancient Egyptian, and Hebrew. In Kabbalistic texts, Samael is described as the "Severity of God," and in Gnostic texts his name stands for "the Blind God."

Archangel Samael is one of the Angels of Death (together with Azrael). He symbolizes and manifests darkness and the negative aspect but also healing and enlightenment. He has been regarded as both a good and an evil Angel. In esoteric and spiritual healing arts, Samael is considered to be an Angel of post-death soul liberation, of transitions to other levels, and of change generally. He is also the Angel of healing many internal issues, including the damaged human subconscious, the "shadow" side (lower self, flaws), any negative feelings and thoughts, and all deeply rooted, unconscious fears.

Samael performs the Will of God and dispenses Divine Justice. He is regarded as a punisher and great defender at the same time. In Kabbalistic tradition, Samael is related with planet Mars and the Sephirah Geburah (meaning "severity"), which is the domain of justice, punishment, and security.

Samael is an Angel of matter (in its dense form). In cooperation with the four Archangels (Michael, Gabriel, Raphael, Uriel) and the Four Elements (Fire, Water, Air, Earth), Samael—as the Angel of Earth and minerals—directly controls matter and can materialize and dematerialize. He creates dense matter (providing us with the materials for bones, muscles, and organs of the body) under the watch of natural and Karmic laws. Samael has a prominent role in the maintenance of physical health. He materializes all the thoughts, ideas, and desires of the human soul through the four bodies: spirit, mind, emotion, and matter. Working with Samael may bring about the more intense and direct (possibly miraculous) healing that requires any alteration of matter, such as materialization or dematerialization.

A direct collaboration with Samael can be achieved only by advanced mystics who have been unified or "egofied" (i.e., attuned to the highest level) with the four Archangels of the four Elements, after a long, deep esoteric practice in the art of meditation and visualization.

Samael resides in the Seventh Heaven and helps us to overcome our fear of death.

Archangel Azrael

Archangel Azrael is known as the Angel of Death in both Islamic and Jewish traditions. His name means "whom God helps." In Islam, Azrael is the Angel of Death who separates the human soul from the body at the moment of death and keeps track of the dying by erasing their names. In various sources, he is described as a fallen Angel. Although associated with being the Angel of Death, he is a gentle and comforting Archangel who assists people with grieving. Azrael's Angelic duties include comforting people prior to their physical deaths and helping souls depart from the physical realm and transition to the spiritual realm.

Azrael works in the area of esoteric and spiritual healing arts. He is considered to be an Angel of Post-Death Soul Liberation, of Transitions to other levels, and of Change generally. Just like Samael, he is also the Angel of healing the human subconscious, the "shadow" side, negative feelings and thoughts, and deeply rooted unconscious fears.

Azrael helps us to see what is true and substantial. He rules the planet Pluto, and he is often associated with water and the flow of life.

Archangel Raguel

Archangel Raguel is the Archangel of Justice and Fairness. The Book of Enoch regards Raguel as one of the Seven Archangels who judge those who disrespect God's laws. His name means "friend of God." Raguel oversees the entire angelic realm and all creation to make sure that they all (Angels and humans) work together in a harmonious way according to the Divine Order and Will. He is a leader within the Angelic Order of Principalities and the Archangel of Friendship, Cooperation, Balance, and Orderliness.

Characteristics of Archangels

Below you will find a list with the qualities and characteristics of each Archangel, including their resonance with colors and energies.

The Domains of the Archangels

Michael: Protection, Guidance, Purification, Divine Will

Gabriel: Feelings, Serenity, Peace, Hope, Regeneration

Raphael: Healing

Uriel: Light, Grounding, Balance, Harmony

Sandalphon: Nature, Grounding, Balance, Harmony

Metatron: Enlightenment, Ascension

Haniel: Joy, Psychic Abilities, Emotional Communication

Chamuel: Love, Relationships

Raziel: Rite, Mysteries, Knowledge and Wisdom of the Universe

Ariel: Environment, Wild Nature, Water, Wind

Tzaphkiel: Maternal Energy and Love, Reflection, Angelic Realms

Zadkiel: Justice, Compassion, Forgiveness, Purification, Healing

Jophiel: Beauty, Art, Knowledge, Wisdom

Jeremiel: Compassion, Insight, Prophecy, Dreams

Samael: Transition, Change, Deep Healing, Materialization and Dematerialization

Azrael: Transition, Change, Healing of Subconscious

Raguel: Friendship, Cooperation, Justice, Harmony

The Colors and Energies of the Archangels

Michael: Red (Fire, Purification, Protection) or Blue/Azure (Divine Will) or Gold (Divine Protection and Power)

Gabriel: Blue/Azure (Water, Feelings, Serenity) or Fuchsia (Divine Love, Care, Maternal Energy) or White (Purity)

Raphael: Green/Emerald Green (Body Healing) or Purple/Violet (Etheric Vitality, Life-Force Energy) or White (Light of Life)

Uriel: White or Silver

Sandalphon: Green, Stone/Earthly Colors

Metatron: Platinum

Haniel: Azure, Baby Blue

Chamuel: Pink

Raziel: Deep Blue

Ariel: Pale Green

Tzaphkiel: Turquoise

Zadkiel: Violet

Jophiel: Yellow

Jeremiel: Violet

Samael: Deep Green

Azrael: Deep Red

Raguel: Orange, Yellow

Guardian Angel: All colors (rainbow) or White (purity) or Pink (selfless maternal love and care) or Azure (celestial serenity and protection)

Angels

Angels are substantial spiritual beings, true heavenly creatures. They are immaterial beings of pure consciousness who carry out divine purposes and acts. One of their duties is to transfer messages from human beings to the Higher Power, God (the Ultimate Sublime Reality and Source of everything) and vice versa. Angels are most known to people as messengers of the Divine, and their name comes from the Greek word angelos, which means "messenger." Nevertheless, Angels have countless duties and tasks, attributes and characteristics, qualities and powers: encouraging direct communication between human beings and the Divine and transferring messages, ideas, inspirations, heavenly guidance, spiritual energies, and qualities.

There are countless Angels for every area of life and for everything: Angels of harmony, peace, freedom, faith, joy, mercy, compassion, power, knowledge, beauty, and so on; Angels of arts, sciences, colors, sounds, music; Angels of nature, water, air, earth, rivers, animals, rocks, minerals, and many others. There are also Guardian Angels, Angels of protection, Angels of healing, Angels of purification, Angels of guidance, Angels of illumination, Angels of abundance, and Angels of love, romance, family, and all relationships. Angels guide each person individually. They are our heavenly siblings!

Two distinct and special Angelic Orders

There are celestial beings of superior angelic energy and power that are not part of the known nine Orders of the Angelic Hierarchy. These are spiritual entities of the highest light, such as Elohim and Shekhinah. There is not much information available about these primordial and transcendental cosmic forces because humanity cannot attune with such high levels of consciousness and being.

Elohim

The Elohim are Sons of God. They are not part of the known Angelic Hierarchy; they are viewed by esoteric traditions and sources as higher spiritual entities of Divine consciousness and infinite light. It is believed that seven or twelve Elohim exist. They are the primary essence of the Creator in form; they are makers of dimensions, universes, and worlds. Elohim are the hands and creative forces of God. They are emanations of the Divine Source that serve as the Highest Angelic Creators. They might be connected with other ancient systems of twelve deities or forces, such as the twelve Olympians. In the Old Testament, the Hebrew word Elohim is commonly used to refer to God.

Shekhinah

Shekhinah is a mystical embodiment of the feminine aspect of God—the Feminine Principle of Existence and the Infinite Divine Being. She is also called the bride of God. She is the Divine Source's hidden presence made manifest. In Kabbalah, the Shekhinah is the archetype of the Divine female, and she is represented as Sephirah Malkut, "the daughter of God." She is also symbolized by the moon, which reflects the light of the sun. Shekhinah is the Divine Presence, the Divine Source of Life, the Divine Mother. She is the female counterpart of Archangel Metatron. Shekhinah is the connection from Earth to Heaven, and Metatron is the connection from Heaven to Earth. Shekhinah and Metatron are different aspects of the Divine. The Gnostics say she is Pistis Sophia. Shekhinah is believed to be the Mother of Angels.

Guardian Angel

The Guardian Angel belongs to the Order of Angels. Stylianos Atteshlis (known as "Daskalos") taught that the Guardian Angel belongs to the Order of Thrones. The Guardian Angel is the most important Angel and the one closest to us, the most immediate, direct, and personal—the most loving and beloved—among all celestial spiritual beings.

Each Guardian Angel is connected directly to the soul and the personality of one person. Every soul has a Guardian Angel assigned and attuned to it for its protection and guidance. A Guardian Angel is a divine blueprint, an angelic "duplicate" of a human being's soul. A Guardian Angel is a person's celestial "other half."

Each human being has a Guardian Angel assigned by God to watch over him. The Guardian Angel assigned to each person is unique, though it is possible to connect to more Guardian Angels as we advance and evolve spiritually. A Guardian Angel accompanies, protects, supports, and guides a person through his entire life; listens to his prayers, comforts him; loves him deeply, wholly, totally, and unconditionally. He is love in its most angelic form, the angelic aspect of our Higher Selves. A person and his Guardian Angel are spiritually united, eternal beings existing in the bliss and completeness of the Divine Source.

The Guardian Angel cannot bypass our free will to reach greater maturation and self-discovery through the various separations, conflicts, and sorrows we experience in our lives. Guardian Angels minister to human beings (souls on Earth) as our guides and protectors, always according to the wishes of our higher selves—the intentions, choices, and plans of our wise souls. The Guardian Angels appear at our rescue only when that action is in accordance with the deepest wishes of our souls and with the karmic laws. They will not stop us from learning the hard way what we have chosen to learn, but they will rescue us if we are in danger and it is not our time to die. Our Guardian Angels will guide us to places, directions, or people we are supposed to find, necessary for our development. They will inspire us and answer our questions, once we are ready and open to higher truths.

As we lovingly call upon our Guardian Angels (even by just thinking of them), we connect with them energetically and build a relationship that helps us advance in our spiritual and everyday lives. The greatest wish of each Guardian Angel is to help us grow and stay on the path of harmony.

The Guardian Angel is the most precious gift from Heaven, from the Divine Source, from God to humanity, to each one of us. That great, unique, personal, close, and intimate gift is the love of Heaven and of Spirit—the Divine Love!

Abadie, Marre Jeanne. *The Everything Guide to Angels*. MA: Adams Media, 2001.

Atteshlis, Stylianos. *The Esoteric Practice*. Cyprus: The Stoa Series, 1994.
The Esoteric Teachings. Cyprus: The Stoa Series, 1992.
Joshua Immanuel the Christ. Cyprus: The Stoa Series, 2001.
The Parables. Cyprus: The Stoa Series, 1991.
The Symbol of Life. Cyprus: The Stoa Series, 1998.
Words of Truth. Cyprus: The Stoa Series, 2009.

Briggs, Constance Victoria. *The Encyclopedia of Angels*. NY: Plume, 1997.

Bunson, Matthew. *Angels A to Z*. NY: Three Rivers Press, 1996.

Cooper, Diana. A Little Light on the Spiritual Laws. UK: Findhorn Press, 2007.
A New Light on Angels. UK: Findhorn Press, 2009.
A New Light on Ascension. UK: Findhorn Press, 2004.
Angel Answers. UK: Findhorn Press, 2007.
Angel Inspiration. UK: Findhorn Press, 2007.

Cortens, Theolyn. *Working with Archangels*. UK: Piaktus Books, Ltd., 2007.

Courtenay, Edwin. *The Archangelic Book of Ritual and Prayer*. Germany: The Prince of the Stars, 2006.

Cresswell, Julia. *The Watkins Dictionary of Angels*. London: Watkins Publishing, 2006.

Davidson, Gustav. *A Dictionary of Angels*. NY: The Free Press, 1967.

Giuley, Rosemary Ellen. *The Encyclopedia of Angels*. NY: Checkmark Books, 2004.

Gregg, Susan. *The Encyclopedia of Angels, Spirit Guides, and Ascended Masters*. USA: Fair Winds Press, 2008.

Paolino, Karen. *The Everything Guide to Angels*. MA: Adams Media, 2009.

Prophet, Elizabeth Clare. *How to Work with Angels*. USA: Summit University Press, 1998.
I Am Your Guard. USA: Summit University Press, 2008.
Violet Flame. USA: Summit University Press, 1998.

Raven, Hazel. *The Angel Bible*. London: Godsfield Press, Ltd., 2006.
The Angel Experience. London: Octopus Publishing, 2010.

Theotoki-Atteshli, Panayiota. *Gates to the Light*. Cyprus: The Stoa Series, 1996.

Virtue, Doreen. *Angels 101*. Carlsbad, CA: Hay House, 2006.

Angel Medicine. London: Hay House, 2004.

Angel Therapy. Carlsbad, CA: Hay House, 1997.

Angel Visions. Carlsbad, CA: Hay House, 2006.

Archangels 101. Carlsbad, CA: Hay House, 2010.

Archangels & Ascended Masters. Carlsbad, CA: Hay House, 2004.

Daily Guidance From Your Angels. Carlsbad, CA: Hay House, 2008.

Earth Angels. Carlsbad, CA: Hay House, 2008.

Goddesses and Angels. Carlsbad, CA: Hay House, 2006.

How to Hear Your Angels. Carlsbad, CA: Hay House, 2007.

Healing With The Angels. Carlsbad, CA: Hay House, 1999.

Messages From Your Angels. Carlsbad, CA: Hay House, 2002.

Realms of the Earth Angels. Carlsbad, CA: Hay House, 2007.

The Miracles of Archangel Michael. Carlsbad, CA: Hay House, 2009.

The Healing Miracles of Archangel Raphael. Carlsbad, CA: Hay House, 2010.

Virtue, Doreen and Charles Virtue. *Signs From Above*. Carlsbad, CA: Hay House, 2009.

Angel Words. Carlsbad, CA: Hay House, 2010.

Webster, Richard. Gabriel: *Communicating with the Archangel for Inspiration & Reconciliation*. USA: Llewellyn Publications, 2005.

Michael: Communicating with the Archangel for Guidance & Protection. USA: Llewellyn Publications, 2004.

Raphael: Communicating with the Archangel for Healing & Creativity. USA: Llewellyn Publications, 2005.

Spirit Guides & Angel Guardians. USA: Llewellyn Publications, 2004.

Uriel: Communicating with the Archangel for Transformation & Tranquility. USA: Llewellyn Publications, 2002.

The Encyclopedia of Angels. USA: Llewellyn Publications, 2009.

Books by Georgios Mylonas (Geom!*)

Healing, Spiritual and Esoteric Meditations

Angelic Invocations

Angelic Symbols

The Golden Codes of Shamballa

How to Cleanse the Energy of Your Space

Higher Abundance

Higher Love

Energy Circles

Divine Healing

Esoteric Answers: The Red Book

Abundance Symbols